{The Concise}

ENTERPRISE INTERNETWORKING AND SECURITY

Kyle Cassidy and Joseph Dries III

201 W 103rd Street
Indianapolis, IN 46290

Kyle Cassidy and Joseph Dries III

The Concise Guide to Enterprise Internetworking and Security

Kyle Cassidy and Joseph Dries III

International Standard Book Number: 0-7897-2420-0

Library of Congress Catalog Card Number: 00-109003

Printed in the United States of America

First Printing: December 2000

03   02   01   00   4   3   2   1

Trademarks

Warning and Disclaimer

Associate Publisher
Jeff Koch

Acquisitions Editor
Maureen A. McDaniel

Development Editor
Maureen A. McDaniel

Technical Editor
Aaron Rogers

Managing Editor
Thomas F. Hayes

Project Editor
Leah Kirkpatrick

Copy Editor
Julie McNamee

Indexer
Cheryl Landes

Proofreader
Benjamin Berg

Team Coordinator
Vicki Harding

Interior Designer
Trina Wurst

Cover Designer
Rader Design

Production
Darin Crone

About the Authors

Kyle Cassidy, MCSE, has a degree in English Literature from Rowan University though he was never naïve enough to think he could earn a living that way. He's a network engineer at the University of Pennsylvania's prestigious Annenberg School for Communication. He's been writing about technology since 1986, most recently as a frequent contributor to *Windows NT Systems* magazine and in Que's *Special Edition Using Windows 2000 Server*. When not working on fascinating projects at the Annenberg School, he can often be found writing pithy blurbs about himself in the third person for the inside covers of books like this one. He lives in Philadelphia with Linda Harris the fine art painter, Thunderbelly the wonder cat, and Saturn, their VAX 4000/300. In his spare time he actually likes to listen to clever 78s on his Victrola and snaps the occasional photograph.

Joseph Dries has been working in Information Technology since 1983. He received his computer science degree, along with mathematics and physics minors, from Rowan University. In 1998 he left his position at Lockheed Martin as senior network engineer to start DCsquared, a consulting company specializing in network security, network engineering, and NOS architecture. Learning is a lifelong passion, and he received a full dose of it coming up to speed to run his new company. While full of technical knowledge and esoterica, it wasn't until he met Kyle that he put his pen to paper for others to learn from. He lives in southern New Jersey with his two cats, Milla and Tatiana, conducting RF experiments on his neighbors. Were there to be any spare time, it would be spent looking for quality scuba diving experiences.

Drop us a line:

We'd love to hear from you, though please keep in mind the volume of mail we get prohibits us from trying to diagnose technical problems:

```
joseph@dries.org
kylecassidy@asc.upenn.eduv
```

Dedication

To Christian Xavier Heim

Acknowledgments

Writing this book was like trying to hold down a 30-foot squid with a pair of barbecue tongs. Somehow it seemed like a simple enough thing to do when we started the project but an enormous amount of the oddest difficulties started popping up all over the place once we'd taken it on. Were it not for a dedicated team of individuals from Macmillan/Que this book would never have been written, or at least it wouldn't have been nearly as well organized or attractive. The author's job is only one part of the total package; it was up to others to barrage us with voice and electronic mail messages reminding us that our deadlines were not, in fact, merely suggestions. We did our best to cause premature aging to several members of the Que team—most prominent among them our acquisitions editor Maureen McDaniel from whose life expectancy we've no doubt subtracted 18 months, also our team coordinator Vicki Harding and project editor Leah Kirkpatrick. We'd also like to thank Jenny Watson for getting the ball rolling. Aaron Rogers was our technical editor on this project and provided continued valuable advice, though any remaining errors or admissions are entirely our own. We owe them all a case of Butterskotch Krimpets. We'd also like to thank a bunch of other people. (You can stop reading now unless you think your name might be in here.)

Kyle and Joe would like to thank:

Bill Mattson, Jimmy Drnek, Frank, Janeen and Pete Macgregor, Bill Obst, Chuck Diem, Jim Burwell, and Chris Freas.

Kyle would like to thank:

Linda Harris, Thunderbelly, and some other people:

The people who picked up the slack at work while I was writing this: Rich Cardona, John Strommer-Galley, Aaron Simmons, Mario Giorno, & Lizz Cooper. Also my boss, Dr. Kathleen Hall-Jamieson, who gave me the time, encouragement, and invaluable advice, including fiercely negotiating my contract.

Friends and coworkers at the Annenberg School for Communication: Laura Jane Kordiak, Josh Gesell, Dr. Paul Messaris, Dr. Carolyn Marvin, Deb Porter, Deb Williams, Patrick and Bob Jamieson, and David Graper. Kip Forstoffer from Dell.

Rabbit's Friends and Relations: Mom & Dad, Heather, John, Oakes & Sawyer. Chris & Bonnie Heim, Charles Kershenblatt & Dylan. Rob Ditto and Michael Greve at Wharton. Carley Jane, Madison & Delaney, the Harris family. Dr. Sean Heim, Paul Knox.

From Rowan University: Dr. Jay Chaskes, Dr. Richard Mitchell, Dr. Terry Donohue, Dr. Michael Berman, Jon Maslow, Jonathon Maslow, Bruce Klein, Ken Denton, Karlton Hughes, Clare Lafferty, Dr. Jack Cimprich, and Leigh Weiss.

Jessica Bunnell & my friends in PhillyGoth; Nikki, Jennyfur, Gary, Vince, Patrick, Jef & Cass, Spyndal, & Helen.

From someplace else: Kevin Craft, Lorie Sporer, Laura Carney, Cindy Gretchen Ovenrack & Doris, Jim Shulman & John Williams. Kim Stevenson. Ward & Scott at Marston. B.D. Colen, Johnny Deadman, & the various curmudgeons in the LUG.

And of course all those people in my CD player: Tapping the Vein (you should all go download *Beautiful* from mp3.com), Carfax Abbey (ditto with downloading *Ketamine*), Museum, Leah Mikel, Nicole Blackman, The Empire Hideous, Jef & Torsion, The Fields of the Nephilim, and of course, Karen's Sisters of Mercy bootlegs without which I would still be mired somewhere in chapter 6.

Joseph would like to thank:

Jennifer Drechen for her love and patience, Milla and Tatiana for their typing assistance, and some other people;

The people who worked while I was writing this: Matt Doughty, Dan Petrin, Doug Cours and Paul Delisi.

Friends and coworkers: Michael Wolk at Apple, Michael Weaver, Denise Basara, Timothy Peterman, Herb Hoppe, Kurt Fischer, Gary Mietz, Greg Gedling, Tom Charlton, Allan Hollowell, Bob Martin, Bruce Ratkevic, Jim Hamby, Tony Wicks, Selvyn Scott, April Duggins, Tom Rassmann, Dan Cushing, Kevin Hamm, Jeff Bishop, Jonathan Bishop, Kaydon Stanzione, Len Oliver, Christopher Zarcone.

Friends and Relations: Dad, Mom, Erik & Angie Dries, Erik Jr., Fred, Pam & Aaron Pesnell, Dr. Sean Heim, Jimmy, Laurie, Brittney and Taylor Dunn, Doug & Amy Finn, Scott, Kathy & Emily Lewis.

From someplace else: Carolyn Gargaro, Lorraine Sporer, Ed Champion, Darrell Aruanno, Maxim Chan, Carmen Grasso, John Desper, Shane Gosdis, Lou Hall, Al Green, Scott Herman, Ken Williams, Paul Knox,

Paul Cassidy, Megan Mulherin, Maria O'Callaghan, Wayne & Karen Quesada, Rich Sezov, J. Brian Waters, Tony Schreidel and Carl Thomas Jr.

And of course all those people in my CD player: Tool, A Perfect Circle, Suicidal Tendencies, Infectious Grooves, The Dead Milkmen, The Offspring, Henry Rollins, VoiVod, Durham Rule, Slayer, David Bowie, Tori Amos, Trent Reznor, Mr. Bungle, Korn, Kronos Quartet, Saint-Saëns, Mozart, and Gwar.

Contents

Tell Us What You Think!

As the reader of this book, *you* are our most important critic and commentator. We value your opinion and want to know what we're doing right, what we could do better, what areas you'd like to see us publish in, and any other words of wisdom you're willing to pass our way.

As an associate publisher for Que, I welcome your comments. You can fax, email, or write me directly to let me know what you did or didn't like about this book—as well as what we can do to make our books stronger.

Please note that I cannot help you with technical problems related to the topic of this book, and that due to the high volume of mail I receive, I might not be able to reply to every message.

When you write, please be sure to include this book's title and author as well as your name and phone or fax number. I will carefully review your comments and share them with the author and editors who worked on the book.

Fax: 317-581-4666

Email: quefeedback@macmillanusa.com

Mail: Jeff Koch
          Que
          201 West 103rd Street
          Indianapolis, IN 46290 USA

INTRODUCTION

About Security

With continued reliance upon the Internet by businesses and individuals, not having a presence on it is extremely counterproductive. In fact, it could be argued that a business without an Internet presence could not survive in today's world.

At the same time, the second you connect your network to the Internet you've opened a door through which the entire world can visit; this is especially true if you attach a WWW server. Some of your visitors will be customers excited about purchasing your product, some will be window shoppers, and others will be the Bored and Unwashed looking to cause mischief.

Intruders can steal, alter, or destroy your data; run commands on your servers; or launch denial-of-service attacks against you. Any one of these can be disruptive or even catastrophic.

Knowing how to design and implement a secure environment for your users is key to the job of maintaining any network in toady's world. This book will help you connect your network to the Internet and do so in a secure fashion.

One of the greatest threats to Internet security today is the incredible ease at which automated hacking tools are available. Even five years ago, an intruder had to have at least a rudimentary knowledge of the arcana of computer systems to pose a viable threat to your security. But today, cracking software is readily available at the click of a couple of links and anybody with malicious intent can start poking around looking for weaknesses.

The key to maintaining your data integrity is by anticipating attacks and preventing them. This is done through vigilant planning and dedicated attention to maintenance and updates. The good news is that you don't need to do all of this yourself. This book outlines where and how to get security services working for you, checking for holes in your network and alerting you of known security flaws.

Additionally, this book provides resources for consultants and those hiring consultants, keys to working with your Telco and ISP in delivering bandwidth to your door, the secure implementation of TCP/IP and its various constituent components, and concepts of security design such as firewalling, hardening, and DMZs.

Layout of This Book

This book consists of five different sections: Learning, Planning, Implementing, Testing, and Maintaining. These correspond directly with the five distinctly different types of work you'll be doing when connecting your network to the Internet. You'll notice that these sections aren't uniform in size, and neither are the concepts. We've spent a lot of time on Learning and Reference because you'll be going back to those sections throughout the building of your Internet connection; we spent correspondingly less time on the Maintaining section. The bulk of your work will be in the planning and installing. After the connection is up and running, maintaining it will seem easy.

Throughout the book, we tried to remain as platform independent as possible but we assume that you will probably be using some magic mix of UNIX, Windows 2000, and Macintosh computers and periodically we will mention implementations specific to those operating systems.

Learning/Reference—Chapters 1–4

The first part of this book consists of learning and reference materials that make up the underlying base of knowledge you will use later. In these chapters, you learn about TCP/IP and related protocols (that is, where UDP/IP would be used instead of TCP/IP); the various types of bandwidth delivery technologies that you'll be dealing with; concepts of security; and a hardware overview that describes many of the components you'll be working with.

In Advance: Planning and Designing Your Network— Chapters 5–9

Upon the completion of every network, there is some amount of forehead slapping and exclamations of "Why didn't I…" (often in the form of something like "Why didn't I check to make sure all those outlets were on different circuits!" or "Why didn't I know that Accounting needs to install remote dial-in services on its workstations?"). It's inevitable, but it can be minimized by careful planning, outlining, and interviewing.

The second part of this book deals with the preplanning stages of putting your network on the Internet: defining your connection requirements, choosing an Internet service provider, and dealing with consultants and contractors. Because we're assuming that some of you *are* consultants and contractors (maybe even the majority), this chapter deals with both sides of the coin. In these chapters, you'll learn what to ask your consultant and what a consultant should be able to answer. This includes questions such as "How will you guarantee the safety of my data?" and "Is there a cheaper way to do all this?" You'll also find design considerations, such as wiring difficulties, and the types of modifications you'll be making to each of your client workstations. Finally, we'll talk about assessing your security needs. Obviously, security is not applied in blanket form and deciding what level of security needs to be achieved will be based upon surveys of your users and careful consideration of the importance of your data.

In Practice: Implementing Your Network— Chapters 10–11

There are two chapters on assembling your hardware and software and plugging them in; Chapter 10, "Getting Connected," and Chapter 11, "Implementing Security." In this section, we'll talk about selecting and connecting the hardware devices that physically bring the signal into your building and configuring the hardware and software you'll be using to manage its security.

In Earnest: Testing Your Network—Chapter 12

After your network is up and running, you'll need to ensure that everything is functioning properly. This not only means making sure that your users can log in, but also that your data is safe from outside predation.

In Hindsight: Maintaining Your Network—Chapter 13

After you've installed and connected your network, it won't run itself. As is the nature with such technology, your Internet connection requires constant attention and upgrades. New software comes out daily, virus scanners become obsolete, and new types of attacks become popular. There are also concerns of the changing network habits of your users and planning for emerging technologies.

Where to Go for More Information

RFCs are the white papers that define various Internet technologies. They contain everything you want to know about a particular technology and then some. They're available from
`http://www.faqs.org/rfcs/`.

1

TCP/IP AND RELATED
PROTOCOLS

"All parts should go together without forcing. You must remember that all the parts you are reassembling were disassembled by you. Therefore, if you can't get them together again, there must be a reason. By all means, do not use a hammer."

-IBM maintenance manual, 1925
(displayed in the Chicago Museum of Science & Industry)

TCP/IP and its related protocols and applications (FTP, TFTP, SNMP, DNS, Finger, Telnet, and so on) form the backbone of Internet communications. TCP/IP is actually two different but tightly interdependent protocols: the Transmission Control Protocol and the Internet Protocol. They go together like water and fish—where you find one you usually find the other. Based originally on the Internet Layered model and later shoehorned into the OSI model, TCP and IP together handle the breakdown, sequencing, addressing, transmission, and reassembly of data across a network.

How Data Travels Across Networks

A network is a collection of devices connected together; for all intents and purposes, at least some of these devices need to be computers, although others can be printers, disk drives, scanners or video cameras. An internetwork is a collection of networks connected together via gateways. The Internet is made up of a collection of voluntarily interconnected networks. There is no central authority that regulates and ensures those connections are error free or reliable. Some networks, by design or circumstance, might have intermittent connectivity.

A block of your data is generically referred to as a datagram. And the process of breaking apart, addressing, and transmitting your data is referred to as packetizing your datagram.

The Internet Procotol, IP, is designed with two basic functions. The first is addressing the datagram with the source and destination addresses. The second is fragmenting and reassembling the datagrams when traveling over networks of different packet sizes. IP makes no attempt to provide facilities for end-to-end reliability, sequencing of delivery, or flow control. Those responsibilities are the domain of TCP.

The Monolithic Versus Layered Method of Application Design

As early as the 1970s, programmers were edging away from what is known as the monolithic method—one piece of software that acts as a sole translator, guide, and guardian of data as it moves between point A and point B (like Virgil taking Dante through all nine circles of hell). This was abandoned in favor of a layered solution, in which numerous smaller applications each handle specific parts of the translation and transportation (like the ghosts of Christmas past, present, and future passing Ebenezer Scrooge between one another). In this way, individual layers can be rewritten or replaced as needed without having to rewrite the entire monolith. The OSI model is the most famous layered approach to networking. TCP/IP is the most famous application of network layers. As you will soon see, they're not entirely compatible. Oh well.

The OSI Model

Realizing the need for a networking standard to avoid considerable brewing confusion, the International Standards Organization (ISO), or as it likes to call itself, the Organization Internationale de Standards (OIS), came up with a seven-layer model for network communication called the Open System Interconnection (OSI). In doing so, it created a lot of confusion with all those letters but avoided a lot more trouble by nailing down a method of network intercommunication that has been going strong for nearly 30 years. And in this industry, anything 30 years old has considerably proven longevity. The idea behind the OSI model's layers was that no longer would programmers need to write gargantuan network protocols for each device they wanted to attach to each other device. Programmers need only write clients for whatever layers of the OSI networking standard they wanted to access.

One notable thing about the OSI model is that in practice with the actual implementations on the Internet, it is rarely fully represented. However, many successful internetworking protocols (such as TCP/IP) owe considerable ancestry to it.

The seven layers are as follows:

- Layer 1: Physical
- Layer 2: Data Link
- Layer 3: Network
- Layer 4: Transport
- Layer 5: Session
- Layer 6: Presentation
- Layer 7: Application

The Physical layer is the most primitive (closest to the hardware of the network) and the Application layer is closest to the user.

The Physical Layer

The Physical layer defines the way in which bits of data are encoded and how that data is to travel across the transmission media (wire, fiber, or otherwise). The physical level is where electrical or mechanical functions take place.

The Data Link Layer

The Data Link layer specifies how "frames" are sent. A *frame* is a block of data prefixed with a header and post-fixed with a frame check sequence (FCS). The header is composed primarily of the data link control (DLC) which contains the source MAC address (SA) and the destination MAC address (DA). Any additional header information is dependent on the networking technology used to send the frame.

The Network Layer

Both addressing and routing are handled in the Network layer. The network protocol makes sure that data is properly addressed and gets to its final destination. IP operates at the Network layer.

The Transport Layer

The Transport layer is responsible for "end-to-end control," meaning that it checks to make sure all the data has arrived and arrived uncorrupted. Both TCP and the related UDP (User Datagram Protocol) operate at the Transport layer.

The Session Layer

The Session layer allows different processes to talk to one another. The ports and sockets used to identify the processes and services are analogous to asking to speak to a particular person after you've dialed a phone number.

The Presentation Layer

The Presentation layer provides translation functionality. It may translate ASCII to EBCDIC, for example. TCP/IP has no defined functionality in this OSI layer.

The Application Layer

The Application layer provides Application layer access to the network. Again, TCP/IP has no defined functionality in this OSI layer.

TCP/IP and the Internet Layer Model

The Internet doesn't use the OSI model; however, it uses the four-layer Internet model. While traveling from one computer through a network to another machine, data passes through four Internet protocol layers. At each layer, the data metamorphasizes as header information is added.

The following are the four layers of the Internet:

- Application
- Transport
- Network
- Datalink and Physical

In each layer, a block of data takes on various header information and a different name. The following table shows these:

Layer	Name
Application	PDU
Transport	Segment
Network	Packet or Datagram
Datalink and Physical	Frame

A block of data in the Application layer is called a PDU (Protocol Data Unit). As it descends into the Transport layer (where TCP functions), header information is added and the PDU becomes a "segment." Further down, as it is passed to the Network layer (where IP functions), further header information is added and it becomes a "datagram," or "packet." It is then passed to the Datalink and Physical layer (these two OSI layers are merged in the TCP/IP model, remember), dubbed a "frame," and transmitted as bits.

When the packet arrives at the router, it is peeled open like an artichoke, and the router takes a look at the IP header to see where the packet belongs. Reading the IP address out of that header, it is repackaged at the Datalink and Physical layer, made back into a frame, and sent on to its final destination where it is received and does not turn into a butterfly.

Mapping TCP/IP to the OSI Model

The OSI model has seven layers; TCP/IP has four. TCP/IP maps to the Network and Transport layers of the OSI model (see Figure 1.1). IP covers packet delivery and translation between different data-link protocols (if any exist).

Application	FTP, Telnet, SMTP, HTTP…
Presentation	
Session	
Transport	TCP, UDP
Network	IP, ICMP
Data LInk	Ethernet, Token-Ring, FDDI, ATM, Wireless…
Physical	Copper, Fiber, DSSS, FHSS…

Figure 1.1   TCP/IP maps to the OSI model.

Each of the first four layers are important because they represent useful information about networking, network design, and security. How important, and specifically how important they are pertaining to TCP/IP varies according to your timeframe and lust for knowledge.

The Physical layer is important to know for proper network design, because that defines the physical constraints on the layout of your network. Knowing that Gigabit Ethernet over multi-mode fiber normally has a distance limitation of 500 meters is vital to planning which components to purchase. TCP/IP, and other Layer-3 protocols, such as IPX and AppleTalk, are neither defined nor have any implications when working at this level.

The Data Link layer, although closer to TCP/IP in the model, usually isn't that important to typical operations of TCP/IP. The Data Link layer really comes into play when you have some LAN analyzers and are troubleshooting Local Area Networking problems.

The Network layer is obviously important to TCP/IP, because that is where IP is defined. Additional knowledge of Layer-3 protocols influences a great deal about overall network layout and design, not to mention security considerations.

Transport and Session are one and the same because they are tightly coupled in the normal TCP and UDP world. Knowing which services you need to provide and protect is vital. Coupled with the Network layer, an in-depth knowledge of Layers 3 and 4 will help you design, implement, and troubleshoot your network.

The Basics of Layer 2

Keeping in mind both the OSI and Internet models, each block of data must first pass down through the layers to be transmitted. So, for two nodes on a network to talk to each other, they must encapsulate the IP packet into a Layer-2 frame, usually Ethernet or Token Ring. The frame is addressed with a 48-bit address known as a Media Access Control (MAC) address, a supposedly unique address burned into the controlling firmware of the network interface card. All actual communication on LANs is done at Layer 2, so even though your computer is speaking IP to your printer, behind the scenes they are talking Ethernet or Token Ring.

When transmitting data on LANs, two different addresses are used—the IP address is encapsulated in the IEEE 802.x frame, usually Ethernet. Generally, most traffic on the wire is between two nodes, such as when your workstation grabs a document off the file server or sends a print job to a printer. This is normally referred to as unicast traffic.

However, there are other types of traffic in which it's important that multiple, or all, network nodes are involved. It would be inefficient, and sometimes impossible, to address all those nodes individually. This kind of traffic is referred to as multicast (multiple nodes) and broadcast (all nodes) traffic.

To summarize using a network convention analogy:

- Unicast packets are put on the wire with a single destination address. Traffic is transmitted one-to-one. This is the equivalent of talking to a vendor at its booth. The vendor is speaking directly to you about your need for its wares on your network.

- Broadcast packets are put on the wire using a special address that all network nodes listen to. Traffic is transmitted one-to-all. This is the equivalent of attending a keynote speech. The keynote speaker is addressing everyone in the room at the same time.

- Multicast packets are put on the wire using a special address that only some subset of the network nodes are listening to. Multicasting is a specialized form of broadcasting that targets only a select group of network nodes. Traffic is transmitted one-to-many, but not necessarily all. This is the equivalent of attending a special-interest working group. Only those members of the audience that attend the working group get that information.

Address Resolution Protocol (ARP)

ARP is used when a sending computer knows the IP address of a destination computer but needs the OSI Layer-2 (MAC) address. Most local area networks use Ethernet or Token Ring as their transports. RFC 1042 defines Transmission of IP and ARP on IEEE 802.x networks, of which Ethernet (802.3) and Token Ring (802.5) are members.

ARP protocol defines several fields that identify the protocol type, hardware address (Media Access Control, or MAC), the protocol address length, and whether the ARP is a request or a reply.

Because ARP is a broadcast protocol, when a computer ARPs, every computer on the network hears the ARP. Each computer compares the ARP request to its IP address, and responds if there is a match. In a fully functioning network, only the requested computer responds.

ARP requires that the IP network broadcast address (the binary equivalent of the network address with the host portion filled with 1s) be mapped to an IEEE broadcast address of all 1s. The individual format for frames on the various 802 network media is beyond the scope of this book. However, in logical operations, 1s are wildcards and generally mean anything or anyone.

ARP also defines the network byte order, generally referred to as *big endian*.

Keep in mind, even though the network nodes are speaking IP as a Network layer protocol, the actual addressing and transmission on the wire happens at Layer 2. Before two IP network devices can talk on the same wire, they must ARP for each other's MAC address.

Connection Versus Connectionless Communication

Data can travel across an IP network in either a connection or connectionless form.

Connection-oriented, or circuit-switched, communication negotiates a dedicated path of communication before data is transmitted. After the path is established, all data follows that path. This is similar to a telephone call, in which handshaking is done in the form of dialing a number, establishing a private circuit, and then talking to your party at the other end without any additional dialing.

Connectionless communication, on the other hand, sends each block of data into the world with all the information it needs to reach its destination independent of all other blocks of data. Each datagram finds its own way and can arrive via another route or out of sequence with its brethren.

Connection-oriented communication is distinguished by the following:

- A dedicated communication path established through the network
- Limited addressing
- Feedback on whether packets were delivered

Connectionless communication is distinguished by the following:

- No select path chosen for data transmission
- Complete addressing of each block of data
- Network has no ongoing knowledge of the connection
- Data can be rerouted on-the-fly if network difficulty arises
- No inherent delivery notification or guarantee of data

Although connection-oriented communication might be analogous to a telephone call, connectionless communication is similar in many respects to the postal system. Numerous letters can be sent through the mail, arriving out of sequence, independent of one another. They may take alternative routes to reach their destination, and upon receipt can be reassembled into the proper order by the recipient.

Connectionless transmission places fewer demands on both the clients and the network (data is capable of circumventing damaged components or nonexistent paths), but it is far slower due to the redundant addressing in the header and the need to determine whether packets have been dropped.

TCP/IP

TCP/IP is a connection-oriented form of network communication—it is a pair of protocols used to transport data across a network. TCP, the Transmission Control Protocol, is in charge of breaking up messages into blocks. These broken-up messages are placed into IP envelopes containing addressing and numbering information. The whole thing is then sent across the wire and reassembled on the other side.

TCP/IP has been the de facto standard for internetwork data transmission since the mid-1970s. By 1983, it became a requirement for all computers on the newly emerging Internet. One thing that led to this was the intentional distribution of the TCP/IP source code. The move baffled many people at the time; why turn over valuable computer code to competitors and anyone who asked for it? Companies were used to holding such cards very close to try to maintain an edge. The result was that people began to use TCP/IP in droves rather than spend grueling hours and dollars to reinvent the wheel. TCP/IP is firmly entrenched in computer networking and shows no sign of leaving in the near future.

Making TCP Connections

The Internet is not a connection-based network. So, when applications require a connection to a remote service, and want those connections to be robust and as error free as possible, they use TCP to communicate. The TCP communication between application and service from start to finish is known as a *session*.

TCP establishes a connection by using a three-way handshake. The handshake ensures that the remote service is reachable, ready, and able to send and receive data. Various bit-flags in the TCP header signal the appropriate steps in the handshake.

The first packet sent from host to server has the SYN bit set to 1, ACK (as in *ACK*nowledge) set to 0. The SYN bit, or Synchronize Sequence Numbers, tells the remote host that the Sequence number in the header is the Initial Sequence Number. This allows the server to resequence packets that arrive out of order, or not at all.

The server replies with SYN set to 1, ACK set to 1. The SYN bit is set so that the client synchronizes the sequence number of the server. The ACK bit tells the host that this is a reply to a session that is (or is being) established.

The host replies to the server with the SYN bit set to 0, and the ACK bit set to 1. From now on, all packets between host and server will have the ACK bit set to 1.

After the connection is ready to be torn down, the host sends a packet with the FIN bit set to 1, as well as the ACK bit set to 1. The FIN bit, or Finish, tells the server to tear down the connection and release the resources allocated. The server responds with a packet with the ACK bit set to 1.

IP Addressing

More technically known as IPv4, there are 32 bits of address space usually represented in a decimal dotted-quad notation; each decimal represents 8 bits of the 32-bit address space. (There is a more advanced IPv6 that we'll talk about later in this chapter.) In generic terms, an IP address is a number that represents a destination for information. An IP address can represent an individual node or host, an entire collection of hosts or network, or all hosts on a specific network.

The host address represents an individual network node. The host address is usually just represented by the IP address in dotted-quad notation. An example host IP address is 192.168.71.200.

The network address represents an individual network. There is a second component to the network address known as the *network mask*. The network mask is a 32-bit number in which the network portion has all binary 1s, and the host portion has all binary 0s.

The network address for any given node can be determined by doing a logical AND of the node's IP address with the network mask. The binary 1s will not change the values in the network portion of the address, and the binary 0s will zero out the host portion, giving you the network address.

The network mask can either be represented in dotted-quad notation like the IP address itself, or in the preferable netmask notation, which is a slash followed by the number of 1s in the mask. The network address using a common network mask for the host address used previously could then be represented by either 192.168.71.0 netmask 255.255.255.0 or 192.168.71.0/24.

If you are unfamiliar with binary math, logical operators, and the full IP addressing rules, they are unfortunately beyond the scope of this book. However, those concepts and more can be found in any number of TCP/IP-specific books.

The broadcast address is a network address that addresses all hosts on a single network. Like the network address, there is a second component associated with the broadcast address. The second component is the host mask, the logical counterpart to the network mask. The host mask has all binary 0s for the network portion, and binary 1s for the host portion of the IP address.

The broadcast address can be determined by doing a logical OR of the host or network address with the host mask. The binary 0s will not change the network portion of the address, and the binary 1s will make the host portion all 1s.

The resulting broadcast address is generally just represented by a single dotted-quad address. The host mask is also represented in dotted-quad notation, but generally is never used except by some network vendor's equipment. The broadcast address for the previous sample network is 192.168.71.255. The host mask is 0.0.0.255.

IP Address Classes

You might often hear people who work with IP networks talk about Class A, B, and C networks. You might even hear of Class D and E networks. What are they, exactly?

Classes were originally conceived as a logical way to break up the IP address space for allocation to Internet community groups of different sizes. There weren't a whole lot of Internet community members at that time, so the artificial partitioning made more sense than it does now. The following are the classes summarized:

- Class A networks have addresses that start from 1 through 126. Each Class A network could support 16.7 million hosts.
- Class B networks have addresses that start from 128 through 191. Each Class B network could support 65,534 hosts.

- Class C networks have addresses that start from 192 through 223. Each Class C network could support 254 hosts.
- Class D networks were reserved for multicasting applications, and usually start with the number 224.
- Class E networks were reserved for experimental use.

Looking at this list, you might be wondering what happened to 127 and who came up with those ranges?

Well, the 127 network is the internal address used by IP-connected hosts. The localhost or loopback address is 127.0.0.1, and is usually used to talk to services running on the local node.

The seemingly odd breakup of the ranges has more to do with how binary math works. Basically, every time one of the most significant bits changed from 0 to 1, a new network class is defined:

- 0000:0001 through 0111:1111 is 1–127
- 1000:0000 through 1011:1111 is 128–191
- 1100:0000 through 1101:1111 is 192–223

Looking at the network/host allocations, you might come to the conclusion that it seems to be both awfully wasteful and a little restrictive. And you would be right. The authorities at IANA, the Internet Assigned Numbers Authority, thought so as well.

One of the methods they used to rectify the situation is to hand out more appropriately sized address blocks. These blocks are commonly referred to as Classless InterDomain Routing (CIDR, but pronounced cider) blocks.

Additionally, companies that were allocated large network spaces divided them up by using a technique known as subnetting. *Subnetting* allows you to increase the number of logical IP networks by extending the network mask of the allocated network space. Each additional bit of subnet mask doubles the number of IP networks and halves the number of hosts.

Routing

Now that you have a number of subnets, logical groupings of network nodes, how do you get them all to communicate? A network node that transmits packets between networks is generically called a gateway, but more commonly referred to as a *router*.

The router peels away the layers of information put on by the datagram's journey through the OSI layers like an onion. The router does this to examine the source and destination IP addresses. The router then decides what the next leg of the packet's path will be, wraps it all back up, and sends it on its way. The routing table determines where to send the packet.

Routing Table

A router builds a table of destination IP networks to forward packets to. The forwarding table is built from routes both learned by the router via routing specific protocols, and routes statically added by the network administrator.

In actuality, all IP-connected nodes have routing tables, not just routers. Most hosts have very basic routing tables, just enough to get the packet on the wire to a router which should know where to send it.

Table 1.1 shows an example of a small routing table that you might find on any host or small router.

Table 1.1   Sample Routing Table

Destination	Mask	Gateway	Metric
0.0.0.0	0.0.0.0	192.168.5.1	1
10.0.0.0	255.0.0.0	192.168.5.1	1
192.168.5.0	255.255.255.0	192.168.5.150	1
192.168.7.32	255.255.255.255	192.168.5.20	1
209.0.0.9	255.255.255.255	192.168.5.150	1

Let's take a quick look at the terms used in Table 1.1:

■ **Destination**—The host or network address the packet is intended to reach.

■ **Mask**—The 32-bit mask component of the host or network address. A network mask for a host address is always all 1s, as can be seen in the last two table entries.

■ **Gateway**—The IP address of the router to send the packet to. This is also known as the *next hop*.

■ **Metric**—The number of routers between this node's network and the destination network. This is also known as the *hop count*.

When a router receives a packet on one of its interfaces, or when a host or router looks to transmit a packet, it first tries to match the destination IP address from the routing table. Generally, it's a fairly simple matching algorithm. Check to see whether there is an exact match for the IP address in the table. If there isn't, check to see whether there is a match against the network address.

If there is no exact or network address match, the host or router uses the *default gateway*. The default gateway for a host is normally a router. The default gateway for a router is normally a router at the Corporate data center or your ISP. The default gateway, or the gateway of last resort as some vendors refer to it, allows you to forward packets to an upstream router that has more knowledge of the Internet than you want, or need, your router to have.

If no default gateway is defined, and no route is defined for the destination IP address, the router drops the packet and normally sends a `destination unreachable` message back to the sending host. This message is delivered via ICMP, or the Internet Control Message Protocol. ICMP is discussed later in this chapter.

Packet Trace

The router handles passing data over the WAN link, making sure it arrives at the proper destination. For example, Figure 1.2 shows the path data takes when your boss sends email to your local printer.

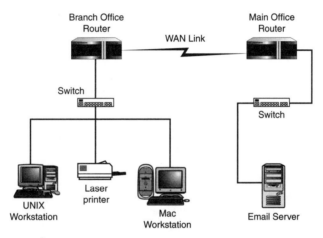

Figure 1.2   The data path.

Retrieving your email requires your workstation to contact the email server at 172.16.100.100. Because your workstation's routing table does not have a route to 172.16.100.0/24 directly, it uses the default route to 172.16.1.1. Because you have not retrieved your email yet today, you must first ARP for 172.16.1.1. After you have the MAC address for the router, your workstation encapsulates the IP packet destined for 172.16.100.100 in a frame addressed to the router's Ethernet interface.

The Branch Office switch receives the packet, inspects the MAC address, and determines which port to send the packet on. If it does not have an entry for which port has the MAC address of the router, the packet is sent on every port; otherwise, it is just sent to the port the router is on.

The router receives the packet on its Ethernet interface, strips away the Layer-2 information, and sees that the packet is destined for 172.16.100.100. The Branch Office Router has a routing table entry for 172.16.100.0/24 with a next hop of 192.168.1.1, so the router re-encapsulates the packet and transmits it over the WAN connection.

The Main Office Router receives the packet on the WAN interface, strips away the Layer-2 information, and sees that the packet is destined for 172.16.100.100. The Main Office Router has a routing table entry for 172.16.100.0/24 with a next hop of 172.16.100.1, so the router checks its ARP table to get the MAC address of the email server, re-encapsulates the packet, and transmits it over the Ethernet interface directly to 0a:00:20:af:be:cd.

The Main Office switch examines the MAC address and bridges the frame to the appropriate port that the email server is on.

The reply packets follow the same path, in reverse. After your email client has the email message, and you click Print, the process follows a similar path.

First, your workstation checks the destination IP address against its internal routing table, and sees that the printer, 172.16.1.21, is on the same network. The workstation then checks the ARP table to see whether the matching MAC address for 172.16.1.21 is already known; if not, it proceeds to ARP for the IP address 172.16.1.21. After your computer receives a reply, it encapsulates the IP packet with a destination MAC address of 08:00:09:f1:e2:d3.

User Datagram Protocol (UDP)

UDP was defined in RFC 768 way back in 1980. It functions in a manner similar to TCP, which is to say, usually in conjunction with IP. When it does, it's known as UDP/IP. It, like TCP, resides in Layer 4 of the OSI model, the Transport layer. The main difference between TCP and UDP is that UDP provides far fewer services, which translates into far less information in the header, which translates into less bandwidth overhead at higher speeds. Or, as the RFC states, it transmits data with a "minimum of protocol mechanism."

The content of the header is extremely simple: Source port, destination port, length, checksum, and data. TCP headers on the other hand, contain a gross addition of information in the headers. UDP does provide port numbers and does provide optional checksum error detection.

UDP does not do the following:

- Break the data up into manageable parts
- Provide flow control
- Reassemble data at the receiving end
- Provide sequencing information
- Respond to packet losses

You would use UDP in the following situations:

- You have a reliable network connection.
- You have a small amount of data to transmit.

- You broadcast or multicast your data to multiple computers simultaneously.
- You have an application capable of providing the reassembly services that TCP usually provides.

Examples of places where UDP is used or useful include the following:

- The Trivial File Transfer Protocol (TFTP)
- Simple Network Management Protocol (SNMP)
- Domain Name Service lookups (DNS)
- Internet Name Server Protocol (INSP)
- Sending video or audio

IP Packet Headers

The packet header contains the routing information necessary to get the packet to its destination (see Figure 1.3).

0		1		2		3	
0 1 2 3 4 5 6 7	8 9 0 1 2 3 4 5	6 7 8 9 0 1	2 3 4 5 6 7 8 9 0 1				
Version	IHL	Type of Service	Total Length				
Identification			Flags	Fragment Offset			
Time to Live		Protocol	Header Checksum				
Source Address							
Destination Address							
Options				Padding			

Figure 1.3   A disassembled IP header.

The information is as follows:

- **Version (4 bits)**—The version of IP being used (that is, 4 or 6).
- **Internet Header Length (IHL) (4 bits)**—The length of the IP header in 32-bit segments, ranging from 5 to 60 words. This includes anything in the options fields.
- **Type of Service (TOS) (8 bits)**—TOS includes things such as minimum delay, maximum throughput, precedence, and reliability. This allows you to set a lower precedence for a file transfer program, such as FTP, and a higher precedence for a Telnet session, assuring smooth operation of the relatively low-bandwidth Telnet sessions, while file transfers in the background are given second priority.

- **Total Length (16 bits)**—Length in bytes of the datagram including headers. Some networks require that all frames be the exact same length, which sometimes requires padding of smaller packets. The total length field is used for that purpose.
- **Identification (16 bits)**—A unique identifier used for reassembly.
- **Flags (3 bits) and Fragment Offset (13 bits)**—If a datagram arrives at a gateway and is too large to pass through, it can be fragmented. These fields contain the information necessary to reassemble fragmented frames.
- **Time to Live (TTL) (8 bits)**—A counter that records the number of routers that a datagram has passed through (called a hop counter). When the maximum number of routers is achieved, the datagram is discarded as being too old. Upon its nonarrival, the sender is notified and the datagram re-sent. This keeps datagrams from wandering the Internet like Flying Dutchmen never arriving at their destinations.
- **Protocol (8 bits)**—Tells what protocol the datagram is destined to be passed off to at the destination, usually TCP or UDP, but it could be any number defined in RFC-1700.
- **Header Checksum (16 bits)**—Checksums are generated by hashing out the datagram and providing a number based upon the values of the datagram's header and data. Upon receipt, if the checksum and the datagram don't match, the receiving machine assumes the datagram has become corrupt and discards it. No error message is sent, but when it turns up missing, it is retransmitted.
- **Source Address (and Destination Address) (32 bits)**—IP addresses of the sending and receiving machines.
- **Options (variable length)**—Can be things such as security or time stamps.
- **Data (variable length)**—Your message here.

Common IP Services

IP is actually a "suite" of protocols, when you get IP, you get a lot of stuff with it, such as the familiar Telnet and HTTP, as well as Ping and SMTP. Versions of all these services have been written for just about every operating system for which IP is available. You can see a list of some of them in Table 1.2.

Table 1.2   Components of TCP/IP: Their Names and Common Ports

Description	Service Name	IP Protocol	Port
World Wide Web	HTTP, HTTPS	TCP	80, 443
File Transfer	FTP, FTP-DATA	TCP	21, 20
Electronic Mail	SMTP	TCP	25
	IMAPv4	TCP	143
	POP2, POP3	TCP	109, 110

Table 1.2 Continued

Description	Service Name	IP Protocol	Port
Domain Name Lookup	DNS	UDP, TCP	53
Usenet News	NNTP	TCP	119
Terminal Emulation	Telnet	TCP	23
Encrypted Telnet	SSH	TCP	22

Telnet

The Telnet protocol was at one time used to a much greater extent than it is today. Telnet exists for logging onto and using remote computers from a command line. This was the de facto method of computer use in the '70s, '80s and early '90s, but with the increased use of GUI interfaces, users became less willing to type commands. Microsoft and other companies were quick to provide dial-up services such as RAS (Remote Access Service), which allow people to use their GUI from a remote location. Strangely enough, however, Microsoft's Windows 2000 Server now comes with a Telnet host, perhaps as part of its new serious investment in TCP/IP.

HTTP

The Hypertext Transfer Protocol is possibly the most widely used protocol on the Internet today. It is, in fact, the protocol that drives the World Wide Web, the veritable killer app that brought the Internet into everyone's homes. HTTP is a method by which text and graphics can be hyperlinked and distributed across any number of networked computers making for a convenient and easy-to-use method of sharing data. HTTP reads documents written in HTML, the Hypertext Markup Language.

SMTP

The Simple Mail Transfer Protocol is one of the most popular protocols in the TCP/IP stack. But you don't need us to tell you that. SMTP is usually located at port 25.

Mail sent to an SMTP mailer is "spooled" or queued; this allows for mail to be backed up during peak hours without a larger investment in bandwidth or users having to sit at their terminals waiting for their mail to be delivered. SMTP handles mail on a first-come, first-served basis. When mail is being sent by one SMTP device, a connection is negotiated with the receiver either with or without authentication (not requiring authentication leaves you open to spammers relaying mail through your gateway—unpleasant when you receive 200 angry emails from spamming victims who think you're trying to sell hormone supplements to them).

FTP

FTP is an extraordinarily powerful tool for transferring files between remote computers. FTP uses TCP port 21, but FTP is different from many other protocols because it uses multiple connections to accomplish its task.

In addition to multiple connections, there are two flavors of FTP:

- **Active**—Active FTP uses a Telnet session for the control and commands. The data channel, however, is initiated from the FTP server back to the client on port 20, otherwise known as FTP-DATA. This causes a variety of problems that are discussed in Chapter 8, "Assessing Your Security Needs," and Chapter 10, "Implementing Security."

  The following is an example of an active FTP conversation between a client and a server:

  ```
  Client---->Server "get foobar.baz"
  Client<----Server SYN=1, ACK=0, Source Port=20
  Client---->Server SYN=1, ACK=1, Destination Port=20
  Client<----Server SYN=0, ACK=1, Source Port=20
  Client<----Server "here is foobar.baz"
  ```

- **Passive**—Passive FTP opens a second connection from the client to the server for the FTP-DATA connection. This is not negotiated on a well-known port, rather the server provides a port above 1024 in the reply to the PASV command. Because the connection is created from client to server, it is much easier to handle through firewalls and other security devices.

  The following is an example of a passive FTP conversation between a client and a server:

  ```
  Client---->Server "get foobar.baz"
  Client---->Server SYN=1, ACK=0
  Client<----Server SYN=1, ACK=1
  Client---->Server SYN=0, ACK=1
  Client<----Server "here is foobar.baz"
  ```

DNS

Until 1983, computer names were resolved into IP addresses through the use of files called "hosts," which contained mappings of all computer IP addresses and their names. Even in 1983 with the limited number of computers on the Internet, this was becoming unwieldy. The result was the development of DNS or the Domain Name System. DNS is a hierarchical naming system that allows local administrators to administer their own computer names and propagate those changes upstream.

The hierarchical method of domain naming starts from the current seven top-level domains:

- **.com**—A commercial domain.
- **.gov**—Government organizations.

- **.edu**—Educational facilities.
- **.arpa**—ARPAnet.
- **.mil**—Military outfits.
- **.org**—Usually nonprofit organizations.
- **.con**—Countries using the ISO abbreviations for their names. Recently Tobago (.to) sold a huge block of domain names to American entrepreneurs with clever names like go.to.

These domains are broken down into subdomains, as in macmillanusa.com or whitehouse.gov. These subdomains themselves can be broken down further into subdomains, such as sales.macmillanusa.com.

DNS is another quirky and troublesome protocol from a security perspective. DNS lookups from clients are different from DNS lookups from servers, which are different from DNS zone transfers.

Client DNS lookups are UDP based with a source port above 1024, with a destination port of 53. Server DNS lookups are also UDP based with a source and destination port of 53. Finally, DNS zone transfers between DNS servers are done on TCP port 53.

Internet Control Message Protocol (ICMP)

IP has no facility to report or correct errors. Therefore, it must rely upon something else to do so. That something else is ICMP. ICMP lives on the host or on a gateway and works as a partner to IP. When an error occurs, ICMP reports the error. It does this by burrowing into an IP packet and being transported across the network like a remora on a shark.

ICMP doesn't make IP work better; it only lets you know how badly it is working. TCP is responsible for error correction.

Figure 1.4 shows the ICMP format.

The following is a list of the ICMP messages and what they mean:

- **0**—Echo reply.
- **3**—Destination unreachable.
- **4**—Source quench.
- **5**—Redirect.
- **8**—Echo request.
- **11**—Time exceeded.
- **12**—Parameter problem.

- **13**—Timestamp. There are three timestamps: originate, receive, and transmit. They're used as you would expect. RFC 792 insists that timestamp values be in milliseconds after midnight Universal Time.
- **14**—Timestamp reply.
- **15**—Information request. This allows the host to find out specific information from the network, namely the IP address of the host and destination machines. Use of this has been largely replaced by RARP (Reverse Address Resolution Protocol).
- **16**—Information reply.

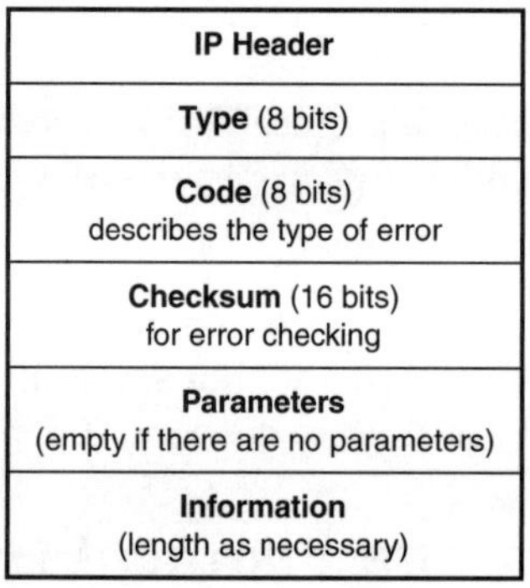

IP Header
Type (8 bits)
Code (8 bits)   describes the type of error
Checksum (16 bits)   for error checking
Parameters   (empty if there are no parameters)
Information   (length as necessary)

Figure 1.4   The format of an ICMP message inside an IP packet.

Ping

Ping is used to check the status of a remote computer. It basically just says "Hey, are you awake?" Although there are GUI ping clients for various operating systems, it's still usually typed at a command prompt in the form of the following:

```
ping www.macmillanusa.com
```

This would return (depending upon the configuration of the receiving computer) something like the following:

```
www.macmillanusa.com is alive.
```

There are numerous flags you can use along with the ping command for various types of troubleshooting. The flag -v will give a "verbose" response with more information. A typical verbose response would look more like this:

```
(/home/cassidy)% ping -v www.mcp.com
PING www.mcp.com (63.69.110.193): 56 data bytes
64 bytes from 63.69.110.193: icmp_seq=0 ttl=245 time=14.0 ms
64 bytes from 63.69.110.193: icmp_seq=1 ttl=245 time=21.2 ms
64 bytes from 63.69.110.193: icmp_seq=2 ttl=245 time=17.9 ms
64 bytes from 63.69.110.193: icmp_seq=3 ttl=245 time=12.0 ms
64 bytes from 63.69.110.193: icmp_seq=4 ttl=245 time=11.7 ms
64 bytes from 63.69.110.193: icmp_seq=5 ttl=245 time=15.5 ms
--- www.mcp.com ping statistics ---
6 packets transmitted, 6 packets received, 0% packet loss
round-trip min/avg/max = 11.7/15.3/21.2 ms
(/home/cassidy)%
```

This shows the average round-trip time (in microseconds) between the sending and receiving computers.

Ping uses the Internet Control Message Protocol (ICMP) to accomplish its magic. ICMP is IP protocol 1 as defined in RFC 792. There are several important ICMP types—one of these is traceroute.

traceroute is used to determine the route that a packet of data takes between its source and its destination. For example, if I wanted to find out how data was getting to the Macmillan USA site from my computer, I could use traceroute:

```
/home/c/cassidy/Mail>traceroute www.macmillanusa.com
traceroute to www.macmillanusa.com (63.69.110.193), 30 hops max, 40 byte packets
 1  brain.phl-core.fe0-0-100M.netaxs.net (207.8.186.81)  2 ms  1 ms  1 ms
 2  borgcube.phl-core.f0-0-0-100M.netaxs.net (207.8.186.85)  7 ms  7 ms  2 ms
 3  phl-gw.pennsauken.h2-0-45M.netaxs.net (207.106.2.206)  4 ms  3 ms  3 ms
 4  192.157.69.10 (192.157.69.10)  8 ms  7 ms  6 ms
 5  sl-bb12-pen-3-3.sprintlink.net (144.232.5.65)  7 ms  6 ms  6 ms
 6  sl-bb10-pen-10-0.sprintlink.net (144.232.5.154)  6 ms  6 ms  6 ms
 7  sl-gw12-pen-0-0-0.sprintlink.net (144.232.5.86)  7 ms  7 ms  7 ms
 8  sl-dnetny-1-0-T3.sprintlink.net (144.228.165.14)  34 ms  34 ms  36 ms
 9  216.90.236.210 (216.90.236.210)  37 ms  37 ms  38 ms
10  web05.ot.hdmss.net (63.69.110.67)  37 ms  43 ms  *
```

The primary function of traceroute is to find errors or bottlenecks. If you weren't able to reach a particular computer, running a traceroute would show where along the line the packet got held up. It's also useful for finding out who's "upstream" (providing service) for spammers.

Internet Protocol Version 6 (IPv6) and ICMPv6

When IP was designed, its creators didn't give much thought to the possibility that IP addresses would someday be in danger of running out, but they are. Mostly because of oddities in the way that addresses were initially distributed, huge portions of the available addresses were wasted. Documented in RFC 1752, the newest version of IP, version six (dubiously called by its creators "IPng" for "Internet Protocol, Next Generation"), addresses this issue by increasing the address space from 32 bits to 128 bits while maintaining backward compatibility with version 4 addresses. If 128 bits of address space doesn't impress you, consider the following factoids of IPv6 address size floating around the Internet:

If all the IPv6 addresses were evenly distributed across the Earth's surface, there would be roughly 423,354,243,695,259,002,656 per square inch.

There are 340,282,366,920,938,463,463,374,607,431,768,211,456 IPv6 addresses. That's roughly 313 million addresses per every cubic millimeter of Earth.

173 bits would be enough to address every proton and electron on Earth; 192 bits would be enough to address every proton and electron in the Solar System.

As with IPv4 initially, available addresses will not be a problem. Efficient address allocation will be the challenge. Hopefully, ICANN has learned from the past and as adoption of IPv6 occurs the allocation and waste of IPv4 will not be repeated. IPv6 will replace IPv4.

The following are some of the new features of IPv6:

- **Simplified header**—Although IPv6 addresses are longer, the header size is smaller and more efficient. This has been done by removing some of the header data fields and making others optional. The IPv6 header format is also considerably less complicated than the older version 4 header (see Figure 1.5).

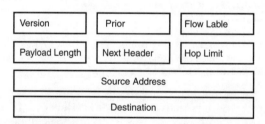

Figure 1.5 The compact IPv6 header.

- **Increased Addressing**—Increasing from 32 bits to 128 bits is enough to give every grain of sand on the planet its own IP address.
- **Authentication Capability/Privacy Capability**—IPv6 defines extensions that allow for authentication and privacy.
- **Quality of Service (QOS) Features**—Packets can be prioritized into particular lanes of traffic to ensure speedy delivery of time-sensitive data.

- **Version**—4 bits, defines the IP version of the packet. In this case, version 6. This is used to distinguish old IPv4 packets from IPv6 packets.
- **Priority**—4 bits, defines the priority of the packet.
- **Flow Label**—24 bits.
- **Payload Length**—16 bits, unsigned, defines the length of the data (in octets) following the header.
- **Next Header**—8 bits, defines the type of header that follows the IPv6 header. This uses the same data types as the old version 4 "protocol" field.
- **Hop Limit**—8 bits, unsigned, similar to "time to live." Each time the packet is forwarded, the value is decreased by one. When the value reaches zero, the packet is discarded.
- **Source address**—128 bits. The address of the origination of the packet.
- **Destination Address**—128 bits. The address of the destination of the packet. This could possibly be the address of a router rather than the final destination of the packet.

The new version of IP also gets rid of some infrequently used ICMP messages. There are 14 different messages available in the latest version of ICMP; these are broken down into two types:

- **Error Messages:**

  1 Destination Unreachable
  2 Packet too large
  3 Time exceeded
  4 Parameter problem

- **Informational Messages:**

  128 Echo request
  129 Echo reply
  130 Group membership query
  131 Group membership report
  132 Group membership termination
  133 Router solicitation
  134 Router advertisement
  135 Neighbor solicitation
  136 Neighbor advertisement
  137 Redirect

If you're interested, you can read all about this in RFC 1885.

2

UNDERSTANDING WAN BANDWIDTH DELIVERY

"We are in great haste to construct a magnetic telegraph from Maine to Texas; but Maine and Texas, it might be, have nothing important to communicate...as if the main object were to talk fast and not to talk sensibly."

Henry David Thoreau, Walden

Introduction to Bandwidth Delivery: How the Computer Crashed into the Telephone

There has been an electronic bandwidth infrastructure in this country since the 1800s when Samuel Morse's invention allowed messages to be sent long distances over copper wire nearly instantaneously. Since that time, there has been significant change in the way data is encoded and transmitted. These changes, and the inherent differences between *voice* and *data*, have created technology that is often at odds with one or the other. Because voice transmission has long been the goal of the telephone company (or *telco*), it is the transmission of data that usually suffers.

From the beginning, this communications infrastructure was torn between digital and analog. The initial form of communication over wire, Morse code, was digital in theory. Binary information was designated by short or long pulses (a dot being 0, a dash being 1), however, the transmission media was analog. The pulses were sent as voltage changes along copper line.

Later it was discovered that information could be sent significantly faster in a wholly analog form and voice transmission over wire took over. After all, who wants to tap out Morse code when you can talk instead? Very fast Morse code operators can send about thirty words a minute—how fast can you talk?

After many people began using voice over wire, the phone company became concerned that they would eventually run out of copper, or places to hang it. A town with 20 telephone owners could well afford 20 copper wires running from individual houses to the telco, but a city of 50,000 or half a million certainly could not.

The goal of transmitting multiple analog signals over a single piece of copper wire became absolutely necessary for telephone expansion to continue. Eventually, some clever person discovered *frequency division multiplexing* which allowed several conversations to be transmitted over a single pair of wires.

How does that work? Well, like many technological miracles, it uses methods that have existed since the beginning of history. In the same way that you can tune into one voice at a cocktail party and carry on a conversation with that one person while dozens of other people are talking, frequency division multiplexing allows computers to distinguish between multiple conversations going on at once by listening only for signals of a higher or lower frequency than the others.

To a certain extent, that's also the way it's done in frequency division multiplexed data signals. Now, you certainly don't want to be in a telephone conversation where you can hear a half dozen other people talking in the background, so the signals have to be separated at the telco, before they get to you. But how? It would be extremely difficult for any equipment belonging to the phone company to figure out what voice belongs with which conversation, so the signal is modified before it's bound to other signals. This is done by "painting" the signal to change its characteristics.

For example, you have the following four streams of numbers you want to send along the same wire:

6	12	9	3
8	9	12	21
6	6	14	9
17	11	3	7

If you just toss them on the wire, it will be impossible to sort them out, because the numbers are all very similar. However, if you add 100 to each number in column two, 200 to every number in column three, and 300 to every number in column four, you get numbers that are easy to separate at the receiving end:

6	112	209	303
8	109	212	321
6	106	214	309
17	111	203	307

So by adding a known quantity to the frequency of the signal, they're made unique. They're decoded at the telco and the proper conversation is sent to your house along your dedicated phone circuit. Figure 2.1 shows how it might look as sound waves.

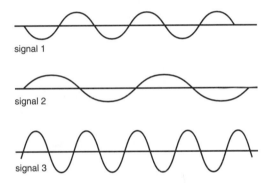

Figure 2.1 Frequency division multiplexing allows multiple signals to travel over a single wire.

Packet Switched Versus Circuit Switched Networks

Data transmission can either be Packet Switched or Circuit Switched. There are advantages to each.

Packet Switched

Large blocks of data are broken down into smaller parts, called *packets*. Each of these packets contains all the addressing information to get it from point A to point B. The packets take whatever route is available; there is no fixed path.

Circuit Switched

A path from point A to point B is negotiated at the beginning of the transmission and kept open until the end of the transmission. During that time nothing else can use that pipe.

The best example of circuit switched networking is a telephone call. You dial your best friend and a circuit is opened between your phone and hers. As long as you have the phones off the hook, that data pipe belongs to you. No one else can use it. If someone calls your house, they'll get a busy signal. A circuit switched network connection is the fastest and most reliable, but it suffers because no one else can use the line. If you were to take a one-hour phone conversation and add up all the fraction of seconds where there is silence on the line, you'll be left with a lot of silence. Every time you're transmitting silence, you're wasting bandwidth. Unlike people, computers only talk when they have something to say, so their conversations are much more direct. Hence, packet switched.

The Telco Engineers Versus the Network Engineers

When computers crashed into the phone company, there was some carnage. From the outset, telco engineers and computer network engineers were at design odds with one another. After all, they have entirely different goals. The primary goal of the telco is to deliver real-time voice transmission. This can be done at the expense of cost and accuracy. Cost is passed on down the line to the consumer, and accuracy...well, the assumption is that if there's a distracting noise in the background, people will retransmit themselves, usually in the manner of "Huh? What did you say Bob? There was a bus passing by just then." Network engineers are more concerned that data will be accurate and less concerned that it will be real-time. If faulty wiring causes a handful of static to be thrown into a telephone conversation, most people won't notice, but that same static could alter critical data in the transmission of a computer file resulting in errors.

What we are left with is a telephone infrastructure designed for analog voice through which digital computer data must be sent. There is a push today for an entirely digital telco that can serve both voice and data. To an extent, this is already happening. Much of the innards of the U.S. telephone system is digital; what remains is known as the "last copper mile", or the *local loop* of wiring between a consumer's house and the telco building. The investment in that wiring and telephones compatible with it is extensive and expensive, and its replacement will be hard fought.

For this reason, we have an amalgamation of technologies providing service in, sometimes, rather strange and kludgy ways.

Analog Modems

Analog modems are devices that provide a data connection over the *POTS*, or *plain old telephone service*. Today, the fastest analog modem, v.90, is 56Kbps—about the speed of the telephone company's internal digital connection. Although the modems are commonly referred to as 56Kbps, they can't send faster than 53Kbps because of FCC restrictions on maximum power transmission. Because of this and line noise problems inherent with analog modems, it's not likely that they will get any faster any time soon. This means that organizations looking to connect faster than that will need to look to other technologies for their future Internet connectivity needs.

At the low end of the Internet connectivity spectrum, small offices are making the choice between single or multiple analog modems and digital offerings such as ISDN, cable modems, or xDSL. Modems are still popular because of the ready availability of telephone lines, the relative ease of connecting a modem, and the fact that local calls are often included in local billing. The other options, ISDN, xDSL, and cable modems, have the advantage of being digital and therefore less prone to spurious noise. One problem with any new technology is that if it doesn't become widely adopted, chances are high that it will suffer the fate of the BetaMax and the Commodore Amiga.

Hierarchy of Dedicated Digital Services

Dedicated Digital Service (DDS) is a class of digital services ranging from 56Kbps leased lines to T3 trunks and beyond. It encompasses ISDN and the various incarnations of T. DDS represents the infrastructure of the telco, which, apart from the last copper mile, is almost entirely digital.

Physical Properties

Typically, DDS runs over two sets of twisted copper pair cable. There are two types of DDS: Short Haul Cables, which can run about 660 feet, and Long Haul Cables, which can run about 6,000 feet. After these distances, attenuation takes its toll and the signal must be repeated with an aptly named T1 repeater. Higher speed DDS, such as SONET/SDH, is available via fiber only.

Signal Encoding

There are several telecommunication-specific terms that we will use in following sections. We'll pause to define them here.

Signaling is the process of exchanging information between points that set up, control, and eventually terminate a call. There are two common methods of embedding the signaling: in-band and out-of-band.

In-band signaling sends control signals embedded in the same channel as the telephone call itself. In telecom parlance, a channel is just a path, real or virtual, through which signals can flow. *Out-of-band signaling* uses a dedicated channel just for control of the telephone call.

Signal encoding is the process of electronically transmitting the signal on the wire in a specific format. The telecom industry generally uses Return to Zero Bipolar Signaling or Alternate Mark Inversion (AMI). The signaling is synchronous and clocked. The term *synchronous*, in telecom, means that data can always be found in the same position at the same time. This is yet another reason for the all-important clocking and synchronization.

A 0 is signaled by no voltage on the line. Deviation, either positive or negative, indicates a 1 (hence the need for clocking). Typically, pulses alternate in polarity to maintain a 0 volt direct current on the line. If the signal didn't spend an equal amount of time above or below 0 it would eventually saturate the transformer. The alternating positive and negative voltage also serves as a form of error detection.

A *bipolar violation* occurs when two consecutive pulses in the same polarity are received; this is an indication of one or more bit errors. Bipolar violations are sometimes created intentionally because the bipolar error can be used as a third signal of sorts.

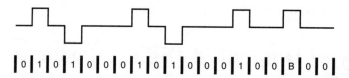

Figure 2.2   The signal is clocked, so every hash mark represents a number. Either positive or negative deviation from 0 represents a 1 bit. No voltage is a 0. A bipolar error (B) occurs when two like signed 1s occur in a row. This signals a transmission error. Sometimes, however, bipolar errors are performed intentionally for signaling purposes.

To maintain the 0 volt average on the line, Return to Zero Bipolar signaling has a requirement for "ones density"—at a minimum, there must be 12.5% (one bit in every eight) 1s to 0s ratio.

In other words, each 8-bit time slot must contain at least a single 1. So what do you do when you need to send a large block of 0s? There are several answers.

The first method is affectionately known as B7ZCS, Bipolar 7 with Zero Code Suppression. This is a form of bit-stuffing, adding bits to the data stream to ensure synchronization. The equipment sets a known bit (the Least Significant Bit) to 1. A voice listener would never be able to tell the difference, but it would really bug a computer. This encoding standard reduces the overall bandwidth to 56kbps rather than 64kbps.

ZBTSI, Zero Byte Time Slot Interchange, is a complicated method of encoding extra 0s by buffering part of them and moving them to a different channel. This method isn't commonly used because of the expense of the buffering hardware.

B8ZS, Bipolar with 8-zero Substitution, encodes a string of eight consecutive 0s into a series of 1s, 0s, and a specific pair of bipolar violations. B8ZS does not reduce your overall bandwidth, and thus is required for all "clear channel" 64kbps transmission rates (see Figure 2.3).

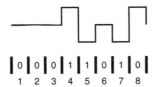

Figure 2.3   To code a string of eight 0s, B8ZS sends three 0s, two 1s, a 0, a bipolar error, and a 1.

In the basic DDS definition, because there's no separate signaling data channel, all signaling is done in-band; other line conditions such as idle, out of service, and loopback are also encoded using non-accidental bipolar violations.

DS0: The One True Standard

The DS0 is the building block of the telco. It is used both by itself and in aggregate forms. DS0 is the only DDS that is the same in the United States, Europe, and Japan.

The DS0 is the basic rate of 64Kbps used to transmit individual telephone calls; it is the building block of the telco's voice and data structure. Actual available bandwidth depends on the signal-encoding standard used. (Some signal encoding technologies, for example, allow multiple bits per baud, which can give a higher overall bit rate.)

The DS0 is different from those faster versions in that it doesn't use a framing format. Anything above 56Kbps is usually a fractional or full T1.

The data transport capability of the telco is based on variations of the DS0, as shown in Table 2.1.

Table 2.1   Speeds of Dedicated Digital Services

Name	Speed	Consists Of
DS0	64Kb/s	1 DS0
DS1	1.544Mb/s	24 DS0s
DS2	6.312Mb/s	96 DS0s
DS3	44.736Mb/s	28 DS1s

The following sections look at some of the more popular iterations in more detail.

DS1: the Ever Popular T1

The T1, in typical American trunk line voice/data networking terminology, is the bulwark of the phone system. Prior to 1983, T1 lines were only available to Bell Telephone internally, but with the breakup of AT&T, these lines became available to the public.

The bit rate of a T1 line is 1.544Mbps, 1.536Mbps of which is available for payload, the remaining 8Kbps is used for framing. A T1 is the aggregate of 24 64Kbps DS0s.

Although the T1 line consists of only two sets of twisted pairs (one transmit and one receive upon which there can be *zero* bridge taps), data is transmitted as though the T1 were actually physically made up of a group of 24 DS0s (referred to now as channels), which are Time Domain Multiplexed, meaning that data is first sent to one logical DS0, then the second, and so on based upon the clock sequence.

The same basic rules of the 56Kbps DDS apply to the T1. It uses the same Return to Zero Bipolar pulse stream that the 56Kbps DS0 uses.

Each T1 channel is like a line of soldiers marching in a parade. A drill instructor at the telco can use a DS Splitter to have some of the solders march off of their T1 and join another unit (this happens frequently when several partial T1s are combined). To make sure that all the data arrives at the destination at the right time and in the right order, it's not only imperative that each DS1 be synchronized with its own channels, but each must be synchronized with the channels of all the other DS1s as well. The synchronization must be consistent throughout the entirety of the telco. If each of the troops is marching to a different drummer, none of them will arrive at the same time and their formation will suffer, troops will get lost, or they'll show up after the battle or before the food. For this reason, a single clock in Hillsboro, Missouri pounds out a 1.544MHz drum beat which all the DS1 traffic in the country listens to, sending in as nearly perfect synchronization with it as is machinely possible.

The T1 Framing Format: Two Standards

This is the reserved 8Kbps control overhead that turns your 1.544Mbps T1 into a 1.536Mbps line. There are two framing format standards—D4 (superframe) and extended superframe.

Superframe (D4)

The control overhead in a D4 configured T1 circuit is purely to provide *frame synchronization*. A dozen frames make up a "superframe." The framing bits line up in a particular pattern (100011011100). The recipient uses this known pattern to discern which 8 bits belong to which channel.

Extended Superframe (ESF)

One thing vendors never seem to grasp when naming technology (perhaps because sales departments end up naming products) is that you should never call anything "super" or "advanced" or anything else with a similarly inflated moniker because a year later it's going to be yesterday's trash. Superframe was soon replaced by Extended Superframe, which added some new features. ESF has error correction in the form of Cyclic Redundancy Check (CRC6 specifically, the 6-bit version; CRC32 in TCP/IP is normally 32-bit). Additionally, Extended

Superframe allocates 4Kbps of the overhead as a facility data link. The facility data link gives the phone company the capability to interrogate the customer premise equipment for error statistics and line performance to aid in predicting and preventing line outages.

The T1 Frame

T1 frames are 193 bits and are sent at 8KHz. Each of the 24 channels (virtual DS0s) carries 8 bits of data plus a single framing bit ([24×8]+1 is 193). A dozen frames make up a *superframe*. The framing bits line up in a particular pattern (100011011100). The recipient uses this known pattern to discern which 8 bits belong to which channel. This is known as *frame synchronization*.

Extended Superframe also provides error detection and a separate data channel. It's twice the size of an ordinary superframe, 24 193-bit frames. The framing synchronization is provided by every fourth bit.

The following are the 24 framing bits:

```
1 2 3 4 5 6 7 8 9 10 11 12 13 14 15 16 17 18 19 20 21 22 23 24

· c - s · c - s ·  c  -  s  ·  c  -  s  ·  c  -  s  ·  c  -  s
```

s bits provide synchronization. c bits provide 6-bit CRC made up of the data in the superframe. Error checking is therefore continuous. - bits make up a 4Kbps auxiliary data channel used for monitoring and supervision of data transmission. Check out Figure 2.4 to see an example of a frame.

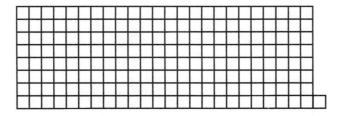

Figure 2.4   24 channels (across) of 8 data bits (up) to which is added a single one framing bit—192 data bits +1 = 193 bit frame. The first vertical row of 8 bits is sent first, followed by the second, on down the line. After the last set of 8 bits is sent, a single framing bit follows, and then the next frame.

T1 consists of 24 channels or "time slots," each 64Kbps (although it's possibly only 56Kbps will be available if "clear channel" is not supported. Clear channel is any signal encoding that does not require bit stuffing, so all 8 bits per channel are available for data payload). Each time slot/channel can be used for either voice or data.

Synchronization is required so that the receiving end can determine the beginning of each frame.

The frame synchronization sequence is odd so that the number won't be accidentally produced by a test tone.

When T1s first became available in the 1960s, they implemented a type of framing known as "D1," in which the frame bits were in a repetitive pattern of 10101010101010. This was confused by the telco's 1KHz test tone, which frequently generated this series of numbers. For this reason, the phone company adopted a 1,004Hz test tone. D1 framing itself was eventually discarded in favor of D4 (Superframe) and finally Extend Superframe (ESF). The complex frame sequence of ESF ensures that the sequence will not likely be reproduced accidentally.

The back channel can be used to see if telephones are on or off hook by reporting line voltages or other supervisory tasks.

For digitized voice over T1 trunks, line supervision is achieved through bit stealing, where on sixth and 12th frames a single bit is retasked to supervision.

Fractional T1

The fractional T1 is actually a whole T1. If you buy, for example, a half T1, the phone company can't actually give you a half a line, they give you a full T1 line and let you transmit and receive over 12 of the DS0 channels; the remaining channels just send 1s. Sound sneaky? It's not, really. After your fractional T1 gets to the telco, it's bundled with your neighbor's fractional T1 and actually fills a whole pipe internally (see Figure 2.5).

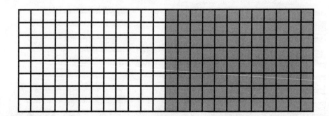

Figure 2.5   When purchasing a fractional T1 you actually get a whole T1. Think of the vertical columns as DS0 data pipes stacked 9 bits high. Some channels are available for data; the others (shaded) transmit nothing but 1s.

T3

T3 is equal to 28 T1 circuits. A T3 can carry 44.736Mbps. A DS3 is actually part of the *Plesiochronous Digital Hierarchy (PDH)* network (plesiochronous means "almost synchronous"). Individual calls cannot be teased out of a DS3 frame, rather the entire frame must be decomposed to its original constituent DS1 frames before individual calls can be added or removed from the data stream.

> **What Is Plesiochronous?**
>
> Synchronous signals are sent in the lock-step of marching fascist troops. The signals are clocked and governed by a super-accurate Primary Reference Clock (PRC). This is usually an atomic clock. There is no room for deviation.
>
> Plesiochronous signals are *almost* synchronous. They might be governed by two different atomic clocks. The signals are still very accurate, but nothing like synchronous. The difference between the two clocks is called the "plesiochronous difference."
>
> Asynchronous signals don't march in lock step at all.

Although PDH is the traditional method of multiplexing on T3s, it's being replaced by SONET (Synchronous Optical Network).

Fractional T3

A fractional T3 is functionally the same as a fractional T1, however the bandwidth is in multiples of T1s, somewhere between a single T1 and 28 T1s (which would be a full T3).

SONET

In 1984, the U.S. telephone carriers (regional Bells) and international phone companies sought a standard to replace their proprietary fiber infrastructure. Deciding upon a standard would allow them all to buy equipment from the same vendor pool, bringing down costs as well as expanding the amount of available equipment.

This task fell to ECSA, the Exchange Carriers Standards Association (now ATIS, Alliance for Telecommunications Industry Solutions) who developed SONET, for connecting disparate fiber networks.

SONET is a circuit-switched method of multiplexing over a fiber network. The multiplexing scheme is called "byte-interleaved." This sends time-divisioned signals from multiple sources over the same medium. The base signal in SONET multiplexing is called Transport Signal level-1, or STS-1. It's a 51.84Mbps signal. Multiplexing takes place at multiples of STS-1 (see Table 2.2).

Table 2.2   SONET Multiplexing Frequencies

Name	Frequency	Comparative DDS Bandwidth
STS-1, 51.840 Mb/s	28 DS1s	(1 DS3)
STS-3, 155.520 Mb/s	84 DS1s	(3 DS3s)
STS-12, 622.080 Mb/s	336 DS1s	(12 DS3s)
STS-48, 2488.320 Mb/s	1344 DS1s	(48 DS3s)
STS-192, 9953.280 Mb/s	5376 DS1s	(192 DS3s)

The STS frame is 90 bytes wide and 8 bytes deep. With 8 bits per byte and sent 8,000 times a second, this is 51,840,000 bits per second, or 51.840Mbps.

Although the Plesiochronous Digital Hierarchy (PDH) is the traditional method of multiplexing channels, it suffers from a number of problems. First, as its name implies, it's not completely synchronous. At rates above the DS1, it's *almost synchronous*. There was no standardization with international telephone systems. And interoperability between different vendors' equipment was not guaranteed, even though they were built to the same standards.

> Multiplexing different data streams together that do not have a single time reference can be a daunting task. This task is complicated by the fact that the data travels at different rates depending on temperature and distance. These factors and more mean that multiplexed DS1 data streams do not align. DS2 and DS3 multiplexed data streams are therefore not synchronous.
>
> Telco engineers worked around this asynchronous transmission problem using "bit stuffing." Adding additional bits here and there makes the multiplexed data streams difficult to address directly. To access a DS0 in a DS3, the DS3 first has to be demultiplexed down to 4 DS2s. Then the DS2 that contains the call that needs to be modified is demultiplexed down to 7 DS1s. At the DS1 rate, individual DS0s can be addressed. This process is expensive, both in terms of processing necessary to drop or add calls, and in terms of equipment necessary to do said processing.
>
> Synchronous transmission is by definition synchronized, and does not use bit stuffing. Therefore it is not as complicated a task to strip one data stream from a multiplexed pipe.

In 1987, Bellcore proposed SONET as a replacement for PDH to the CCITT. This original design of SONET was rejected by the CCITT. One of the main problems was that SONET was originally defined to transmit at 49.9Mbps, which works great with North American DS3s, but it does not accommodate European CEPT standards.

See the digital hierarchy in Figure 2.6.

Hierarchy Level	North American Bit Rate	Channels	European Bit Rate	Channels	Japanese Bit Rate
0	64	1 DS0	64	1 64 Kbps	64
1	1,544	24 DS0s	2,048	1 E1	1,544
2	6,312	96 DS0s	8,448	4 E1s	6,312
3	44,736	28 DS-1s (672 DS0s)	34,368	16 E1s	32,064
4	139,264	n/a	139,264	64 E1s	97,728

Figure 2.6   Plesiochronous Digital Hierarchy and comparative bit rates.

You can compare this to the SONET/Synchronous Digital Hierarchy (SDH) in Figure 2.7.

SONET Signal	Bit Rate Mbit/s	SDH Signal	SONET Capacity	SDH Capacity
OC-1 (STS-1)	51.84	STM-0	28 DS-1s or 1 DS-3	21 E1s
OC-3 (STS-3)	155.52	STM-1	84 DS-1s or 3 DS-3s	63 E1s or 1 E4
OC-12 (STS-12)	622.08	STM-4	336 DS-1s or 12 DS-3s	252 E1s or 4 E4s
OC-48 (STS-48)	2.488.22	STM-16	1344 DS-1s or 48 DS-3s	1008 E1s or 16 E4s
OC-192 (STS-192)	9,953.28	STM-64	5376 DS-1s or 192 DS-3s	4032 E1s or 64 E4s

Figure 2.7   The SONET/ Synchronous Digital Hierarchy.

Believe it or not, the Americans, the Europeans, and the Japanese were each able to make concessions and the CCITT (*Comité Consultatif International Téléphonique et Télégraphique*—now, after a 1992 reorganization, known as ITU, the International Telecommunication Union) produced a nearly unified Synchronous Digital Hierarchy (SDH) standard. Two major concessions were made to reach consensus. First, the Americans increased the basic rate of SONET from 49.92Mbps to 51.84Mbps. Second, the Europeans gave up on having their CEPT-2 and CEPT-3 PDH rates directly supported.

SDH is the proper international name for SONET/SDH networks. Although many people use SONET and SDH interchangeably, there are minor differences between the two, and SONET and SDH networks do not interoperate without conversion equipment. This equipment is trivial compared to that which was necessary for the PDH network.

SONET differs from the legacy PDH in many ways. Most important is that SONET synchronizes at bit rates faster than DS1. The capability to address individual DS0 channels without first having to demultiplex a DS3 several times is a multibillion dollar savings for the telco. Individual calls could be dropped or added without all the additional processing and equipment at each central office.

SONET transmits using a highly stable reference-clocking source for the entire SONET network. Because there is no need to synchronize clocks or align data streams, there is no need to do bit stuffing. In instances in which data might vary, pointers—similar in concept to pointers in the C programming language—in the SONET frame header are used to determine the exact offset of the data within the frame payload. This allows, for example, data in a DS1 to be directly accessed without first demultiplexing.

SONET itself is nothing more than a fast direct method of transporting data which is costly, but resistant to delays. SONET can carry many upper-level protocols: legacy PDH DS-3 and CEPT-4 circuits, FDDI, and, of course, ATM. The most important, at this point in time, is the support for legacy PDH technologies. This allows the telecom companies to deploy SONET while maintaining connectivity for their customer base, thus allowing a gradual phase-out of the aging PDH technology.

ISDN

Integrated Services Digital Network, or ISDN, is a digital connection that consists of two full duplex 64Kbps circuits called *Bearer channels* (or "B" channels), and one 16Kbps *Delta channel* (or the "D" channel), which is used for control and management. You could say that ISDN is a mutt of PSTN technologies (the dedicated B channels) and PSDN technologies (the packet-based D channel).

The B channels are used for carrying the digital information, whether computer data, digitized voice, or motion video. The D channel is dedicated between the phone company and you and handles out-of-band circuit management. This eliminates inbound management traffic from the B channels, generally providing you with a full 64Kbps bandwidth.

The D channel uses packets to establish phone call connections, send billing information, enable caller ID, enact charge reversal requests, and perform other nifty telco features.

A requirement of ISDN is that your office must be within 18,000 feet (about 3.4 miles or 5.5 km) of the telephone company central office for BRI (Basic Rate Interface) service; beyond that, expensive repeater devices are required, or ISDN service might not be available at all.

Originally an ISDN connection was difficult to install, configure, and troubleshoot. Although many advances in ISDN equipment have made inroads toward easing the installation and initial configuration of ISDN, it is still significantly more difficult to troubleshoot than other WAN technologies. That is mainly due to the way that ISDN was developed, nearly stillborn by committee. ISDN was first proposed in the late 1970s, and spent more than 10 years in the definition and approval process.

In 1988, after ISDN had been fully defined and approved, the world had changed. In North America, AT&T had been broken up, and it was no longer cost effective for the Regional Bells to foot the conversion bill necessary to get end-to-end digital. Only where entire telephone infrastructures were being rebuilt, such as those in Germany and France, was ISDN an attractive choice for the incumbent phone company.

Like many other networking protocols, ISDN covers the bottom three of the standard ISO levels: the Physical, Data Link, and Network Layers.

As expected, ISDN's Physical layer is oriented toward telephone wiring. There are two basic versions of this Physical layer interface that the public can choose from. These are the Basic Rate Interface (BRI) and Primary Rate Interface (PRI).

Basic Rate Interface (BRI)

BRI is designed to run through the last copper mile, or subscriber loop, of twisted pair wires running from your office to the local telephone exchange.

The subscriber loop is a twisted pair of 22 to 26 gauge copper wire that was designed to handle a rather narrow band of frequencies. The original specifications called for handling a range of 20–50 volts with frequencies less than 4,000 hertz. This isn't enough to carry a single channel of 64,000bps.

The interesting thing with ISDN is that there are three logical circuits. Two, each rated at 64,000bps, are known as B channels. These are called bearer channels because they carry the actual digitized data. The third channel in Basic Rate is the D channel. ISDN BRI service is often referred to by its designation of 2B+D.

Although most ISPs describe ISDN as 128Kbps, this is misleading. There are two separate 64,000-bit channels and no official specification for concatenating them into a single 128,000bps channel. There are, however, two competing industry standards for making use of both B channels to achieve 128Kbps throughput:

- Bandwidth On Demand Interoperability Group, called *BONDING*, is a set of protocols that lets you simultaneously use more than one of ISDN's 64Kbps B channels. BONDING is often referred to as multilink, channel aggregation, channel bonding, and load balancing.
- Multilink-PPP is a method for splitting, recombining, and sequencing datagrams across multiple logical data links. RFC-1717, the original specification for Multilink-PPP was defined in 1994 and later obsoleted in 1996 by RFC-1990. Although ISDN was the original motivation for Multilink-PPP, it's not specific to ISDN and can be applied to any number of multiple-link technologies.

The two B channels can be used independently of one another, to handle two different voice/data calls at once or to provide bandwidth on demand.

In the case of Basic Rate D channel, the bandwidth is 16Kbps. The channel is, in practice, used exclusively by the telephone companies for telephony signaling. Although the D channel can be used to carry data as well as control information, the capability to carry data on the D channel is generally vendor specific.

NT-1

The NT-1 is a relatively simple device that converts the two-wire U interface into the four-wire S/T interface. Today, many devices have NT-1s built into their design. This has the advantage of making the devices less expensive and easier to install, but often reduces flexibility by preventing additional devices from being connected.

Technically, ISDN devices must connect through a Network Termination 2 (NT-2) device, which converts the T interface into the S interface (the S and T interfaces are electrically equivalent). However, virtually all ISDN devices now include an NT-2 in their design. The NT-2 communicates with terminal equipment, and handles the Layer 2 and 3 ISDN protocols. Almost all ISDN devices expect either a U interface connection (and thus have a built-in NT-1), or an S/T interface connection.

S/T Interface

The S/T interface supports multiple devices (up to seven devices can be placed on the S/T bus) because, although it is still a full-duplex interface, there is now a pair of wires for receive data, and another for transmit data. The S/T interface is on the customer (user) side of the NT-1.

Devices that connect to the S/T (or S) interface include ISDN capable telephones and fax machines, video teleconferencing equipment, bridge/routers, and terminal adapters. All devices that are designed for ISDN are designated Terminal Equipment 1 (TE1). All other communication devices that are not ISDN capable, but have a POTS telephone interface (also called the R interface), including ordinary analog telephones, fax machines, and modems, are designated Terminal Equipment 2 (TE2). A Terminal Adapter (TA) connects a TE2 to an ISDN S/T bus.

Outside the United States, the telephone company supplies the NT-1 and the customer is provided an S/T interface.

U Interface

In the United States, the telephone company provides its BRI customers with a U interface. The U interface is a two-wire (single pair) interface from the phone switch on the far (switch) side of the NT-1. It supports full-duplex data transfer over a single pair of wires, therefore only a single device can be connected to a U interface.

The U interface is directly connected to the NT-1. This makes physical installation nearly as convenient as connecting an analog telephone.

Primary Rate Interface (PRI)

The Primary Rate Interface is designed explicitly for the American T1 and European E1 long-distance phone circuits. In the case of T1, the PRI supports 23 B channels at 64,000bps, and one 64,000bps D channel for at total of 24 channels. Not coincidentally, this is the exact number of channels in a North American T1. The European E1 version uses 30 B Channels each at 64,000bps and one 64,000bps D channel. The remaining E1 channel is still used for timing.

Unlike Basic Rate Interface, there are officially defined methods to aggregate several B channels to form larger capacity channels in PRI. These methods are the H channels:

■ H0=384Kbps (6 B channels)
■ H10=1472Kbps (23 B channels)

- H11=1536Kbps (24 B channels)
- H12=1920Kbps (30 B channels)—International (E1) only

These 6, 23, 24, and 30 standard B channels are designed to work either on the American T1 (H0 and H11) or the European E1 (H0 and H12) cables.

ISDN Layer 1—Physical

The ITU I-series and G-series documents specify the ISDN Physical layer. The U interface provided by the telephone company for BRI is a 2-wire, 160Kbps digital connection. The mojo used to provide 160Kbps over the last mile is powerful. Powerful invocations of Echo cancellation are used to reduce noise. Data encoding schemes (2B1Q in North America, 4B3T in Europe) permit this relatively high data rate over ordinary single-pair local loops.

2B1Q

2B1Q (2 Binary 1 Quaternary) is the most common signaling method on U interfaces (see Table 2.3). This protocol is defined in detail in the 1988 ANSI spec T1.601. In summary, 2B1Q provides the following:

- Two bits per baud
- 80,000 baud per second
- Transfer rate of 160Kbps

Table 2.3   2B1Q Signaling Interface Values

Bits	Quanternary Symbol	Voltage Level
00	-3	-2.5
01	-1	-8.833
10	+3	+2.5
11	+1	+0.388

This means that the input voltage level can be one of four distinct levels (0 volts is not a valid voltage under this scheme). These four voltage levels are called Quaternaries. Each level represents 2 data bits, and because there are four possible ways to represent 2 bits, that works out to be a clever implementation.

Frame Format

Each U interface frame is 240 bits long. At the defined data rate of 160Kbps, each frame is therefore 1.5 milliseconds long. The frame header is shown in Figure 2.8.

Sync 18 bits	12 * (B1 + B2 + D) 216 bits	Maintenance 6 bits

Figure 2.8   The U interface frame format.

The Sync field consists of nine Quaternaries (2 bits each) in the pattern 1010 0000 0010 0010 00.

(B1 + B2 + D) is 18 bits of data consisting of 8 bits from the first B channel, 8 bits from the second B channel, and 2 bits from the D channel.

The Maintenance field contains CRC information, block error detection flags, and additional maintenance commands used for loopback testing without disrupting user data.

Data is transmitted in a Superframe format consisting of 8 240-bit frames for a total of 1,920 bits (240 octets). The sync field of the first frame in the Superframe is inverted (that is, 0000 1010 1000 1000 10).

ISDN Layer 2—Data Link

The ISDN Data Link layer is specified in the ITU Q-series documents Q.920 through Q.923. Link Access Protocol-D channel (LAP-D) is defined in Q.921. LAP-D is almost identical to the X.25 LAP-B protocol.

LAP-D works in the Asynchronous Balanced Mode (ABM). This mode is totally balanced (that is, no master/slave relationship). Each station can initialize, supervise, recover from errors, and send frames at any time. The protocol treats the DTE and DCE as equals.

Figure 2.9 shows the structure of a LAP-D frame.

Flag	Address	Control	Information	CRC	Flag

Figure 2.9   The structure of a LAP-D frame.

The following are the bits and pieces of the Lap-D frame:

- **Flag (1 octet)**—This bit pattern is always 0111 1110. To ensure that this pattern never occurs in the data portion of the frame, bit stuffing is used. You can see this in Figure 2.10.

Address (2 octets)							
8	7	6	5	4	3	2	1
SAPI (6 bits)						C/R	EA0
TEI (7 bits)							EA1

Figure 2.10   Bit stuffing keeps the bit pattern 0111 1110 from accidentally occurring in nature.

- **SAPI (Service access point identifier)**—This is a 6-bit field that identifies the point where Layer 2 provides a service to Layer 3 (see Figure 2.11).

SAPI	Description
0	Call control procedures
1	Packet Mode using Q.931 call procedures
16	Packet Mode communications procedures
32-47	Reserved for national use
63	Management Procedures
Others	Reserved for Future Use

Figure 2.11   The Service Access Point Identifier.

- **C/R (Command/Response) bit**—Indicates whether the frame is a command or a response. Frames from the user with this bit set to 0 are command frames, as are frames from the network with this bit set to 1. Other values indicate a response frame.
- **EA0 (Address Extension) bit**—Always set to 0.
- **EA1 (Address Extension) bit**—Always set to 1.
- **TEI (Terminal Endpoint Identifier)**—7-bit device identifier. TEIs are unique IDs given to each device (the Terminal Endpoint) on an ISDN S/T bus (see Figure 2.12). This identifier can be dynamically assigned by the ISDN switch or the value can be assigned statically when the device is installed.

TEI	Description
0-63	Fixed TEI assignments
64-126	Dynamic TEI assignment (assigned by the switch)
127	Broadcast to all devices

Figure 2.12   Terminal Endpoint Identifiers identify the end points of an ISDN device.

- **Control (2 octets)**—The frame level control field indicates the frame type (Information, Supervisory, or Unnumbered) and sequence numbers, control features, and error tracking.
- **Information**—Layer 3 protocol information and user data.
- **CRC (2 octets)**—Cyclic Redundancy Check is a low-level test for bit errors on the user data.

ISDN Layer 3—Network

The ISDN Network layer is specified by the ITU Q-Series documents Q.930 through Q.939. The Networking layer of ISDN is used for the establishment, maintenance, and termination of logical network connections between two devices.

SPIDs

The Service Profile Identifier, or SPID, is used to identify the ISDN device to the telephone network, much as an Ethernet address uniquely identifies a network interface card. A SPID (or more than one, if necessary) is assigned when you order the ISDN Basic Rate Interface (BRI) from the phone company. Although optional, without a SPID ISDN devices won't work on most lines. If an ISDN line requires a SPID, but it isn't correctly supplied, then Layer 2 initialization will take place, but Layer 3 will not, and the device will not be able to place or accept calls.

Beginning in 1998, most phone companies began to use a generic SPID format. In this format, the SPID is a 14-digit number that includes your 10-digit telephone number, a 2-digit Sharing Terminal Identifier, and a 2-digit Terminal Identifier (TID). With the introduction of the generic SPID format, the installation of an ISDN line was simplified because the SPID could easily be communicated to users.

Information Field Structure

The Information Field is a variable length field that contains the Q.931 protocol data (see Figure 2.13):

Information Field							
8	7	6	5	4	3	2	1
Protocol Discriminator							
0	0	0	0	Length of Call Reference Value			
Flag	Call Reference Value (1 or 2 octets)						
0	Message Type						
Mandatory & Optional Information Elements							

Figure 2.13   The structure of the Information Field.

- **Protocol Discriminator (1 octet)**—Identifies the Layer 3 protocol.
- **Length (1 octet)**—Indicates the length of the next field, the Call Reference Value. The Call Reference might be one or two octets long depending on the size of the value being encoded.
- **Call Reference Value (CRV) (1 or 2 octets)**—Used to uniquely identify each call on the user-network interface between the device making the call and the ISDN switch. This is an arbitrary value assigned at the beginning of a call and allocated for the entire call duration.
- **Message Type (1 octet)**—Identifies the message type. This determines what additional information is required and allowed.
- **Mandatory and Optional Information Elements (variable length)**—Options that are set depending on the message type.

Digital Subscriber Line (XDSL, aDSL, sDSL)

xDSL ranges from 6.1Mbps to 155Mbps incoming and from 600Kbps to 15Mbps outgoing. The "x" is a wildcard that can be aDSL (asynchronous) or sDSL (synchronous). xDSL uses digital encoding to provide more bandwidth over existing twisted pair telephone lines. (POTS). Many iterations of xDSL allow the phone to be used for data communication at the same time it's being used to transmit data. This is because phone conversations use frequencies below 4KHz above which xDSL tends to operate. Several types of xDSL modems come with "splitters" for using voice and data concurrently.

xDSL connections use frequencies of over 4,000KHz to achieve their great bandwidth. This comes at the expense of attenuation. The two most popular types of line coding, CAP and DMT, use lower frequencies and therefore are able to support longer loops between the user and the phone company. You can see a breakdown of their capacity in Figure 2.14.

Type of Connection	Maximum Transfer Rate	Maximum Distance from the Phone Company
56 K Analog Modem	56 kbit/s	None
ADSL	1.5 - 8 Mbs/s Downstream Up to 1.544 Mbit/s Upstream	3.4 miles
HDSL	T1 - 1.544 Mbs/s (2 twisted pair connections) E1 - 2.048 Mbit/s (3 twisted pair connections)	2.2 miles 3.4 miles
SDSL	T1 - 1.544 Mbs/s E1 - 2.048 Mbs/s	2 miles
VDSL	13 - 52 Mbs/s incoming 1.5 - 2.3 Mbs/s outgoing Up to 34 Mbs/s if symmetric	2.2 miles 3.4 miles
R-ADSL	1.5 - 8 Mbs/s incoming Up to 1.544 Mbit/s outgoing	3.4 miles

Figure 2.14   Bit rates of the various xDSLs.

ADSL

Asymmetric Digital Subscriber Line (ADSL) is asymmetric because of its relatively high capacity to download data when compared to its lower upload capacity. ADSL allows you an 18,000-foot loop from the phone company and is capable of transmitting at speeds of up to 8Mbps over ordinary twisted copper pairs. ADSL allows for a splitter box that lets users talk on the telephone at the same time data is being transmitted. The asymmetric speed of ADSL is appropriate for home users who typically draw more from the Internet than they send out to it. ADSL uses Carrierless Amplitude Phase Modulation (CAP) or Discrete Multi Tone (DMT).

R-ADSL

The speed of a Rate Adaptive Digital Subscriber Line (R-ADSL) is dependent on the capacity of the twisted pair it's running over. R-ADSL allows for on-the-fly determinations of proper transmit and receive speeds based upon the quality of the connection, length of the loop, and type of wire being used in the loop. It should be used in situations in which the quality of the line connection is variable or affected by weather. R-ADSL also allows for a splitter. It transmits data using CAP.

HDSL

HDSL (High-Speed Digital Subscriber Line) is the result of early 1990s research into approaching T1 and E1 speeds (1.5- and 2.0Mbps respectively) over POTS. HDSL uses the same encoding methods employed by ISDN and employs two sets of phone lines. It also employs a higher number of bits per baud. The incoming and outgoing speeds of HDSL are identical.

IDSL

ISDN Digital Subscriber Line (IDSL) technology ports ISDN functionality to DSL. It permits data speeds of 128Kbps over ordinary twisted pair phone lines in loops of 18,000 feet. IDSL is capable of using the same hardware as ISDN. IDSL has the advantage of being able to use any transport protocol that ISDN can, such as PPP or Frame Relay. IDSL uses the same 2B1Q line coding that ISDN does. IDSL does not support voice transmission.

VDSL

Very High Digital Subscriber Line (VDSL) suffers from extremely high attenuation, resulting in loop lengths of only about 3,000 feet.

SDSL

Symmetric Digital Subscriber Line (SDSL) is symmetrical in that the incoming and outgoing bandwidth is the same. SDSL can duplicate T1 or E1 speeds over normal twisted pair (copper) phone cable for distances up to 11,000 feet (looped, so you must be within about one wire mile of your telephone company). SDSL uses Carrierless Amplitude Phase modulation (CAP).

Splitterless DSL or DSL-Lite

DSL-Lite has no splitter box and is less expensive than other forms of DSL. It provides data-only communication and requires no interventive hardware setup on the user end. Because it isn't cost effective to replace the copper wire infrastructure with fiber, there has been a great leap to trying to send more data across the existing wire. Both Carrierless Amplitude Phase Modulation (CAP) and Discrete Multi Tone (DMT) use the unused high frequencies of the phone line to encode multiple bits of data in each signal.

Carrierless Amplitude Phase Modulation (CAP)

CAP is a variation on Quadrature Amplitude Modulation (QAM), which has been used in analog modems for several years. CAP divides the frequency spectrum into the POTS spectrum (0–4KHz), downstream data, and upstream data.

QAM is a method for encoding digital data on an analog signaling system. QAM uses a combination of amplitude and phase variations to provide more than one bit per signal, or baud. Generally QAM is represented by a map that lays out a bit pattern on a coordinate axis (see Figure 2.15). The combination of amplitude and phase will always map to a certain number of points.

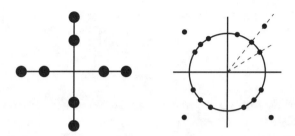

Figure 2.15   Changes in amplitude modulation (left) and phase shift (right) allow for one baud (signal) to have multiple meanings. This allows for significantly faster data transmission.

Take for example the simple QAM of two possible amplitudes and four possible phase shifts. Combining the two possible amplitudes and the four possible phase shifts gives you a total of eight possible wave forms. This can be mapped out in a table rather easily (see Figure 2.16).

Bit Value	Amplitude	Phase Shift
000	1	none
001	2	none
010	1	90
011	2	90
100	1	180
101	2	180
110	1	270
111	2	270

Figure 2.16   Bit values of phase and amplitude shift.

It is quite convenient that this example has eight possible wave forms, as that can easily be represented by 3 bits. Using Figure 2.16, say you wanted to transmit the following data:

```
001010100011101000011110
```

You would first break it down into 3-bit representations. You can see how each 3-bit value maps to a specific wave combination:

```
001-010-100-011-101-000-011-110
```

The whole point is to transfer more than one bit of data per signal.

There is no carrier frequency transmitted in CAP. Three channels are allocated: POTS, upstream data, and a high-speed downstream data. Each channel is separated in the frequency domain.

Data modulates a single carrier and is transmitted down a phone line. The carrier is removed before transmission and added again at the receiving end.

Discrete Multi Tone (DMT)

Copper lines distort heavily at the high frequencies used by ADSL circuits. DMT is particularly good at overcoming this. DMT was developed by Amati Communications in collusion with Stanford University. Originally, it was intended for sending video over copper. Actually a form of Frequency Division Multiplexing (FDM), Discrete Multi Tone is a multicarrier modulation that divides the available channel into individual subchannels called tones. Each of these tones has the same bandwidth, but is modulated on a separate carrier. There are 256 different tones that range from 20KHz to 1.024MHz at 4KHz intervals.

DMT dynamically adjusts to compensate for line noise, allocating subcarriers with a high signal-to-noise ratio to the highest spectrum.

Loading Coils

Some telephone lines are equipped with induction devices called *loading coils*. The loading coil is designed to improve voice transmission over POTS when the local loop is more than 18,000 feet (the last three copper miles). It does this by compensating for the capacitance of the wire and raises the frequency. This is nice for voice transmission; however, a side effect is the distortion of high frequency signals. This distortion will annoy xDSL. Ask your telephone company about its procedure for removing loading coils from xDSL connections.

Cable Modems

Cable data modems are a recent entry into the data bandwidth delivery arena. Only in the last several years have any real standards emerged in cable modem interoperability. Whatever the cable provider was using for equipment, you had to use as well. (This is somewhat common in the IT business.)

CableLabs created an interoperability standard known as Data Over Cable Service Interface Specification (DOCSIS). CableLabs also is responsible for interoperability and conformance testing of cable data modem products.

Cable companies realized when the Internet started to become popular that they had an enormous opportunity to expand their revenue bases. New media-rich services available on the Internet required more bandwidth than the plain old telephone system could deliver. The telephone companies were having difficulty, or lack of vision, in deploying ISDN. The raging hot new xDSL technologies were not even on the reading edge of trade rags. There was definitely a bandwidth void that needed to be filled.

The cable companies had broadband wire already in the ground to a large percentage of the population of North America. All they had to do was upgrade their infrastructure to ensure data reliability; after all, some snow in your cable TV reception is significantly different than lost data in a computer transaction.

First order of business for the cable companies was to upgrade the cable from coaxial to fiber at the Head End, the endpoint at the cable provider's facility. With the installation of fiber there, and coaxial at the customer's premises, the cable plant network became known as hybrid fiber-coaxial, or HFC networks.

Digital data is carried over radio frequency (RF) carrier signals on the HFC network. Cable Data modems convert digital information into a modulated RF signal and convert RF signals back to digital information. The conversion is performed by a cable modem at the subscriber's premises, and again by Head End equipment handling multiple subscribers.

Shared Network Technologies

Broadcast video is highly bandwidth intensive. If you recall, telephone quality voice requires only 3KHz of frequency spectrum to be reproduced. CD-quality stereo audio requires 44KHz of the frequency spectrum. Current broadcast video requires 4.2MHz, which is ten times more. The next generation of broadcast video, HDTV, requires 30MHz for *each* color signal. That would be 90MHz were it not for high compression ratios, inter-frame differential predictive encoding, and other niceties found in the MPEG-2 standard. After HDTV is compressed and encoded, it fits neatly into the 6MHz allocated for channels by the See Federal Communications Commission>Federal Communications Commission (FCC).

For normal television operation, the customer's television receiver selects the channel to watch by tuning to a 6MHz portion of the assigned spectrum. The FCC allocated frequency channels in such a way to prevent interference with each other. The end result of this allocation scheme is that most of the terrestrial broadcast television spectrum is vacant.

Between the poor allocation of the terrestrial broadcast television spectrum and the burgeoning number of available channels to watch, there is insufficient spectrum to accommodate the appetite of today's viewer. The large number of available channels on cable television is made possible by the use of coaxial cable. Coaxial cable is able to separate the frequency spectrum from the terrestrial broadcast spectrum while maintaining the properties of the spectrum that allow it to work with existing equipment. This means that a television receiver connected to a cable signal will behave as it does when connected to an antenna. The frequencies that are, in the broadcast world, reserved for use by air traffic, commercial, and military communication are now available to carry additional channels because those frequency channels are limited to the coaxial cable and do not interfere with the terrestrial broadcast television spectrum.

A single 6MHz channel can support multiple data streams or multiple users through the use of shared network technologies. Different modulation techniques can be used to maximize the data speed that can be transmitted through a 6MHz channel. Modulation techniques that you're already aquainted, if not familiar, with are Quadrature Phase Shift Keying (QPSK), Quadrature Amplitude Modulation (QAM), and Vestigial Side Band (VSB) amplitude modulation. VSB-AM is an artifact of the NTSC broadcast protocol and the fact that the original televisions were built using expensive tubes.

More on Sharing

Sharing usually implies taking a whole product and dividing it up equally among all participating members. This same reasoning does not apply to the world of shared bursty packetized data networks. Five users sharing a 10Mbps Ethernet do not effectively have 2Mbps of throughput each. Ethernet networks, LANs, and data communications in general would not scale very well if this line of reasoning held true.

A data over cable shared access network provides roughly 30Mbps burst capacity. If you remember from Frame Relay, the capability to deliver requested data at the port speed is known as the network's burst capacity. On standard telecom dedicated circuits, such as a 64Kbps DS0, there are only 64Kbps of throughput burst capacity available to a single user. It is impossible for that user to borrow additional unused capacity from other idle users.

Contrast that with a shared access network. A user can use the full bandwidth of the shared resource, and then release that resource for allocation to the other users. If you remember, as with Frame Relay and ATM, the ability to use a resource only when needed provides great performance benefit, as well as inherent economic benefit to both the service provider and the customer.

The portion of bandwidth reserved for upstream traffic (from the customer to the cable network) is usually in the 5–40MHz portion of the spectrum. This portion of the spectrum can be subject to interference, so if you see snow or other interference patterns on your lower six channels, most likely your data is also being affected. Upstream bandwidth is usually asymmetric to the downstream. Most cable providers provide 128–768Kbps upstream bandwidth to a nominal 3Mbps downstream bandwidth. This situation should eventually change after cable companies convert the rest of their cabling and equipment infrastructure to accommodate the return traffic. This is obviously driven by demand, so if customers don't demand fast or at least symmetric sending speeds, the cable companies are not likely to provide them.

Frame Relay

Frame Relay uses the Public Switched Data Network (PSDN), and is thus a packet-switching technology that is in common use for WAN connectivity. Frame Relay differs significantly from the circuit-switched point-to-point technologies, such as the North American T1. The most significant difference is that Frame Relay networks consist of many nodes sharing the same physical network.

The Frame Relay node at the customer location talks to a network switch. This connection is a private line between the customer and the Frame Relay network. The remote location mirrors this configuration.

Circuit Switched Versus Packet Switched

Circuit-switched technology provides dedicated bandwidth between endpoints. This makes it significantly easier to provide quality of service (QoS) in terms of voice quality and delay. This same attribute, dedicated bandwidth between endpoints, means that use of network resources is poor.

Packet-switched networks are more economic in resource use. Because there is no dedicated channel that might not be carrying any traffic, the full bandwidth of the circuit is available to carry the packetized data. Unfortunately for real-time communications, the variables of congestion and delay can seriously affect the quality of service of voice and video traffic.

Advantages of Frame Relay

There are some immediately obvious advantages to considering Frame Relay, for both the customer and ISP.

First and foremost, it is generally less expensive than traditional point-to-point circuits. There are several reasons for this. Consider the following:

- You are purchasing a shorter dedicated circuit. The private line between the Customer Premises Equipment (CPE) and the Frame Relay network switches at the local telco.
- The ISP can be much further away. Because Frame Relay uses packet-switching technology and not dedicated circuit-switching technology, Frame Relay is not billed per mile. You are now free to pick the ISP with the best service and price without being limited to local only choices.
- Usually, the ISP already has an existing CPE. If the ISP already offers Frame Relay, they do not necessarily have to purchase new equipment as they would if supporting a dedicated point-to-point circuit.
- The ISP can aggregate many customers onto a single physical circuit. Generally speaking, 40 56Kbps Frame Relay connections can be handled over a single DS1 rate circuit.

The Max Burst rate permits data to transmit as fast as the circuit's capacity. This works out quite well for short bursts of traffic.

Frame Relay is also widely deployed, which is a major concern for newer technologies such as xDSL and Cable.

All these advantages don't come free, however. There are disadvantages to Frame Relay, but they might not affect your requirements for a circuit. The major disadvantage of Frame Relay is caused by the same design that provides the advantages. Because Frame Relay is a packet-switched technology, latency is introduced in the processing of each packet at every Frame Relay switch. This should be negligible for short distances, but it adds up over long distances. A rule of thumb is that for every 1,000 circuit miles expect 20ms of latency.

Frame Relay is available in any combination of fractional DS1 rates. Common Frame Relay capacities include 128-, 256-, 384-, 512-, 768-, 1024-, and up to 1,544Kbps for North American T1 and 2,048Kbps for European E1.

Components of Frame Relay

There are five major components of Frame Relay: the Data Link Connection Identifier (DLCI), the Permanent Virtual Circuit (PVC), Switched Virtual Circuit (SVC), the Committed Information Rate (CIR), and Local Management Interface (LMI).

Data Link Connection Identifier (DLCI)

In every packet-switched network, including Frame Relay, each packet must know its source and destination addresses. This is similar to the Layer-2 Data Link Media Access Control (MAC) address used in modern LAN technologies. In Frame Relay, the addressing information is contained in the packet header as the DLCI.

The Data Link Connection Identifier, or DLCI, is attached to data frames on the Frame Relay network. This information is used to route the frames within the telecom network.

Another use of the DLCI is to differentiate between virtual connections on the same physical port. Packets for several different virtual ports are statistically multiplexed onto the physical port to be transmitted. The aggregated logical connections can co-exist on a single physical port because it's the DLCI that logically binds the data to the connection.

Permanent Virtual Circuit (PVC) and Switched Virtual Circuit (SVC)

If you've been paying attention thus far, you know that in a Frame Relay architecture you have a physical dedicated circuit between your CPE and the telecom's network switch. The same configuration exists at your ISP's location. Because between those two network switches the data is packet switched, there is no guarantee that the path the data travels is consistent. This is why Frame Relay networks are generally represented by a cloud in diagrams. In reality, the data generally travels the same path; it would only travel different routes if there were significant amounts of congestion or hardware failure.

The path between the telecom switches is commonly referred to as a *virtual circuit*. This is an apt description, because there is no actual dedicated circuit, and your data can travel over many physical paths and switches. Because variety is the spice of life, there is of course a choice of virtual circuits.

The Switched Virtual Circuit (SVC) is constructed when there is a need to pass data. After some defined threshold has been reached (such as no traffic for the past 30 seconds), the virtual circuit is torn down. This acts in many respects like the normal analog phone system.

The Permanent Virtual Circuit (PVC), shown in Figure 2.17, is preconfigured to connect to specific DLCI. The circuit is always available and always connected. Most ISPs deploy Frame Relay using PVCs.

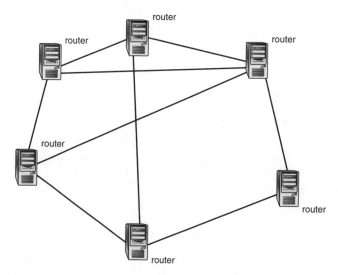

Figure 2.17   In a Frame Relay PVC mesh, each router has at least two connections set up in a ring. It's fast, but the problem is that you're paying for each of these lines.

Using PVCs, the ISPs can now use the DLCI to define logical connections to virtual ports in the routers over a single physical circuit.

An extremely useful application of PVCs can be demonstrated when you want to connect multiple sites together directly, but cost-effectively. Frame Relay does not have to be deployed in strictly a point-to-multipoint configuration. There are several applications of deploying a mesh of PVCs between remote locations, providing multiple virtual paths and direct routes between remote locations without having to first travel through your ISP's router. You have to pay for each PVC defined through the Frame Relay network, but the performance tradeoff might be worth the additional expense. Figure 2.18 shows an example of a mesh of PVCs.

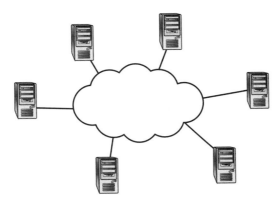

Figure 2.18   In a switched virtual circuit, numerous connections exist within the mesh; they are created and destroyed as necessary.

Committed Information Rate (CIR)

The second major difference between Frame Relay and dedicated point-to-point circuits is how the circuit capacity is described. Dedicated point-to-point circuits are just that: dedicated. If you send no data, the channel timeslots are still allocated to your circuit.

Remember that Frame Relay is a shared network using packet-switched technology. The intent is to use the full capacity of the circuits, whether or not you're transmitting any data. Therefore in a shared environment, there needs to be some provisions to make sure that you get what you're paying for.

The Committed Information Rate (CIR) has been described as the worst-case throughput that the Frame Relay network provider attempts to guarantee.

The physical port speed is the absolute maximum data rate accepted by the Frame relay network provider. The port speed is generally twice that of the CIR.

Frame Relay uses the LAPF variant of HDLC as the transmitting protocol used to physically put frames on the Frame Relay network. HDLC is a synchronous protocol, meaning that it is synchronized to a clock source. LAPF and HDLC are defined at Layer 2 of the OSI model. When data is transmitted, the whole frame is transmitted at the clock speed, thus bursting over CIR because there is no way to slow down the data.

The difference between the guaranteed CIR and the Port speed is available on a best-effort-only basis.

Local Management Interface (LMI)

Local Management Interface (LMI) is a keep-alive mechanism to periodically check to make sure the interface is still active. Additionally, it is used to give the end user circuit status information such as whether the link is congested.

There are three versions of LMI:

- **LMI**—The Frame Relay Forum Implementation Agreement (IA) FRF.1, which has been superseded by FRF.1.1.
- **Annex D**—As defined in ANSI T1.617.
- **Annex A**—ITU 933 as referenced in FRF.1.1.

Unfortunately LMI is the generic term used to describe all protocols rather than specifically IA FRF.1. As with practically all standards, the three versions of LMI are not interoperable. LMI is fairly ubiquitous. Most vendors support Annex D, although very few vendors support Annex A.

Congestion and Delay

Delay and congestion are a direct result of the shared nature of packet network resources. Each piece of the packet-switched data network introduces delays because of the processing that occurs at each node to determine the next hop for the packet.

Delay is synonymous with *latency*, which is the time required for transmission from origin to destination. Latency is usually measured in milliseconds. The threshold for delay interval intolerance for humans is roughly 250ms.

Delay is not a problem in circuit-switched networks because each call uses a reserved circuit. Congestion exists in circuit-switched networks only when all available timeslots are used. You might be familiar with the phrase "All circuits are busy." In a circuit-switched network, this is easily addressable by adding network capacity in appropriate locations.

Shared packet-switched networks are much more dynamic and bursty. Frame Relay networks aggregate multiple PVCs onto a single physical circuit. When there is more aggregated data in the network than there is bandwidth, you have congestion. This is similar to merging five lanes of traffic into two lanes over a bridge. This normally doesn't cause a problem for 20 hours a day, but during rush hour it seems to have an effect on people's blood pressure.

The Frame Relay Forum has defined several mechanisms to handle the congestion problem. Several bits are defined in the Frame Relay header that allow network switches to notify other switches or Frame Relay end-nodes of impending congestion (see Figure 2.19).

The Forward Explicit Congestion Notification (FECN) bit is added to a congested frame. The receiving Frame Relay network router detects that congestion is occurring when it receives the FECN from the network switch.

Extension Bit: 1 bit
Discard Eligibility Indicator: 1 bit
Backward Exploit Congestion Notification: 1 bit
Forward Exploit Congestion Notification: 1 bit
Data Link Connection Identifier: 4 bits
Extension Bit: 1 bit
Command/Response Field Bit: 1 bit
Data Link Connection Identifier: 6 bits

Figure 2.19   Part of the Frame Relay header deals with congestion.

The Backward Explicit Congestion Notification (BECN) bit is added to a frame returning to the router that is causing congestion. The transmitting Frame Relay network router detects the congested states when it receives the BECN from the network switch. It then reduces the transmitting rate to the maximum or below CIR until the congestion in the network is reduced. Normal transmission is then resumed.

The Discard Eligibility bit is a self-elective way of saying "if you have to, you can discard this frame." One method of electing what can be discarded is via prioritization. Prioritization allows the end-node to define which traffic is more important and must go through. An example of this might be prioritizing interactive traffic such as Telnet or SSH over non-interactive traffic such as FTP or HTTP.

Asynchronous Transfer Mode (ATM)

Asynchronous Transfer Mode is the progeny of both the telecom world and the computer-networking world. The successful combination of the ideologies, much less the technologies, of these two very different worlds has taken quite a while to mature. The ATM specification is still being refined, although most of the changes now refer to LAN-specific features such as ABR (Available Bit Rate), MPOA (Multi-Protocol Over ATM), and LANE (LAN Emulation).

From the telecom point of view, the network was a way to link two individuals together from different locations for short periods of time. You paid for the privilege of access to the telecom network, and you paid per-connection charges.

Contrast this to the data networking ideology, in which the media was shared by groups of people all working at once. The data was important; the network was just a resource allowing people to browse Web sites, send email, and transfer files. If it took 2 seconds or 20 to transfer the data, it did not matter as long as the data transferred uncorrupted.

Changes occurred to both the telecom and data networking industries, however. The need for additional media formats, such as audio and video, has increased the bandwidth requirements. Real-time audio and video conferencing over data networks has created a need for the same real-time, Quality of Service guarantees that the telecom industry has enjoyed since the inception of digital telephony.

It's All About Timing

So, what is it that makes ATM so different from all the other telecom technologies? The most obvious is that it is asynchronous, as in Asynchronous Transfer Mode. But what does that mean, exactly?

Asynchronous, in the context of ATM, means that sources are not limited to sending data during a set time slot, which is the case with circuit switching, such as the old standby T1. ATM transmits data not in bits, nor frames, but in packets. Actually, in ATM parlance, the packets are called *cells*. Cells are fixed in length and composed of two parts: the header and the payload.

ATM is not totally asynchronous, however. ATM cells are transmitted synchronously to maintain clock between sender and receiver. The sender, however, is not limited to sending data in any specific time slot or channel. Rather, the sender transmits when it has something to send and, when idle, sends empty cells synchronously. In short, data is sent asynchronously and cells are sent synchronously. The synchronous nature of the cells allows both sides of the ATM link to maintain timing reference similar to DS1.

SONET/SDH removed the need for bit stuffing due to the multiplexed and layered plesiochronous digital hierarchy. Remember, plesiochronous services are not synchronized to the same clock source. Although they are arbitrarily close in frequency and precision, over long distances and temperature ranges, plesiochronous signals will be skewed from each other. ATM would allow the enormous SONET/SDH bandwidth to be efficiently used.

Mitosis

The ATM cell is quite simple, which is part of the attraction to ATM. The fixed length of the ATM cell simplifies the transmission and reception of the cell compared to the variable length packets of Frame Relay and LAN networks.

The ATM cell is 53 octets in length and is divided into two portions: the header, which is 5 octets, and the payload, which is 48 octets. You can see this displayed in Figure 2.20.

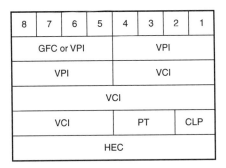

Figure 2.20   Lives of an ATM cell.

The following are the components of the ATM header:

- Generic Flow Control (GFC) was originally allocated for local switch functions such as flow control. *Local* means that the value is not preserved from endpoint to endpoint, and can be expected to change each physical hop in the ATM network.

- Virtual Path Indicator (VPI) is the virtual path through the myriad of ATM switches that a cell must pass through to make its journey through the ATM network. The VPI actually changes from node to node, as the VPI is local to each ATM switch.

- Virtual Channel Indicator (VCI) is similar in concept to a virtual circuit, however it identifies a specific virtual channel on a virtual path. You can think of VPI as identifying the road you're driving on and VCI identifying the lane your car is in. The VCI allows many different virtual channels of data to be transmitted over the same virtual path. Many channels are reserved for overhead, administration, and maintenance of the ATM link. These reserved channels are similar in concept to the D channel for ISDN.

- Payload Type (PT) define features of the overhead, administration, and maintenance of ATM.

- Cell Loss Priority (CLP) allows the ATM switch to prioritize cell traffic by defining which cells are okay to discard if there is a problem. This is very similar in concept to the Discard Enable bit of Frame Relay. If this bit is 1, the cell can be discarded. If it is 0, it should not be discarded, although setting this bit to 0 does not guarantee that the cell will not be discarded.

- Header Error Control is an 8-bit CRC of the first 4 octets of the header.

One thing to keep in mind is that VCIs and VPIs are not addresses. They are explicitly assigned at each segment (link between ATM nodes) of a connection when a connection is established, and remain for the duration of the connection. Together, the VCI and VPI are used to multiplex (and demultiplex) data onto a physical link.

Why 53 Octets?

I'm sure you're asking yourself "Why on earth would anyone pick 53 octets as a standard size of anything?" ATM cells are standardized at 53 octets because it seemed the politically correct thing to do. The United States proposed a payload of 64 octets focusing on bandwidth use for data networks and efficient memory transfer (length of payload should be a power of 2 or at least a multiple of 4). 64 octets fit both requirements.

The French, and eventually most of Europe, proposed a 32-octet payload focusing on voice applications. At cell sizes greater than 152 octets, there is a talker echo problem. Cell sizes between 32 and 152 result in a listener echo problem. Cell sizes of 32 or less overcome both problems.

In the end, the CCITT decided to split the difference, and proposed and settled on 48 octets for payload. Not wanting to impose more than 10% overhead for the header information, 5 octets was agreed upon for the header length. Thus the ATM cell is 48 octets of payload and 5 octets of header, totaling 53 octets in length.

ATM OSI Layers

The OSI model helps descramble protocols or specifications into Physical, Data Link, and Network layers. ATM does not fit well into the OSI model. As a matter of fact, you have a better chance of herding cats than to get a consensus on how to shoehorn ATM into the OSI model.

Many people agree that the ATM standards cover three distinct layers: the Physical Layer, the ATM Layer, and the ATM Adaptation Layer (AAL).

The Physical Layer (corresponding to OSI Physical Layer 1) is usually assumed to be SONET/SDH. This is not the only possibility, however, as there are specifications for running ATM over DS1, DS3, and twisted-pair copper. The PHY specification deals with medium-related issues.

The ATM Layer is responsible for creating cells and formatting the cell header (5 octets). Some argue that it also corresponds to OSI Physical (it deals with bit transport) and others say the ATM Layer corrosponds to the OSI Data Link (formatting, addressing, flow control, and so on).

The AAL is responsible for adapting ATM's cell-switching capabilities to the needs of specific higher layer protocols. The AAL is responsible for formatting the cell payload. Some argue that this layer corresponds to OSI Data Link (data error control, above Physical); others say it corresponds to OSI Transport (it's end to end). ATM is almost a Physical Layer, whereas TCP/IP is a higher layer that gets encapsulated onto a Physical Layer.

Transmitting a TCP/IP frame from one medium to another requires the IP frame to be decoded, and then re-encapsulated onto the new medium. This becomes expensive in implementation costs, latency, and complexity. To transmit from a local Ethernet to an FDDI backbone to a WAN via DS1, the frame must be processed four times.

The attractiveness of ATM is that an ATM cell *is* an ATM cell. After an ATM cell is created, it does not get changed (except for the VPI, which is local to the ATM switch). ATM cells might get grouped together in the conversion to DS1 or DS3 frames, but the cell itself does not need to be processed.

ATM Adaptation Layers

The four ATM Adaptation Layers (AAL) that have been defined are as follows:

- **AAL1**—Designed to support connection-oriented services that require constant bit rates and are sensitive to timing, delay, and error detection. Sequence numbers are associated with each cell similar to TCP/IP. Because cells always arrive in order, this allows for easy determination of lost cells and a request for retransmission. One octet of the payload is used for the sequence number, which leaves 47 octets for data payload. Sample candidates for AAL1 are constant bit rate services such as DS1 or DS3 transport.

- **AAL2**—Designed to carry voice and video over ATM. AAL2 consists of variable size packets encapsulated within the ATM payload, but does not require the constant bit rate. AAL2 is otherwise similar to AAL1. Because of the variable length data stream, three octets of the payload were used: 1 bit for sequence, 6 bits for length, and 10 bits for CRC-10. This only leaves 45 octets for actual data payload.

- **AAL3/4**—This AAL is intended for both connection-oriented and connectionless (AAL3, AAL4 respectively) variable bit rate services. AAL3/4 was designed for computer data that is sensitive to loss, but not necessarily timing or delay. AAL3/4 does not support real-time or timed connections. The final nail in the coffin for this specification is that it takes 4 octets of overhead, leaving only 44 octets for data payload.

- **AAL5**—Supports variable bit rate data services. AAL5 is essentially a raw cell, 48 octets of pure payload. Compared with AAL3/4, you lose error recovery and built-in retransmission, however this can be handled at upper protocol layers, such as TCP/IP. Because sequence numbers and CRCs did not need to be calculated, this simplified processing and implementation.

Guaranteed Service Levels

One of the original design goals of ATM was the capability to efficiently provide bandwidth to both time- and delay-sensitive services, such as voice and video, and to loss-sensitive services, such as computer data. To guarantee those levels of Quality of Service (QoS), several service classes for ATM have been defined.

Consistent Bit Rate (CBR)

The CBR service class is intended for real-time applications, those applications sensitive to delay and delay variation, as would be appropriate for voice and video applications. Time

Division Multiplexed traffic is extremely sensitive to delay and delay variation. Any cells that are delayed beyond the value specified by cell transfer delay (CTD) are assumed to be of significantly less value to the application.

Real Time VBR

The real-time VBR service class is intended for real-time applications that are sensitive to delay and delay variation, such as interactive compressed voice and video applications. Sources are expected to transmit at a rate that varies with time, that is, bursty traffic. Cells that are delayed beyond the value specified by CTD are assumed to be of significantly less value to the application.

Non–Real-Time VBR

The non–real-time VBR service class is intended for non–real-time applications that have *bursty* traffic. Those applications that are bursty are slightly less sensitive to delay, such as video playback, video training, and so on. Non–real–time VBR is used where interactivity is not an issue; some types of conversations are insensitive to delay while others are very sensitive. An electronic mail message, for example, can be held up for 20 or 30 seconds along the way without terrible consequence. A telephone conversation, on the other hand, is very sensitive to delay; a 20 second wait between the time you spoke and the time the listener heard you speak would make the medium unusable. For those cells that are transferred, VBR expects a bound on the cell transfer delay.

Unspecified Bit Rate (UBR)

The UBR service class is intended for delay-tolerant or non–real-time applications that are not sensitive to delay and delay variation, such as traditional computer communications. Sources are expected to transmit in short bursts of cells. UBR service is known as a "best effort service" that does not specify bit rate or traffic parameters. There is no guaranteed QoS with UBR. UBR is subject to increased cell loss and the discard of whole packets.

Available Bit Rate (ABR)

ABR, like UBR, is also a best effort service, but differs in that it is a managed service, based on minimum cell rate (MCR) low cell loss.

Wireless

IEEE standard 802.11 include two major Physical-Layer standards: direct-sequence (DS) spread spectrum and frequency-hopping (FH) spread spectrum. Both operate in 83.5MHz of unlicensed spectrum in the 2.4GHz band.

The Strange History of Frequency Hopping
Oddly enough, the idea of frequency hopping was patented by 1940s Hollywood heartthrob Hedy Lamar as a way of preventing American torpedoes from being jammed by Japanese ships. She and composer George Anthiel hold U.S. Patent number 2,292,387, dated June 12, 1941, describing the technology using piano tones. They called it a "secret communication system." Its most common application today is to secure cell phone conversations.

Although it is frustrating for the industry to deal with two 802.11 radio standards, there are sound reasons for them. FH systems provide greater scalability and better protection from radio-frequency interference, while DS systems provide about 20% better per-station performance and slightly greater transmission range.

DS has the lure of a fast-emerging upgrade to the existing 802.11 standard that will deliver a data rate of 11Mbps. Note that while vendors might tout these products as offering Ethernet speeds, you shouldn't be confused by the difference between data rate and throughput. This technology offers throughput that is only 60% of Ethernet's, however, it is likely to improve in the future.

FH uses a predetermined method of rapid frequency switching to facilitate secure transmission.

Hardware Requirements for Different Networks

Obviously, network needs are variable from place to place and user to user. A small office with a dozen power users might need more bandwidth than an office three times that size full of people who use nothing but Telnet. These, however, are some guidelines for purchasing bandwidth based upon the size of your network:

- **1–10 workstations**—Recommended bandwidth: 56Kbps–128Kbps. The following are your options:
  - **Low:** 56Kbps modem connection
  - **Middle:** ISDN
  - **High:** IDSL
- **11–50 workstations**—Recommended bandwidth: 128Kbps–256Kbps. The following are your options:
  - **Low:** ISDN
  - **Middle:** ADSL or Cable
  - **High:** Frame Relay
- **50–100 workstations**—Recommended bandwidth: 256Kbps–512Kbps. The following are your options:
  - **Low:** Frame Relay
  - **Middle:** Frame Relay, SDSL, or Cable
  - **High:** Frame Relay

- **100–500 workstations**—Recommended bandwidth: 512Kbps–1.5Mbps. The following are your options:
  - **Low:** Frame Relay
  - **Middle:** SDSL or HDSL
  - **High:** T1
- **Over 500 workstations**—Recommended bandwidth: 1.5Mbps–45Mbps and up. The following are your options:
  - **Low:** T1
  - **Middle:** Fractional T3 or HDSL
  - **High:** T3

3

SECURITY CONCEPTS

The only justification for our concepts and systems of concepts is that they serve to represent the complex of our experiences; beyond this they have no legitimacy.

—Albert Einstein

Who Is Threatening Your Data?

Blackhats. Crackers. Hackers. Script kiddies. Bad guys. Cyber terrorists. Agents of information espionage. Those are some of the many names that the media and the computer industry at large have given to individuals who attempts unauthorized access or use of your computing infrastructure.

Regardless of their designs, we'll call anyone breaking into your system an "intruder" and anyone who is trying to get in an "attacker." Most commonly, attacks come from within, from current or former employees.

Common Types of Attacks

There are several things an intruder could do when he gets to your site. These are the most common.

Web Defacement

Web defacement can take several forms, some subtle, others obvious. Most companies today have an Internet presence. Either it's hosted by an ISP or you're doing it yourself.

In building your Web site you have the copywriters rewrite your introduction and business model a dozen times just to get the language right. You've gone through at least as many revisions of your company logo and Web site art, not to mention the weeks you've spent tweaking the numbers so you can provide competitive products and services online.

Subtle defacement could take the form of altering your prices to make them 5% higher than your competitors or mixing up the product descriptions and prices.

Obvious defacement could be replacing your entire Web site with an image the intruder has hacked together of your CEO clubbing a baby seal. Another obvious defacement could be putting a message on your site describing how non-existent the security on your site was, and how no one ought to trust you with a customer's credit card information. Obviously, either of these could have a serious and significant impact on your business.

Unsolicited Commercial Email (UCE or Spam)

You don't have to be told that spam annoys a lot of people. It annoys the people who get it, it annoys the system administrators who spend a lot of time trying to block it, and it annoys the ISPs who are paying to store all these email messages on their servers.

If your mail server is configured to allow relaying of spam (by permitting unauthenticated mail to be relayed), not only does it place a burden on your mail server having to deliver all that additional email, but it could blacklist your domain. (We'll talk about how to guard against this later.)

Blacklisting is exactly what it sounds like. Most modern mail servers use several anti-spam controls, one of which is the Real-time Blackhole List or RBL. The Real-time Blackhole List prevents mail coming from known spamming domains from reaching your users. It does this by comparing the IP address of the sender with a list of known spammers. If the IP address is found, the mail is rejected.

The Real-time Black List is maintained by MAPS, the Mail Abuse Prevention System, a non-profit corporation at http://maps.vix.com/.

Allowing spam through your mail server could end up preventing your user base from sending valid email to anyone implementing spam control on their mail servers.

Spoofing

Spoofing an IP address is the act of replacing the real source address with a different source address. Because when the intruder uses a different or invalid IP address as the source, he won't see the reply, it's natural to wonder why he would bother. However, many attacks, such as Denial of Service (DoS) attacks, do not need to see the reply, they just need to get traffic to the intended target.

There are many reasons an intruder would spoof her IP address. First, you will not see the real IP address that the attack is coming from. Additionally, if the intruder uses an IP address internal to your network as the source address, your existing safeguards might allow that packet to pass.

If an intruder discovers an open security hole in your systems, he can then exploit that vulnerability to break into your system. This is quite different from an intruder breaking into your house. Unlike the home intruder, who must rush through your house before the movie is over, the intruder breaking into your system will usually take more time. Typically an intruder takes days or weeks to break into your system rather than hours. The extended break-in is used to obfuscate the attack in the background of otherwise normal activity.

The intruder gains access to your system usually by installing a series of Trojan-horse programs collectively known as a *root kit*. In the UNIX vernacular, *root* is the account with full, unbridled system privileges. Installing the root kit accomplishes two goals:

- The Trojan programs allow normally untraceable access, so there is not as much sanitizing that the intruder must do to cover his tracks.
- The intruder does not want to rely on a security vulnerability that you might eventually discover and close. The root kit allows him to create a more "legitimate" form of entry.

After the intruder has compromised one of your systems, he will often expand the attack by attempting to exploit any trust that system has with others and invade those as well. Frequently the intruder has no interest in your system other than to launch an attack onto another system and hide its origin.

Denial of Service (DoS)

A denial of service attack is a simple, but often extremely effective, attack that is difficult, if not impossible, to prevent. The goal of a denial of service attack is to deny access to your particular services, effectively preventing your organization from operating. A denial of service could be launched against any part of your Internet connectivity and network infrastructure.

Flood Pings

An attacker could target your Internet connection, for example, with a DoS attack. By sending a simple *flood ping*, which barrages the target with ICMP Echo Request packets as fast as possible without waiting for replies, an attacker can cause more traffic than your Internet connection is capable of handling. This effectively prevents you from receiving or replying to legitimate requests. (ICMP is the Internet Control Message Protocol which is used to report errors to devices, usually routers. An echo request packet asks for an ICMP reply; sent continuously, your machine will get bogged down sending ICMP replies.)

Mail Bombing

Another type of Denial of Service attack can be caused by mail bombing, in which an attacker targets your email system by sending overly large email messages to users such as postmaster or Webmaster. This not only affects your Internet connection bandwidth, but also your mail server's capability to handle other email. An attack such as this could easily fill up your mail server's mail store drive, preventing you from sending or receiving new email.

TCP SYN Scan

Another common type of attack is the TCP SYN attack. Typically, when a TCP connection is initiated, the sending machine sends a SYN request, which is acknowledged by the recipient machine with an ACK, and the sending machine responds itself with an ACK. This three-way handshake sets the stage for a normal TCP connection.

Figure 3.1 shows a typical TCP connection.

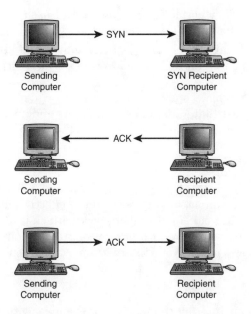

Figure 3.1 TCP's three way handshake: a request, an acknowledgement, and then another acknowledgement.

The recipient computer uses memory resources waiting for the third part of the handshake, the ACK from the sender. A TCP SYN attack exploits this by providing a "spoofed" unreachable

IP address in the SYN. Therefore the recipient computer responds with its ACK to a non-existent machine that never responds to the ACK:

Figure 3.2 illustrates a TCP SYN attack.

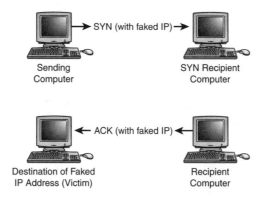

Figure 3.2   The SYN spoof: The receiving computer is asked to send an ACK to a false IP address. A connection is then left open waiting for the third handshake which never arrives.

A TCP SYN scan performs large numbers of SYN connections in rapid succession against your servers, never sending the ACK response. This leaves hundreds, if not thousands, of connections half-open.

Distributed Denial of Service Attacks (DDoS)

Recent forms of distributed, coordinated, mass denial of service attacks have focused on the larger Internet targets such as financial companies, search engines, and government agencies. An intruder breaks into a large number of systems and leaves a root kit and client installed. Prepackaged denial of service "hacker tools" such as Trinoo/Tribal Flood, Stacheldraht, and Mstream are controlled remotely, allowing the attacker to later contact and coordinate attacks at will. When the attack comes, it will be from multiple innocent machines at once.

These distributed denial of service (DDoS) attacks cannot be prevented by the company being attacked. Individual companies, universities, and ISPs connected to the Internet are responsible for securing their networks. It is your duty to ensure your systems are not being used to attack others.

Important Security Terminology

There are four main concepts of data security. They are pervasive throughout different models and serve as a basis for constructing a secure system. These concepts are authentication, authorization, integrity, and encryption.

Authentication

Authentication is verifying who you are. There are numerous ways to implement authentication; each has pros and cons. The most widely implemented authentication mechanism is by password. Various other authentication mechanisms are as follows:

- Digital Certificate, such as those used in the X.509 format. This is when a message is encrypted with a private key. The message can be decrypted by a public key and validated against a certificate of authority. Unfortunately, the private key is usually protected by a symmetrically encrypted key, specifically, a password.

- Hardware token, such as SecurID. The hardware token generates a random number at a specified time interval using a proprietary algorithm. This number is synchronized with an authenticating server, and combined with a personal PIN composed of alphanumeric characters. The randomly generated number expires after the next number is generated preventing its reuse.

- Biometric Technologies such as voice pattern recognition, Iris/Retina scanning, and fingerprinting are the new wave of authentication technologies. Problems such as losing or forgetting your hardware token, password, or digital certificate become a thing of the past.

Authorization

Authorization is granting or denying access to a service based on who you say you are. Authorization is often tightly integrated with authentication, and thus often confused with authentication. Authorization depends on being able to authenticate an identity, but checks that identity against an access control list to grant or deny access.

The access control list can be stored in a configuration in a file, in non-volatile RAM, or in a distributed database such as LDAP, Active Directory, or NetWare Directory Services.

Integrity

Integrity is the process of validating that the data provided by an authenticated source has not been changed. This is often done by running an algorithm over a set of selected data to produce a hash or message digest. This value is then protected by encrypting it and attaching it to the original data. The process of computing the hash, encrypting it, and attaching it to the original data is called digitally signing data.

To validate that the integrity has not been compromised, a new hash or message digest is computed and compared to the decrypted value. If they match, there is no way the data could have been modified without the key used to protect the data originally. Theoretically, only the original person/company would have access to that key. This allows you to validate the digital signature on the data.

Encryption

Encryption is the process of transforming the data so that the original meaning remains confidential. Often the unprocessed data is called clear text, and the processed data is called cipher text. The reverse of encrypting a message is decryption, transforming a processed set of data back to its original clear text form. The value used in the transformation process is known as the encryption key.

Of Public Keys and Private Washrooms

Cryptography has been around for centuries, used mainly to secure communication between governments or military officials. For cryptography to work, both the sending and receiving party must use the same process to encode and decode the data. Cryptographers refer to this as "symmetric key cryptography."

The keys used for cryptography must be guarded closely, because anyone who has the key has the ability to decrypt the data. Keys are therefore usually transferred "out-of-band," meaning they are not sent via the medium (in our instance the Internet) they are meant to protect. Transmission of the keys usually would be done via a telephone conversation, the postal system, or some other physical means, such as a floppy disk.

Immediately you can see several problems with symmetric key cryptography. Any data guarded by the key is at risk if the key is compromised. Dealing with large numbers of people, such as those within a company, much less the Internet, makes managing the keys impractical. Changing the keys often to protect the transmission of data does not scale well.

A new approach to encryption was needed, and in 1976 two cryptographers changed the world of cryptography. Whitfield Diffie and Martin Hellman developed a public-key cryptosystem outlined in their paper "New Directions in Cryptography."

This new method of cryptography uses a pair of unique keys to encrypt and decrypt information. Both keys are assigned to an individual person, company, or system. One key is kept private, known only to that individual. The other key is public, to be shared and known by anyone who wants to communicate with the person/company that owns the corresponding private key. Data encrypted with one key can be decrypted only by the other key in a pair.

Public keys can be used to encrypt data for a specific individual, because only that individual has access to the private key. Likewise encrypted data sent by that individual can be decrypted only by using his specific public key.

The Diffie-Hellman key exchange then uses the public/private key pairing to securely exchange a secret symmetric key without the need of an out-of-band channel.

X.509 Certificates

X.509 certificates are electronic documents that bind information such as a person's name to her public key. The distinguished name embedded in the X.509 certificate could represent an individual, an individual server, or a whole organization.

After the X.509 certificate is created with the appropriate information, it is then digitally signed by a trusted third party, known as a Certificate Authority.

Now the authenticity and integrity of the third party must be verified. There are several ways to accomplish this; companies such as Verisign and Entrust have set themselves up as global Certificate Authorities. They provide various classes of Certifications depending on the credentials provided proving your identity. Many software vendors have preinstalled the public keys for those certificate authorities in their software products.

Additionally, if your company plans to run its own certificate authority (CA), you can have your CA's public key signed by a trusted CA. This allows you to sign your own employee certificates with your CA's public key, which can be verified by validating the trusted CA's public key signature.

You can also manually install the public key of your company's CA into your software's trusted list of certificate authorities.

The big difference between public-key and normal symmetric key cryptography is that you only need to get one public key of a trusted system out-of-band, and most X.509 capable software has the major CAs preinstalled.

The following are some common uses of X.509 certificates:

■ Web servers use X.509 certificates to authenticate themselves and the organization they belong to for clients connecting to them. X.509 certificates are used primarily in e-commerce applications and other transactions that require security. The HTTP session is encrypted between the client and server via SSLv2.

■ Web browsers use X.509 certificates to authenticate individual users to Web servers. This is a more secure authentication than the default HTTP BASIC authentication using an account and password. The HTTP session is encrypted between client and server via SSLv3.

■ Email clients use X.509 certificates for both authentication and encryption. Authentication is handled via digital signing, and message confidentiality is handled by encryption. S/MIME is a version of MIME designed specifically to address security related issues. MIME, RFC 1521, is a message-based format designed to structure messages for client interoperability. Any S/MIME-capable mail client should be able to handle both digital signatures and encrypted email. S/MIME actually uses the document structure defined in Public-Key Cryptography Standard (PKCS) #7, an industry standard on secure information exchange.

■ Java software run from remote servers can be signed with an X.509 certificate. This authenticates the author or vendor of the software. Authenticated software executed within a Web browser can be granted additional capabilities such as full network and file access.

Pretty Good Privacy (PGP) Keys

Pretty Good Privacy is a variation of the public-key cryptosystem developed by Philip R. Zimmermann in 1991. PGP is available both as a commercially supported program, and as a freeware program. Additionally, there are open-source versions that adhere to the OpenPGP standard. PGP has been very popular to use for digitally signing and encrypting email on the Internet.

PGP is different than normal public-key cryptography in that it uses a faster symmetric key to encrypt the message, and then the slower PGP key is used to encrypt the shorter symmetric key.

Digital signatures with PGP are done similarly to X.509 digital signatures. A hash or message digest of the message is computed, and then encrypted with the sender's private key. People who receive the message must compute the hash and compare it to the decrypted value sent with the message.

PGP differs from X.509 in its trust model. PGP imposes no hierarchical structure for authenticating signatures. PGP allows users to sign other people's certificates. That way if you receive a PGP key that has been signed by a number of people you trust, you can then trust that signature is valid.

Although it might not seem at first that this "Web of trust" model scales as well as its hierarchical competitor, the Web of trust model can be made to emulate the hierarchical trust model.

Currently no major software vendors ship email clients that have native support for PGP, the PGP software itself has plug ins for many of the major email software programs. Email messages are formatted using PGP/MIME, which is different and non-interoperable with S/MIME.

PGP could also be used to encrypt or sign individual files, thus ensuring that even if someone gained access to your private data, its confidentiality would be maintained.

Network Associates, the people who now own the original PGP software, have expanded the original capabilities of the PGP client. They have added the ability to encrypt whole volumes of data transparently via their PGPdisk feature. You can also encrypt network traffic using the PGPnet feature. PGPnet uses the Internet standard IPsec protocol to encrypt traffic on the wire. IPsec encrypts *all* traffic between peers, not just a specific protocol such as SSL.

Public Key Infrastructure (PKI)

Public Key Infrastructure is a collection of components used to enable the management of X.509 certificates. The following are the components of a PKI:

- A certificate authority (CA) issues and validates digital certificates. The CA has a digital certificate with its public key that must be trusted by the client software.

- A registration authority (RA) verifies information for the CA before any digital certificates are issued. Most RAs are operated by your corporate security so they can validate the identity of the requesting individual.

- A directory, usually Lightweight Directory Access Protocol (LDAP) enabled, is used to store the certificates.

- A certificate revocation list (CRL) lists certificates that have been revoked for one reason or another. Revocation can be requested, for example, if your private key has been compromised and you need to get a new certificate. Additionally, if an employee leaves the company, her certificate can be placed on the CRL.

PGP does not use PKI, rather PGP users have key rings. A key ring is a collection of public PGP keys. There are public and private PGP key servers available that provide public PGP key information via HTTP or FTP protocols.

Security Hardware

One common design between PGP and X.509 certificates is that there is a private key that needs to be kept secret. If you use multiple computers, this becomes problematic in that you must take your private key with you. How to move your key with you without leaving copies of it on multiple computers is an issue. One solution to this is as old as the lock on your front door: a hardware key.

Token-Based Cards

Most token-based cards, such as SecurID from SecurityDynamics, Inc., use a technique called two-factor authentication. Two-factor authentication requires some personal, unique information from the user, plus some data generated by the hardware, to authenticate the user. In the SecurID example, it uses a time-based token plus personal pin combined to form a passcode. The passcode combined with the username authenticates the user.

Because the time-based token expires every 60 seconds, intruders are prevented from using the passcode in replay attacks. Additionally, because both a username and a PIN are required, if a hardware token is lost or stolen, it does not automatically grant access to your network.

There are a few drawbacks to the hardware-based token mechanism. First, each user must have his own token. Although not wildly expensive, large numbers of cards can be costly.

Secondly, the user must always have the token with them. If the user forgets the token, or loses it, he has no other means to access the system.

Smart Cards

Smart cards are credit-card sized with a computer chip built in. Usually there is some memory, allowing for a flash filesystem to store information on. X.509 certificates can then be stored on the smart card. Some smart cards even have a Java Virtual Machine built in to run applications.

The smart card solves the problem of having to distribute your private key to every machine you use. Unfortunately, that problem is replaced with the hardware need to have a smart card reader on every machine you want to use your smart card. This can get to be quite expensive. There are many interesting ideas for easily getting card readers into machines. Products that use disk drives, PCMCIA slots, keyboard connectors, and USB connections are all available. If smart card readers ever become standard, this will be a very convenient method of authenticating your identity.

Security Through Obscurity

Many people believe that if you hide the details about a device, it will remain secure. This belief has been continuously disproved over the years. If a device is insecure, hiding that fact will only potentially extend the time it takes to exploit the vulnerability. It will not prevent its exploitation.

Passwords are the most prevalent form of security through obscurity. Passwords are used to access most services on networks and the Internet. Theoretically, the password should be known only by its owner. Unfortunately, password-cracking programs such as Crack and L0phtcrack have the capability to brute-force discover passwords on UNIX and Windows NT systems. Additionally, network packet sniffers can discover passwords sent over the network in the clear. Popular protocols such as Telnet, POP3, IMAP, FTP, and HTTP BASIC authentication all pass both user accounts and passwords "in the clear" (which is to say, unencrypted).

World View Versus Internal View

Your corporate network is internal. The Internet and private connections to partners should be considered external.

Normally, internal hosts have access to the full information of the internal network. Perhaps this is why an estimated 80% of information theft is done internally.

When providing the world, and your partners, with information about your internal network, you should give the most limited subset of information about your network that it's possible to give. For example, when Telneting to your server, the following prompt

```
SunOS UNIX (somecomputer.somewhere.com)
```

delivers more information than it needs to. By identifying the operating system (SunOS UNIX), you've given attackers a leg-up to breaking into your system. There is no point in providing a treasure map for intruders to follow through your network.

Different Layers of Security

How much security do you need? The only way to obtain a fully secure system is to disconnect it from the network, from all removable media devices, and from the printer, remove all I/O ports, and lock it in a secured room with a posted guard. Some computer systems warrant such security, and get it. However, that level of security isn't convenient for the normal computing needs of today's enterprises. Absolute security tends to clash with ease of use.

So what does each level of security entail? What is the right mix of levels for you and your userbase? These next few paragraphs will attempt to help answer those questions.

No Security

Some people do this intentionally on certain systems, known as honeypots, that are part of an Intrusion Detection System. This is not the way to run a corporate network in today's Internet environment. Not for any length of time anyway.

In addition to opening yourself up to data theft, data loss, and general mayhem, any system misused to attack other systems opens possible exposure to liability. Your legal department probably has some suggestions for you on that front.

Hardened Security

Hardening is about minimizing risk and increasing robustness. Hardening a server or workstation that is directly Internet accessible includes the following:

- Reducing the number of network services that are running and accessible to the Internet.
- Removing unnecessary software and features, which reduces the overall complexity of the system. This includes removing additional protocols such as IPX, AppleTalk, NetBIOS, DLC, LAT, and DecNET.
- Removing software that allows access to internal system information, such as SNMP.
- Removing insecure remote control software, such as X Window or the ADMIN$ share for remote Windows NT administration.
- Applying all known security updates and service packs. Often times security exploits in necessary software such as DNS are resolved in a simple configuration change or security patch.
- Enabling traffic filters if available. Windows NT and most UNIX systems have built-in or freely available software that allows more control of the kinds and sources of IP traffic that are accepted.

■ Removing unnecessary accounts on the system. Rename existing administrative or root accounts to something unique and hard to guess.

■ Removing unnecessary and overly generous file permissions for both accounts and the file system.

Hardening a server or workstation costs nothing more than the time invested, and perhaps a little research for documents. So there is no additional cost of hardware or software licenses.

Many operating system vendors have knowledge-base articles or How-To documents describing step-by-step how to harden the operating systems and common services such as Web servers. Any capable system administrator should be able to follow those documents. If not, you might need to find new support staff.

Although hardened systems might still be vulnerable to newly discovered system exploits, those vulnerabilities can be plugged.

Firewalls

A firewall is a device or a group of devices that enforce your corporate access control policy on two or more connected networks. Enforcing the access control policy either permits or denies traffic based on various rules you define.

When installing a firewall, you must first have a clear idea of what services you want to expose to the Internet, and what services your userbase requires access to. The policy on access to those services directly determines which rules are implemented on the firewall.

The firewall generally deals with the direction of traffic in relation to the external or internal view. For example, the normal default policy for external traffic inbound to your network is to be blocked. The default policy for internal traffic outbound to the Internet is to be permitted.

When configuring the firewall, you will have to add and modify those rules to match your policy. You should also validate your firewall after making changes to the rule base to ensure that a mistake does not expose your network to possible attack.

Although most people think of a firewall as a dedicated computer running some add-on software, there are many variations of firewalls. Most routers today have embedded firewall software, although most likely you will need to purchase a license to enable those features. Additionally, there is a new breed of network appliances that offer both the Internet connectivity of a router, and the security and performance of a firewall. The correct device, or combination of devices, depends both on your needs and your budget.

Keep in mind that firewalls are not magic pixie dust that you can sprinkle at the entry point to your network and make it all secure. A firewall does not normally perform functions such as scan email for viruses. Although there are add-on products for some commercial firewalls to perform that kind of function, it's good policy to keep things simple. Adding additional functionality creates the opportunity for that functionality to be exploited.

A firewall connecting your network to the Internet does not protect your internal servers from internal attacks.

Finally, a Web or DNS server that has not been sufficiently hardened can still be compromised through a firewall, because you are still allowing external traffic through to that server.

Demilitarized Zone

A Demilitarized Zone (DMZ), as it relates to network security, is a collection of hardened servers, firewalls, routers, and networks that isolate your internal network from the Internet.

The networks exposed on the DMZ are known as Bastion LANs. Bastion LANs are local area networks that are tightly regulated as to what traffic is allowed on, or off, of their segments. A Bastion LAN acts as a buffer between your internal network and the Internet. The Bastion LAN is usually connected to your internal network via packet-screening routers or firewalls. The hardened servers are designed to offer up the necessary exposed services to the Internet, such as an external view of your corporate DNS, externally visible Web server, mail relay, and so on.

DMZs allow you to architect redundancy, scalability, and flexibility into your network connectivity. Even though the DMZ layers of security are not sufficient individually, when combined, those layers hopefully provide a comprehensive strategy and solution to Internet connectivity and security.

Intrusion Detection Systems

Intrusion Detection Systems (IDS) are mechanisms that are put in place to detect when your system is under attack and to take appropriate action. That action is definable by your corporate policy, and could range from doing nothing, to logging the events for later analysis, to proactively creating rules on firewalls to attempt to stop the attack.

There are several components to Intrusion Detection Systems, not all of which need to be implemented to be effective:

- **Network Intrusion Detection Systems**—These sniff packets on the wire to look for suspicious network traffic patterns and attack signatures. NIDS can be agents that run on individual servers, or dedicated systems that monitor network segments of hosts. Packet capture and analysis is CPU intensive, and NIDS that monitor whole network segments are not very useful in high traffic areas.

- **System Integrity Verifiers**—These are programs put into place to validate the integrity of system files on exposed systems. Usually a database is created containing the name of the file with its calculated hash value. This database is usually stored on read-only media such as write-protected floppy disks or a CD-ROM; that way the attacker cannot update the system integrity database.

- **Log File Monitors**—These monitor event logs on Windows NT systems or syslog files on UNIX systems for anomalous events.

- **Decoys or Honeypots**—These are systems specifically left vulnerable to attack so that those attacks can be monitored, logged, and analyzed. It's nice to keep people out, but a more proactive means of security is to know who's knocking on what, and when. There are software packages, deception toolkits, available that assist you in the forensic analysis of the attack. Some of these are Network Associates' Cybercop Sting, NETSEC's Spectre, Network Flight Recorder's BackOfficer Friendly, and Fred Cohen's Deception Toolkit. We'll talk about them in greater detail in Chapter 10 "Implementing Security."

Different Kinds of Access Control

One of the key jobs of a network administrator is to make sure that only the proper people have access to data on the network. This is known as access control. There are several different devices which you can use to keep outsiders away from your data. Some of these are routers, firewalls, and proxies. Each acts in a different manner to restrict access to information. The following sections detail some of the more common methods used to enforce policy.

Packet Screening

Routers are devices that forward traffic from one network to another based on forwarding tables. The first line of defense on routers is the forwarding table. If there is no route to forward the packet to, it is dropped.

Additionally, access control lists add policy filters to traffic. You can forward or drop packets based on such attributes as IP protocol, protocol options, source and destination address, and source and destination port. The router is also the logical place to block spoofed packets.

Although most router access control lists are not as flexible as firewalls, they are quite effective in limiting the types of traffic that reach your network. Almost all routers also do packet filtering, so there is no additional cost to be incurred.

The downside to packet filtering is that the access control looks only at the IP header, not at the payload. Therefore, protocols such as RPC and FTP cannot be easily accommodated by packet filtering.

Circuit Proxies

Many protocols that your userbase might require cannot be firewalled. Multimedia protocols, such as the Real-Time Streaming Protocol or streaming QuickTime, use UDP and cannot normally be associated with a traceable session.

The answer is to use a proxy. A proxy is a software program or device that takes internal client requests, and forwards them to the server on behalf of the client. All communication is between the server on the Internet and the proxy, the client never actually communicates with the Internet connected server.

The most popular proxy of this type is SOCKS5, now under the development of NEC. The downside to using a proxy such as SOCKS5 is that individual software packages must be manually configured to use it, and might require additional client libraries.

Application Gateways

Application Gateways are firewalls that proxy specific protocols, such as HTTP, FTP, RealMedia, email, and so on, on behalf of the client workstation.

The advantage of Application Gateways is that they are transparent to the user configurable clients. The downside is that there are a limited number of application proxies provided with the software. If there isn't an application proxy available for the service you require, you will need to seek a different solution.

Stateful Inspection

Stateful inspection is a combination of packet screening and application gateways. Invented by Checkpoint Systems, most firewalls today use a form of stateful inspection.

Stateful inspection looks at the packet headers to create a state table to track sessions. For protocols that need additional information from the payload, such as FTP, those packets are examined to determine the reply traffic patterns.

Stateful inspection firewalls are faster than pure application gateway firewalls, because they don't have to examine every payload of every packet. Additionally they are more flexible because you can define services and state conditions to expand the existing rulebase.

Network Address Translation

Network Address Translation (NAT) is the process of mapping one IP address to another. NAT is usually implemented to provide an internal private IP address space access to the Internet via a pool of real, routable IP addresses. For the length of the IP session, there is a 1 to 1 mapping between internal and external IP addresses.

Due to the poor allocation of IPv4 addresses, large numbers of IP addresses are generally not allocated to anyone but ISPs. More likely than not, your internal network is using an RFC-1918 defined private IP address space. For these clients to communicate with Internet connected hosts, they must have their IP addresses translated to non-private IP addresses. NAT accommodates this need.

Because RFC-1918 addresses are not routable—meaning most if not all ISPs should drop routes for those networks—using private IP address ranges affords your network an extra layer of insulation against direct attack.

There is one obvious problem with NAT, and that is the 1 to 1 mapping requirement. If you are allocated 32 real IP addresses for your Internet connection, but you have 250 nodes that at any one time need external access, you have a capacity problem.

Luckily there is a variation of NAT known as Network Address Port Translation. It's also known as Port Address Translation (PAT) and IP Masquerading. The basic concept is to map the internal IP address and port to an external IP address and range of ports (such as 60,000 through 64,000) along with the destination IP address and port. This builds up a session table that allows the NAPT device to track communication between client and server, and forward traffic appropriately.

Because there is not a 1:1 mapping of IP addresses with NAPT, it's difficult to near impossible to initiate connections from the outside to internal resources.

4

DEFINING CONNECTION
REQUIREMENTS

The man who sets out to carry a cat by its tail learns something that will
always be useful and which never will grow dim or doubtful.
>   —Mark Twain

Getting an Idea of What Your Users Need

What is the business vision for connecting to the Internet? What applications do your users need to use? It's important to gather your user's requirements, and match those with the business's goals of connecting to the Internet before starting on any design of WAN connectivity.

Unfortunately, there is no crystal ball you can use to determine this—each company's needs are different. However, through careful modeling of the initial design, and monitoring of the network and server resources, you should be able to predict and plan for increasing your capacity. Initially this might seem like a paradox. How can you properly design your connection without usage history and statistics? How can you model what you cannot accurately quantify?

The answer is that you can't. That is why it is important to show due diligence in collecting information both in the form of requirements and expectations from the users and management. This is done both by extrapolating the company's purpose (for example, it's an online stock trading company, therefore a superfast Internet connection is mandatory) and by interviewing people; "What special software, if any, do you plan to use?" Those requirements coupled with your security policy and IT budget will shape your Internet connection.

The following sections address ways to define these initial connection requirements. The most difficult thing about this is that each company is unique. You can have an office with eight people in it, FTPing huge multi-gigabyte image files all day that requires a much fatter Internet connection than another office with a hundred people plinking away on email. Throughout the rest of the chapter, the *terms low bandwidth installations* and *high bandwidth installations* are used to express these extremes. You'll need to plot where your company fits in on this scale. Describing installations in terms of bandwidth needs avoids the misconception that companies with large numbers of employees always need the larger pipes.

Internet Applications Accessed from the Internet

What is the purpose of the Internet connection? Do your users need to browse vendor's Web sites? Will your business live or die by email? Do you need to transfer multi-gigabyte files between customers or other business partners? Are you connecting branch offices using Virtual Private Network technologies? Do you need a secure server for e-commerce?

Having a good grasp on the use of your Internet connectivity goals will help you better design for the present and plan for the future. Either under- or over-designing your network can have drastic results. Over-designing your network makes your users happy but isn't the best use of your valuable company assets. Under-designing on the other hand can leave your users unable to complete their jobs efficiently as they wait for slow file transfers or bottlenecked mail servers.

Table 4.1 lists some common Internet applications and their services, IP protocol, and ports.

Table 4.1   Internet Applications and Their Common Ports

Application	Service	Protocol	Port	Bandwidth Consumption
World Wide Web	HTTP	TCP	80	High
Secure WWW	HTTPS	TCP	443	Low
Electronic Mail	SMTP	TCP	25	Moderate
	IMAP4	TCP	143	Moderate
	POP3	TCP	110	Moderate
Name Resolution	DNS	UDP	53	Low
	DNS	TCP	53	Low
File Transfer	FTP	TCP	20, 21	High

Table 4.1   Continued

Application	Service	Protocol	Port	Bandwidth Consumption
Terminal Emulation	TELNET	TCP	23	Low
Encrypted Telnet	SSH	TCP	22	Low
Usenet News	NNTP	TCP	119	High
Time Synchronization	NTP	TCP	123	Low
Virtual Private Network	IPsec	ESP	N/A	High
Streaming Media	RTSP	TCP	554	High
	RTP	UDP	6970-7170	High

Identifying which Internet applications your users need will help you both size your Internet connection and define your initial outbound security policy.

Application services have specific, well-known protocol and port definitions that allows the client software to connect to the servers providing those services.

Compiling a list of those services, and thus protocol and port definitions, can be used to directly define your security policy. Examples of defining security policies can be found in Chapter 8, "Assessing your Security Needs." Examples of implementing those defined security policies can be found in Chapter 10, "Implementing Security."

Internet Applications Provided to the Internet

The next step in defining connection requirements is to identify which services, if any, you will be providing to the world at large (people outside your organization). At a minimum these services usually include the following:

- Domain Name Services
- Web and e-Commerce services
- Electronic Mail

Domain Name Service works like a phone book. A computer on the Internet seeks to resolve www.yourdomain.com into an IP address. Resolving www.yourdomain.com into an IP address is a distributed, multi-step process (see Figure 4.1).

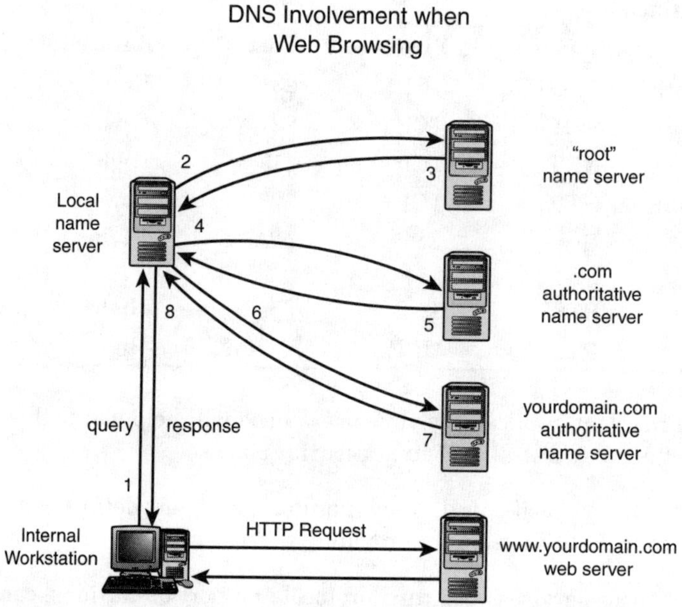

DNS Involvement when
Web Browsing

Figure 4.1   Multiple steps can be involved in the resolution of a domain name into an IP address. Computers that don't know pass the request upstream until an answer is found.

Here's a breakdown of what's happening in Figure 4.1 when your computer asks the local DNS server for the IP address of www.yourdomain.com:

- The local DNS server checks its local cache for the host entry. If the host is not in the local cache, and the local DNS server is not authoritative for yourdomain.com, it queries the ROOT name servers for the authoritative server for yourdomain.com.

- The local DNS server then queries the authoritative DNS server on behalf of the client for the info on the host www.yourdomain.com.

- The authoritative DNS server replies to the referring local DNS server.

- The local DNS server replies to your computer and stores the host entry in its local cache.

- You computer can then cache the result, depending on the application, and then contact www.yourdomain.com.

The process is similar when someone sends email to yourdomain.com:

- Your computer sends an email destined for yourdomain.com to your local mail server via SMTP.

- Your mail server receives an email destined for yourdomain.com. It asks the local DNS server for the IP address of the mail server for yourdomain.com.

- The local DNS server checks its local cache for the host entry. If the host is not in the local cache, and the local DNS server is not authoritative for `yourdomain.com`, it queries the ROOT name servers for the authoritative server for `yourdomain.com`.
- The local DNS server then queries the authoritative DNS server on behalf of the client for the info on the mail exchanger (MX) host for `yourdomain.com`.
- The authoritative DNS server replies to the referring local DNS server.
- The local DNS server replies to your local mail server and stores the host entry in its local cache.
- Your local mail server might then cache the result, depending on the mail server software, and then contact the mail server for `yourdomain.com`.

As you can see, without a working DNS infrastructure people won't be able to find your services. You don't need to be a large corporation with a large staff to own and maintain your own DNS servers. Taking ownership for your own DNS records allows you more flexibility and timely administrative control over your domains. Should you decide to manage your DNS records, you should also have your ISP second your DNS information, which will act as a backup in the event that your DNS servers are unavailable.

Almost everyone is familiar with Web servers, but not everyone necessarily knows how to run a Web server securely. This includes buying a certificate so you can encrypt traffic and knowing the proper Web server configuration settings, file permissions, and dangerous server extensions to disable. These all come with familiarity with the product. Web servers are not terribly complicated. A simple one can be easily maintained by one person. But when you start including dynamically generated content, databases access, e-commerce related transactions, and record keeping, they can rapidly become extremely difficult.

Finally, email is often cited as a company's most critical application. Business is conducted, meetings are scheduled, and work is coordinated all through email. The need to conduct business in that fashion with other people and businesses on the Internet requires that you have an externally accessible mail relay or mail server.

For those businesses staging their installation or not offering any on-site Internet services, the ISP can manage and host DNS, email, and Web services for you. This is often convenient because the ISP already has the infrastructure and personnel to configure, administrate, and troubleshoot the more common services.

If you want to exercise more administrative control or host services on-site, you can start hosting the more sensitive services, such as DNS and email. DNS and email have lower bandwidth requirements than your Web servers and can be more easily hosted on-site without disrupting your Internet services.

Some advantages and disadvantages of locally hosting services are compared in Table 4.2.

Table 4.2   Sample Criteria Comparing Local and ISP Hosting of Services

Locally Hosted Services	ISP Hosted Services
High Sensitivity—Company proprietary email	Low Sensitivity—External Web site
Low Bandwidth—DNS, email	High Bandwidth—FTP and streaming multimedia
Require a local administrative staff	Administrative staff provided by ISP
Immediate administrative control	Administrative changes might take hours or days

Two additional services that are commonly offered to the Internet community are file transfers via FTP and streaming media. Both tend to be bandwidth hogs, and both are difficult to deal with from a security standpoint. Both are also better served by alternate means. There are several companies that offer file and content hosting for large transfers. These distributed content-caching service providers, such as Akamai, Inc., are equipped to handle the bandwidth and disk space requirements involved with streaming media and large file transfers. If, however, your needs are modest, these services will definitely require careful auditing of your systems and security policies.

Hosting any or all of the services listed in Table 4.2 on-site will drive your inbound security policies. Your Internet connection will need to be slightly more complex to ensure that security is maintained. Properly hosting those services on-site requires a DMZ style perimeter network with a firewall. (A DMZ or DeMilitarized Zone is a perimeter network that goes outside of your internal network and shields interior computers from attack.) Otherwise if a server were compromised, the intruder would then have access to your internal networks. Different security implementations are discussed in more detail in Chapter 8.

Sizing your Internet Connection

As technology evolves, bandwidth requirements generally increase. Properly turning your Internet connection requirements into a cost effective, scalable, and secure Internet connection takes experience. That experience can be bought, hired, or earned.

Buying the Skills

There are several software packages available from Optimal Networks, Network Analysis Center, Cisco, and others that allow you to precisely model your network topology, network traffic, application response times, and so on. These packages generally cost in the thousands of dollars. If you are building large distributed applications over a large, complex WAN infrastructure, these applications can be a saving grace. For a company determining the proper WAN connectivity for its Internet connection, they are overkill.

Hiring the Skills

Your ISP most likely will have staff network engineers that, for a fee, will help you turn your requirements into a properly sized WAN connection. If you are concerned that the ISP might use its in-house engineers to better their monthly sales figures, look elsewhere. Many consulting companies, such as CACI, specialize in network engineering or Internet connectivity, and you can use their skills to provide an objective recommendation. Consulting companies often offer these services:

- Analysis of your bandwidth needs
- Recommendation of a connectivity solution
- Independent analysis of local ISP performance and SLA compliance—this means overall performance, not just bandwidth, throughput, and uptime. Customer service response, administrative skills, 24-hour coverage, and engineering support must all be considered.
- Referrals to other customers who have utilized the services of the ISP you're considering, as well as customers who have used other ISPs. An unsatisfied customer will willingly tell you what's wrong with their ISP. A good ISP will inspire their clients to recommend them.

For more in-depth information regarding evaluating and the hiring the right outside help see Chapter 6, "Consulting, Consultants, and Contractors."

Earning the Skills

Earning the experience necessary to model Internet connections requires a lot of up-front data collection, educating yourself as much as possible through books, classes, periodicals, Internet browsing, and the occasional failure.

The first step in sizing your Internet connection, after requirements collection, is to make a manual estimation of the amount of bandwidth use. You can make this rough guesstimation of the bandwidth consumption by putting pen to paper (or formulas to spreadsheet) and working the numbers. As a working example, take the following scenario.

Low-Bandwidth Inc. wants to connect to the Internet. Its main application is email and it's critical to Low-Bandwidth's business. Proposals are delivered via email, and orders are processed from its Web site that is co-located at the ISP. The email server is also currently hosted by the ISP. Low-Bandwidth has 125 employees who use computers, and email specifically, to conduct business over the Internet.

Each employee receives an average of 20 emails per day, and the average size of the email is less than 15KB. Management has requested that after an email is available on the mail server, it should take less than 1 second to retrieve on a client workstation.

Low-Bandwidth Inc. tries to accommodate its employees by allowing employees to work flex-time, so the workday window of sending email is 10 hours long.

So what do you have? You have the number of employees, 125, who send an average of 15 emails per day, each of which averages 15KB or less, distributed over a 10 hour workday. Using some simple arithmetic and a normal distribution curve from Statistics 101 you can determine the average maximum bandwidth usage (see Figure 4.2).

Users = 125
Workday = 10 h
Emails/User = 15
Email Size = 102400 b or 100kb

Response Time SLA = 1sec.

Emails/Workday = 1,825
Bytes/Workday = 192,000,000
Avg. Max Bytes/Second = 6994.48
Avg. Max Bit/Second = 55,955.9

BW • (20%) = 55,955.9
BW = 279,779.4

$$f(x, m, s) = \frac{1}{2\pi s} e^{\frac{-(x-m)}{2s^2}}$$

m = Mean
s = Standard Deviation

f (1.10, 5.5, 3) =

1 = 0.04317
2 = 0.06733
3 = 0.09397
4 = 0.11736
5 = 0.13115
6 = 0.13115
7 = 0.11736
8 = 0.09397
9 = 0.06733
10 = 0.04317

Figure 4.2 Figuring out the amount of bandwidth you need is simple math you can do on a napkin.

Traffic patterns do not always follow the normal distribution curve, even with a large standard deviation. WAN use often ramps up to the available bandwidth and then flattens out, not because usage is not getting higher, but because the maximum possible throughput has been achieved. Because you have yet to establish a maximum bandwidth threshold, using a normal distribution curve is your best bet at estimating the peak workload.

Calculating peak usage can be done in a spreadsheet or on a napkin. Because network usage is never constant for any length of time, it's important to ensure that your network is scalable.

Multiplying the number of employees by the average number of emails per employee per workday gives you the average number of emails per workday. Multiplying that result by the number of bytes per email gives you the average number of bytes per workday. Multiplying that number by the peak workload via our normal distribution curve, you get the maximum number of bytes per hour. Divide that by 3,600 to get the peak bytes per second.

Of course almost all bandwidth is measured in bits per second, not bytes per second. Multiplying our result by 8 gives us the number of raw bits per second required to handle our requirements.

If this were a perfect world, theoretically a single 56Kbps leased line or a single B channel from an ISDN link would suffice to handle the email traffic of Low-Bandwidth Inc. Of course there would be no additional room for any other Internet traffic—no DNS, no Web surfing, no file transfers, and no multimedia streaming. Because the user's email routines might not follow the normal distribution curve, a few modifications need to be made to the sizing worksheet.

A more scalable method of working this would be to say that the email traffic should not consume more than 20% of the available bandwidth at any time. This allows for scaling up to meet the needs of sending those 10MB PowerPoint presentations, while also allowing other normal Internet traffic.

Doing so changes our requirements from 55.9Kbps to 279.8Kbps. So a 256Kbps or 384Kbps link would be more appropriate to meet these traffic needs.

Bandwidth Doesn't Always Mean Performance

Providing the appropriate amount of bandwidth on its WAN connectivity does not necessarily guarantee Low-Bandwidth Inc. a service level of opening an email in one second or less. Why? Because this model does not take into account overhead—for example, the TCP connection handshake to the server, starting the IMAP4 or POP3 service, authentication, authorization, latency in mail server disk access, current mail server load, adding network and transport layer headers, and checksums on the frames.

A more controlled way of meeting the SLA is to have your own mail server on-site. This allows you to monitor and manage the mail server resources so the load never becomes an issue. You can also keep all mail client traffic on the local LAN, rather than traversing the WAN. This reduces the amount of overall email traffic, as emails destined for multiple recipients are not pulled down over the WAN multiple times. Most mail transfer agents deliver just one message over the wire to a mail server for multiple recipients. The email is then delivered to the individual recipient mailboxes locally. See Table 4.3 for a comparison of the advantages of ISP provided service verses locally hosted service.

Table 4.3 ISP Provided Service or Locally Hosted Service?

Service Type	Advantages	Disadvantages
ISP Provided Service	ISP already has infrastructure in-place. ISP responsible for increasing capacity and otherwise administrating services. ISP maintains backups.	ISP hosts many clients on the same servers. Your data might not be 100% confidential. Some services, such as email, are more efficient locally. ISP might be slower in doing backup restores than you like.
Locally Hosted Service	You have full control over server providing service. Client traffic and passwords stay on your network. Internal, confidential data never leaves your network when sending to internal addresses. If the WAN link fails, locally hosted services still function for internal users.	You have full responsibility over the server providing the service. You must purchase the hardware and software licenses. You must have the support staff to administrate the services. Things such as fire suppression and off-site copies of backups are your responsibility.

Criticality of Internet Connection

Gauging the criticality of your Internet connection is going to depend on many criteria, not the least important being your I.T. budget. There is no black box voodoo magic involved in making your connection to the cyberworld highly available: All it takes is money, equipment, and more than one ISP.

Of course there are varying levels of "highly available," and therefore different solutions. Three solutions are examined here: hosting all servers onsite; critical outbound access, no critical on-site servers; and bandwidth-on-demand—out of speed.

Hosting All Servers On-Site

The first scenario is that you're hosting all servers on-site, and it's critical that traffic reaches its intended destination. Multihoming is the solution you're looking for—permanently connecting your company to multiple ISPs simultaneously, not just multiple connections to the same ISP. Multihoming protects your Internet connectivity; if there is a problem upstream with one

ISP, the other should be able to pick up the slack. Additionally you are protected if there are circuit problems; most likely you will not lose both circuits at once.

Make sure that if you go through all this trouble to maintain constant Internet connectivity that you have two different telecom rooms, hopefully in different buildings, attached to two different power sources. Separating your demarcation points in this way ensures that something as simple and common as losing air-conditioning in your telecom room will not shut down all the network gear and thus your Internet connection.

Critical Outbound Access, No Critical On-Site Servers

The second scenario involves no critical servers on-site, but it's critical that users be able to still access certain services from the Internet. In this situation, a dial-on-demand or a dedicated low-bandwidth backup circuit might save the day. A low-speed frame relay or DSL circuit, or even a dial-on-demand ISDN circuit can often still provide basic services to your company if the main circuit is having trouble.

Bandwidth use can be optimized over the backup link allowing critical traffic only, so if email is the critical application and Web surfing is of secondary importance, you can filter out all other traffic such as FTP, prioritize email, and make HTTP a lower priority. Dial-on-demand ISDN and DSL circuits offer a low-cost solution to certain high availability concerns.

Bandwidth-on-Demand: Out of Speed

The third scenario isn't necessarily about high availability of the Internet connection, rather it is about scalable bandwidth in maintaining application performance. Many vendors' routers offer bandwidth-on-demand—ISDN circuits that are activated when certain traffic use thresholds are crossed. This type of solution is really a stopgap. It does not solve the real problem—insufficient bandwidth for the applications involved over that connection. It doesn't provide real scalability, and it doesn't provide high availability because it is tied to a single piece of equipment.

Some of the concerns relating to Internet connection downtime can be mitigated with Service Level Agreements with your ISP. Other concerns can be mitigated by putting critical services off-site in environments that have 24/7 monitoring and security. 100% uptime of all services is not achievable, but with enough money 99.999%, about 5 minutes of downtime per year, certainly is. An uptime of 99.9%, about 8 hours 45 minutes of downtime per year, should be achievable without any major effort on your part beyond the selection of a reputable ISP, quality components, and careful configuration control policies and procedures.

Additional Services

There are additional services that ISPs offer, or that you might be implementing which will affect your connection requirements. Services such as Virtual Private Networks, Remote Access, Multimedia, Multicasting, and the MBONE.

Virtual Private Networks

Virtual Private Networks (VPNs) are composed of encrypted, strongly authenticated traffic tunneled between mobile users (road warriors), or remote locations. The VPN is logically connected over a physical connection to the Internet that is usually local for the user or remote office.

Remote Access

Many national ISPs offer local dial-up access to their network infrastructure, which can then be tunneled back into your private network via VPN technology. This removes the need for you to manage and maintain local on-site dial-up services for the user population. Obviously as part of a fail-safe backup plan, there must be strongly authenticated dial-up facilities for administrators to access the network in case of a major malfunction.

Multimedia, Multicasting, and the MBONE

ISPs also offer multimedia services, such as access to the multicasting MBONE. Internet Audio and Video stations are available for all sorts of uses, whether listing to radio stations from other countries or watching video clips on your favorite news station. H.323, the standard for videoconferencing over TCP/IP, is also very popular.

Security

The decisions you have made thus far will directly influence your security design. The Internet applications your users need and those you need to offer to the Internet will shape your security policies.

The location of your servers, whether hosted or co-located at the ISP or hosted on-site by yourself, will directly affect the design and cost of your security implementation:

- Servers and services hosted off-site simplifies policy immensely; you need only allow established in-bound sessions.
- The more servers and services you host on-site, the more holes must be allowed through the firewall for in-bound traffic. To prevent compromised servers from having access to your internal network, you must isolate them on a DMZ.
- The more hardware and software required for building a DMZ, the greater the overall cost of connecting to the Internet.
- Multimedia streaming protocols are notoriously difficult to support because they use multiple ports in a range and the connectionless UDP protocol. To support these protocols, you must purchase a firewall that directly supports streaming media.

The simpler your security policies, the more manageable and effective they tend to be. If your design and policies are too complex, you run a much greater risk of error. Any high degree of complexity should be taken as feedback that there is probably a simpler and more secure solution. Simplify the services as much as possible. Meet your stated goals, but enforce your security policy. For instance, if you need to allow in-bound file transfers, which are notoriously insecure, provide a "file drop box," a machine with appropriate disk space dedicated to receiving files on a DMZ. If that machine is attacked and successfully compromised, your other hosted services and internal network will not be affected. Additional examples can be found in Chapters 8 and 10.

Security should also be layered. Security measures fail and can be compromised or even bypassed. Rely on no single point of failure, and you have a much greater chance of succeeding in protecting your company, and its resources, from intrusion.

By defining and refining your Internet stated goals, you will directly affect your design. The more services you host, the more protection you'll need to deploy. The more complex services you offer, the more likely you'll need to rely on a firewall product specifically designed with support for those services. Proper licensing of complex commercial products can be extremely costly, so be sure to take those factors into budgetary account. Of course implementing products without complying with product licensing can be more costly to you and your business.

Cost

In a perfect world, you have an unlimited budget, a fully trained IT staff allowing all your needs and security concerns to be met, and management who understand that everything you ask for the company *needs*. Unfortunately, this is rarely the case. Because of this you will need to prioritize your *needs* and your *wants*. The following sections take a look at some indispensable pieces of equipment.

Customer Premises Equipment

The equipment you will need on your site consists of a CSU/DSU for Leased-line circuits, NT1 for ISDN circuits, and DSL modem for DSL circuits. These devices provide the interface between the bandwidth delivery demarcation and your network. You can easily expect to budget $1,000 for CSU/DSU type equipment. ISDN NT1 equipment is quite a bit cheaper, as are DSL modems. DSL and ISDN modems are in the $300 range.

Routers provide the network layer interconnectivity between your LAN and the WAN that connects you to your ISP or your remote locations. Routers also provide the first layer of defense in the form of packet screening. Routers range from very inexpensive to outrageously expensive. Spending $50,000 on a fully configured high-end router is not uncommon.

Single-port Ethernet to ISDN routers are extremely inexpensive, under $1,000. Most modern ISDN routers include the NT1 necessary to connect directly to the ISDN jack in the wall.

Low-end, single-port Ethernet to T1/E1 speed serial connections start in the $1,500 range. The very low-end routers are fixed configuration, meaning if you want to add a dial-on-demand ISDN link to your remote office, you must purchase a new router. The only consistent thing about technology is change. Therefore, it is worthwhile to look for an upgradable or modular router. Hardware features such as additional RAM, flash RAM, LAN and WAN interface ports, and integrated CSU/DSUs are available for most low-end modular routers. Most vendors also have upgraded software features such as additional non-IP protocol support, embedded fire-walling, and VPN capability. Be aware that the additional software features usually increase the RAM and flash requirements, increasing your base hardware costs.

Firewalls and Servers

Firewalls, properly configured, provide another layer of security to your data and systems. Firewalls often are the connection point between your internal networks, DMZ bastion LANs, and the connection to the router.

If your ISP is not hosting your mail, DNS, or Web services, then you will be purchasing servers to do those jobs. Is one machine enough to handle all those services for your company? That is going to depend on a number of factors, such as bandwidth to the box, expected load per service, encrypted versus clear-text traffic, and dynamically generated versus static content. At the other extreme, is it wise to separate out the services each to a dedicated box? Although it simplifies the configuration and administration of each individual server, increasing the number of servers can complicate your design and certainly increase your hardware costs and administrative overhead. The major impact, as with most design decisions, will be to your budget.

Where to Cut Corners

When working on your designs keep security in the forefront of your mind. The cost of implementing and maintaining a secure network might be a factor in your design, however it should never be the sole driver. When choosing where to cut corners it should never be security because that could eventually compromise your entire business. The following sections look at some places where you might be able to save money.

Evaluate Integrated Solutions

When looking at routers, consider fixed configuration routers if you either know that the needs will not change, or if the price is that insignificant. A fixed configuration router cannot be upgraded or changed in its port configuration. If you buy a single-port Ethernet, single-port ISDN router such as the Cisco 802 it cannot be used to connect multiple Ethernets or connect to an ADSL WAN. Because most fixed configuration routers are so inexpensive, if your needs change they can always be redeployed at a smaller branch office or used as a backup to the main connection.

Many vendors offer integrated WAN interface cards for their modular routers. A WAN interface card is the serial interface and CSU/DSU integrated into a single card. This eliminates having to buy a serial interface, a CSU/DSU, and a cable. Eliminating components simplifies the setup and removes points of failure while cutting your cost. Of course, you might not be able to use integrated components in your application, so you can begin to see how crucial the initial requirements collecting is on the design process.

This process can be taken a step further by not only integrating the CPE into a single piece of equipment, but also collapsing your DMZ and firewall into your router. The two major routing hardware vendors, Cisco Systems and Nortel Networks, both offer modular routers that have integrated CSU/DSUs, additional expandability for additional WAN and LAN ports, and integrated firewall and VPN software.

Using Internet appliances is another popular alternative. Internet appliances are, basically Intel- or MIPS-based computers running a customized operating system (usually Linux or FreeBSD) to control all the embedded services. Internet Appliances are popular because they can not only provide the same WAN and LAN connectivity, firewalling, and VPN services that the routers provide, but also server functionality as well. Because most Internet appliances are running a fully capable operating system, they can run Internet services such as email, domain name resolution, Web hosting, and file/print sharing.

Staged Approach

When connecting your business to the Internet, it's usually to meet a set of stated goals. Meeting those goals usually also involves a schedule and timeframe. Properly designing, procuring, staging, validating, migrating to production, and revalidating all takes time. If your deadlines are unrealistic, completing the goals in stages is a compromise that allows your company to start conducting business on the Internet and your I.T. staff to properly and securely connect to the Internet.

Let the ISP Carry the Load Initially

ISPs often offer extended services. Those services range anywhere from DNS, email, and Web site hosting to co-location of your equipment or even network engineering services to assist you in designing your WAN connectivity.

Making use of those services, at least initially, removes some pressure to have the WAN connectivity done yesterday. Allowing the ISP to host your DNS, email, and Web site gives you an Internet presence while allowing you to design, test, and redesign the components of your WAN infrastructure.

After you have the infrastructure in place, and the staff trained to deal with it properly, you can begin migrating services to your internal servers. You might find that some services, such as HTTP and e-commerce, are best left either hosted or co-located at the ISP. Such decisions can be made based on policy, maintenance issues, and costs rather than on arbitrary schedules.

Reiteration Is Your Constant Companion

Reviewing and revising your WAN connectivity and security architecture is a given, not a sign of poor initial design. Reiteration of the design process does not stop after your company is connected to the Internet. As your users' requirements change, so will parts of your Internet connectivity. As your users find new uses for the Internet, the demand on the bandwidth of your WAN connectivity will change (for example, streaming audio/video, Internet radio, .mp3 swapping, animated Xmas cards, and so on). As intruders find new exploits against your WAN infrastructure, the security policies, software, and perhaps entire configuration of your DMZ will change.

After your Internet connection is up and running, the work is not over. Capacity planning and general performance tuning, troubleshooting, and monitoring of security are daily tasks that need attention. The real art of designing WAN connectivity is allowing an architecture that will scale as your business increase.

Connection Requirements Checklist

First there are Internet applications accessed from the Internet. Which ones will you be providing?

- HTTP, HTTPS
- SMTP
- IMAP4
- POP3
- DNS Client Lookups
- DNS Server Zone Transfers
- FTP
- Telnet
- SSH
- NNTP
- NTP
- RTSP
- RTP

Next come Internet applications provided to the Internet. Again, which ones will you be providing?

- DNS Client Lookups
- DNS Server Zone Transfers

- SMTP
- IMAP4
- POP3
- HTTP / HTTPS
- FTP
- NNTP
- RTSP
- RTP

Which, if any, additional services will you be providing for your users?

- Virtual Private Networks
- Remote Access
- Multicasting, Streaming Multimedia, and MBONE

The following are cost factors for budgeting. Which pieces of equipment will you need to lease or purchase?

- CPE, including CSU/DSU and Router
- Servers to provide services
- Firewall—appliance or server
- Software and licenses
- Switch for building DMZ
- Uninterruptable Power Supply

5

CHOOSING AN ISP

When choosing between evils, I always like to take the one I've never tried
before.

—Mae West

Selecting the Right ISP Is a Critical Decision

Choosing the right ISP ensures your company's foothold on the Internet. A
good ISP won't just connect you to the Internet, but will also work with you
to make your Internet presence the best it can be. ISPs can provide consulting services, advice, equipment, labor, and experts. Choosing the wrong ISP
can leave your business in the lurch at a critical moment.

There are a number of things to keep in mind when choosing the company
that will bring the Internet to your door. Cost and reliability are two of
these things. But you also need to ask questions such as

- **Is critical equipment redundant?** This includes not only the ISP's
  routers, switches, and servers, but its Internet connection as well—
  ideally, the ISP should have multiple, high-speed connections so
  there's no single point of failure.

- **Are you buying guaranteed bandwidth?** A dedicated 100Mbps switched Ethernet port, for example, looks very high, but if you're sharing the upstream riser bandwidth with 240 other companies, your actual speed might be significantly less.
- **How well will the ISP support you both during setup and maintenance of your Internet connection?** Does it have 24-hour support?
- **Will the ISP maintain equipment for you on its site?** Is there an additional charge?

Good ISPs care about your business, will actively court you, and are genuinely concerned with your continued happiness. And why shouldn't they be? A good ISP will get your business for years to come and will be appreciative of recommendations you make to your peers. Even a medium-sized company can spend thousands of dollars on an Internet connection every year. ISPs want the continuation of that business in a mutually beneficial way. There's nothing worse for an ISP than a dissatisfied customer outing their grievances on Usenet, and there's little better than a glowing review. If you don't think your ISP is trying to get that glowing review out of you, then it's not working hard enough.

NSP or ISP?

NSPs, or Network Service Providers, are different from ISPs (Internet service providers) in that NSPs maintain their own Internet connections and typically only sell to large companies with dedicated connections. (They also sell to ISPs.) ISPs, on the other hand, typically sell dial-up services to individual users. This is not to say that your ISP can't sell you a T1, because it probably can. The ISP might not be able to sell you a pair of T3s, however. If you want to resell the service you're getting, check with your ISP first to make sure this is allowable under its contract. If you expect to resell a lot of service, you'll definitely want to get an NSP.

Network Access Point (NAP)

Network Access Points are large switching facilities that ISPs use to interconnect their networks. NAPs are the "inter" part of the Internet. Originally, there were four such NAPs, one each in Washington D.C., New York City, Chicago, and San Francisco. Large ISPs and bandwidth providers generally create peering arrangements in NAPs. A peering arrangement is an agreement to directly exchange high-speed traffic flows between two network service providers in a NAP. Peering arrangements are important when trying to determine your target audience, as you will see later. Peering arrangements of high-speed interconnects between bandwidth providers also explain why geographical distances do not translate well to cyberspace.

Metropolitan Area Exchange (MAE)

Before MCI/Worldcom was awarded NAP status by the National Science Foundation, Worldcom along with smaller ISPs created exchange points that allowed for the interconnections of the ISP networks. Those exchange points are known as Metropolitan Area Exchanges, or MAEs (pronounced "may"). A MAE is similar to a NAP, in that it is a switching facility where ISPs can exchange information at high speeds. The MAE itself does no routing, however, only routers or hosts acting as routers are connected to the switching infrastructure at a MAE.

MAEs, like ISPs, are categorized into two tiers. A Tier-1 MAE has one or more major ISP directly connected to the facility. The ISP uses routers with large CPU and memory capacities for the large routing tables that are required. The two primary Tier-1 MAEs are MAE EAST in Washington D.C., and MAE WEST in San Jose, California.

The Tier-2 MAEs are regional interconnection points. This means that few or no major ISPs are directly connected to the MAE facility. A Tier-2 MAE can grow to become a Tier-1 facility, but there is no guarantee that it will. Several Tier-2 MAEs have since been added in the following cities: Chicago, Dallas, Houston, Los Angeles, and New York City.

The Tiers of Babel

There are two major classes of Internet service providers. The Network Service Provider, or Tier-1 ISP, sells dedicated bandwidth to a large range of customers. The Tier-1 ISP normally does not deal with residential Internet connectivity. Tier-1 ISPs normally sell their bandwidth and connectivity to Tier-2 ISPs.

A Tier-2 ISP is normally either a local or regional ISP that not only resells dedicated leased-line bandwidth and connectivity, but also caters to the SOHO or residential customers.

There is nothing intrinsically inferior about a Tier-2 ISP. On the contrary, a Tier-2 ISP with multiple connection points to multiple Tier-1 ISPs might be better than a Tier-1 ISP. The link can be severed or disabled due to problems to a Tier-1 ISP and your Internet-bound traffic will still flow.

When selecting a Tier-2 ISP, it is important to know who its transit providers are. A *transit provider* is a company paid to re-advertise routes on behalf of the ISP. Transit providers are necessary for those networks your ISP does not peer directly with. Only ISPs at a Tier-1 NAP normally carry or advertise the full Internet routing lists.

Cost

When choosing an ISP, there are several cost factors to consider aside from the obvious cost of the Internet connection, which can be measured in several ways. There is also the cost of purchasing and maintaining your equipment, your software licenses, your e-commerce solution, your mail, your Web reports, and any other special services you might be getting. Your contract will provide a base level of service, such as the speed of your connection to the Internet, a Usenet feed, a level of Web hosting, and email services. The actual level of service, of course, will depend on what type of package you buy from your ISP.

Paying by Bandwidth

One way your ISP might charge is by bandwidth, which is the diameter of your data pipe. This is the most common method; typically this is defined by the type of connection you buy, such as ISDN, T1, or T3—other connection types, such as xDSL and Fractional T1 and T3 come in a variety of speeds that your ISP should outline for you.

Paying by Usage

Another way to pay is by the amount of data you actually pass through your connection. This is most desirable if you have a low amount of traffic but want it to arrive quickly when you do transmit.

Extras

Extras not included in your original contract might include equipment that your ISP buys for you or that you lease from them, or space at their site to house your servers or to perform maintenance on them. Also, an ISP might charge you to provide e-commerce solutions; sophisticated, secure Web hosting; or help desk support.

Reimbursements for Network Downtime

The level of confidence that an ISP has in its capability to provide a continuous level of service is often indicative of its capability to provide that service.

If your ISP is a good one, it will offer a guarantee of uptime in the form of a Service Level Agreement. The SLA will spell out the guaranteed level of service you can expect. Should the ISP fail to maintain those levels of service, you would be entitled to a reimbursement for any time that your network is unreachable as a result of an error on the ISP's part. The reimbursement amounts are also generally detailed in the SLA. If the ISP is not willing to provide you with a SLA, you might want to keep looking.

Reliability/Reputation

Without a doubt, the best way to choose an ISP is based on its reliability and reputation. There's no gain in paying only half the price to a discount ISP with 70% uptime.

Peer Survey

The best way to gauge an ISP's reputation is with a telephone or a few pieces of email. Call your friends and neighbors and ask which ISP they're using; find out what they're complaining about and what they're happy with. Have they ever called the help desk? How quickly are email messages and phone calls returned?

If you don't have any local contacts, flip through the yellow pages and just call the IT departments at companies of a similar size to yours. Most people will take three minutes out of their day to tell you that they love or hate their ISP. In fact, if they're using a really good ISP, they'll be dying to tell you how much they like it.

Things you'll want to ask about:

- Were there any hidden charges?
- How quickly does the ISP respond to complaints or questions and how quickly were these resolved?
- What's the level of network uptime? Is service regularly interrupted or interrupted for long periods of time? Has your network ever been down? (No network is up 100% of the time—service can be interrupted by thunderstorms, power failures, or difficulties at the telco, but an uptime of 99.9% is not unrealistic.)
- Have there been problems with billing?
- Does the ISP have good record keeping? When you talk to them, do they know who you are? Do you have to keep repeating yourself every time you call them?

Capacity (Can Your ISP Meet Your Needs?)

One thing you need to be assured of is that your ISP will be able to provide enough data pipe to your location. Make sure that the Internet service you're getting is scalable in the likely event that your company grows.

Installation and Setup Services ISPs Offer

Shopping for an Internet connection is more complex than just getting a data pipe to your door. There are a host of options you can choose from. No two ISPs are identical; however, many are alike and any decently sized ISP will offer all these options.

Bandwidth Options

The amount of bandwidth you choose will depend on the size of your organization and your Internet habits. For example, if you're serving video off your Web site, you'll have different needs than if you're only sending email.

A small- or medium-sized company might need a 56k or T1 connection; a larger organization with intensive Internet usage might need multiple T1 or T3 connections. Your ISP should work with you to determine the amount of bandwidth you need.

Whatever you get, make sure it's rapidly scalable. The Internet is changing quickly and a 56k connection to the Internet that today seems sluggish was the backbone speed of the entire NSFNET in 1986.

Web Hosting

Web hosting is one of the most common tasks tackled by ISPs. The advantages of having your ISP serve your Web pages are multifold. One is that it's not traveling through your data pipe and competing with your own Internet traffic. Another advantage is that you don't have to maintain a Web server at your site, which is a potential security risk (because you can't put a Web server behind a firewall, it needs to be out in the open). Also, you don't have to maintain a support staff to tend to the Web server. Hopefully your ISP also has better uptime than you do and a faster response to network problems.

Typically, an ISP sells you Web hosting by size or bandwidth. You can pay from $20/month to several hundred depending on the type of services you get, the amount of disk space you need, and the types of additional services you might be using from e-commerce to video streaming.

Some other things that your ISP might provide in its Web hosting are as follows:

- Credit card processing
- Web-creation tools
- Secure Socket Layer encryption for secure transactions and resources to help you use them
- Support personnel to help with your Web site implementation—such things as CGI scripting or database maintenance
- Site management tools, telling you what pages your customers hit, how many times, and how long they looked

Mail Hosting

Rather than run your own mail server, you can have your ISP do it for you. This is a reasonable choice if you have less than 50 or 60 users.

Knowledge Services (Help Desk/Consulting)

No matter how smart you are, your ISP will have to help you with some things. Knowing that the ISP is there 24/7 to answer questions is a good thing. It's also important to know whether you're going to get charged for the call. Any ISP you buy service from should have knowledgeable technicians on call 24 hours a day.

Managing Equipment Lease

There are several ways you and your ISP can handle the equipment used to connect your Customer Premises Equipment (CPE) with your ISP's Point Of Presence (POP). Either the ISP owns and maintains your CPE, which you lease from them, or you own the equipment outright, whether you bought it from the ISP or not. You might sign an agreement with the ISP so that it maintains your equipment in either regard. But keep in mind if you do so, the ISP might need access (either physical or remote) to the equipment at any time. This access might mean giving the ISP keys to closets or dedicated phone/modem lines to access routers or servers.

IP Address Blocks

You'll need an IP address for every computer you want actually on the Internet. It's possible that you'll be using IP masking (hiding your network behind one IP address), but if not, you'll need an IP address for every computer on your network. If you're using DHCP to assign these addresses, it's important that you have a contiguous block or configuring DHCP will become a tedious project. Make sure your ISP has enough IP addresses to cover you. You'll probably pay a monthly fee for each IP address allocated to you, whether you're actually using it or not.

Co-locate: Your Equipment, the ISP's Building

Sometimes called co-hosting, co-location is when your servers are physically stored at your ISP. Co-locate when you want your own dedicated server but you don't have an environmentally controlled location with Halon gas and 24-hour technicians. Usually, a co-location deal involves a server, guaranteed bandwidth, and a support contract. Co-location often can reduce your requirements for a larger connection to the Internet. Pricing is often done by space, the number of bays, cabinets, or square feet your devices take up.

So how do you decide whether to Web host, co-locate, or just get nice big fat pipes to your business? A few answers to some simple questions can help you decide.

What Are You Willing to Outsource?

Which systems are too critical to trust to outside staffing? Which systems are too critical to trust to inside staffing? Obviously, email is considered business critical these days. Static Web servers require little maintenance, but what about dynamic sites, requiring multiple feeds of information, multimedia, and database access? Web sites conducting e-commerce are certainly considered business-critical resources.

As long as you have the IT staffing resources and environment to manage all those systems, there is little need for co-location. However, if you are serving large amounts of multimedia, or a high-volume Web site, then even a large internal connection to the Internet is not a solution.

What Are You Willing to Trust to Someone Else's Expertise?

You might not have the required IT staff to support a number of mail servers, firewalls, and a clustered Web-server environment. You might not have sufficient IT staff to support the desktop computing environment that already exists without the complexities of the Internet.

While you're working to build a core team with the competency and skills to support your business requirements, co-location might provide the migration path.

What Does the ISP Offer?

Does the ISP have a better computing environment? Is it air conditioned properly? Is the air filtered to remove particulates? Is the power conditioned and backed up? Does the ISP have a better IT staff? Does it have Windows NT experience? Does it have UNIX/Linux experience? Is that experience level consistent throughout the 24/7 period you demand?

Can You Afford the Cost of Reliability?

Determine your requirements for a Service Level Agreement. How much would it cost to be down 10 minutes, an hour, a day, two days, and so on? Take that into account when trying to determine if your facilities can meet the needs of your online business presence. Can the ISP co-location environment and staff meet those needs? Will the ISP guarantee that in a SLA?

Co-Location Considerations

If you've concluded that co-location is the right solution for your problem, there are some extended details that you should consider when comparing ISPs that offer co-location.

Don't Use Needy Equipment

Remember that co-location work is done remotely. You don't generally have your staff working on-site at the co-location facility. Therefore, it's important to consider several additional factors when selecting equipment to be used at a co-location environment.

Design and build your equipment to survive better because it is not physically accessible. Buy better equipment rather than cheaper, although that doesn't exclude inexpensive equipment. Higher performance components that push performance thermal limits tend to wear out faster than lower performance components. Overpurchase equipment for capacity, such as larger power supplies and larger number of drives in a RAID array. Purchase a tape autochanger so the tapes are rotated automatically. Your ISP will quickly lose patience with you if you're calling every day to ask it to change backup tapes so you can restore something.

Use the Most Reliable Equipment: Stay Away from the Bleeding Edge of Technology

Be sure to stage all OS and application updates in-house before implementing them in the production co-location environment. In a production environment, run the most stable OS and applications, not necessarily the newest or most feature-rich. Bleeding edge technologies in operating systems don't generally make the most stable systems. The basic principle of security, "Keep it Simple," applies equally well to stability in a remote production environment.

Make Your Systems Remotely Accessible

Run your co-located systems without keyboards and monitors. Serial consoles such as those available from LightWave Communications and Western Telematic make excellent remote control devices. You can telnet to the serial console to control any piece of network equipment or serial-connected server. Additionally, an analog modem in the serial console provides backup access to your environment. This is useful in case of failed access equipment or remote upgrades of the router or firewall.

Locality

Everyone wants to do business with local businesses. It's better for the local economy. Besides, if you have to drive to the facility at 2 a.m., how convenient is it to drive two states over? Keep in mind, however, that sometimes local does not mean convenient. Consider what else is close to the co-location facility. Normal everyday events such as conventions and sporting events can cause havoc if you're co-located near a convention center or a sporting arena. Is the ISP located on a mountaintop prone to lightning strikes? Also don't forget rush hour traffic in and around larger metropolitan areas can impede your travels to the co-location facility. You won't be able to *rush* over to replace a failed NIC card or hard drive at 4:30 p.m. in Los Angeles.

Reduce Single Points of Failure

Reduce or remove all single points of failure in both your servers and your network gear. For your network infrastructure

- Install redundant firewalls with failover capacity.
- Use Layer4 load balancing network equipment. It should be able to not only balance the load, but also monitor the services and remove those failed servers from use.
- Use redundant routers with Virtual Router Redundancy Protocol (VRRP, defined in RFC 2338) or Hot Standby Routing Protocol (Cisco's proprietary protocol).

Your Web servers can be inexpensive boxes that are protected from failure by the load-balancing hardware. For servers that cannot be clustered, however, you will need to build them more resistant to failure. The following are some simple steps:

- Add redundant power supplies.
- Install multiple processors. SMP machines are redundant, not just better for speed.
- Use ECC memory.
- Use RAID arrays to prevent disk failure.

Looking at the list of additional hardware you are purchasing might seem daunting at first. Realize, however, that for true high availability you would need to purchase that hardware anyway. One of the reasons you might be co-locating is because of lack of IT staff or to better distribute the high traffic requirements your Internet connectivity requires.

Targeting Your Traffic with Peering

What is your target network audience? If most of your traffic is targeted to a particular audience, it might make sense to have your servers at an ISP that has better peering or connectivity to your target networks. The following are some common targeted networks that have peering arrangements:

- Broadband networks such as @Home and RoadRunner
- Portals such as Yahoo! and Excite
- Online service providers such as AOL and CompuServe
- WAP networks such as Sprint
- SOHO or residential dial-up users from UUNET or AT&T

If you have no Internet presence now, it might be difficult to know where your customers are, and therefore difficult to target them. You can still get an idea of the capabilities of your ISP by asking who it peers with.

Physical Security

Physical security of your equipment is often overlooked. Equipment located on your site is under your control. Most everyone inside your office is an employee or under the supervision of an employee. Still most businesses physically lock down computing resources. You should ask no less of your ISP for co-location.

ISPs will be housing equipment for many businesses and even individuals. You will want to make sure that you can prevent accidental or intentional tampering with your equipment and its connectivity. You really don't want a bored ISP technician playing solitaire on your Web server while drinking a fruit juice. A quick checklist of some security measures:

- Security staff to monitor access to the facility.
- Client-approved access lists, so the security staff has a measure of control of authorizing access.
- Electronic access via badge, electronic token, or biometric means, so access cannot be accidentally granted to imposters.
- Video surveillance records, for obvious reasons.
- Individually locked cages. It's important that keys to the locks are unique; many ISPs use the same cage/rack vendor, which might use a standard key.

It's important to ensure that you have 24/7 physical access to your equipment. If you have staff that needs to fix a down e-commerce server at 3:00 a.m., you should not be prevented access.

Accessibility Considerations

Almost all equipment in a co-location is rack mounted. The rack could be a stand-up, floor-mounted 19-inch rack, or it could be an enclosed lockdown cabinet to prevent tampering.

Raised floors provide for flood protection, and drop ceilings generally provide space to run cabling. Additional support for running cabling could be in the form of cable trays. Do the ISP's racks, cages, and cable-trays have tie-down support for strapping of equipment? Although this isn't normally a concern in New York City, non-trivial earthquakes do happen in the western half of the United States. Making sure your equipment stays in the racks is the first step in lengthening its useful lifetime.

Inspect the rack mounting for workspace. Try to allow at least 22 inches of clearance for technicians to hot swap components.

Does the ISP provide equipment carts, telephone access for tech support, or chairs to sit in while on hold?

For your remote access modems, be sure that you can get analog circuits installed into the cages or lines run to the rack.

Is there enough space to store spare parts on location, or will you need to bring them from your facility? In addition to spare parts, tools are convenient to store on location as well.

You can conserve some space in racks and cages by using terminal servers/serial consoles and keyboard/video/mouse switches to control your multitude of boxes.

Computing Environment: Heating, Ventilation, and Air Conditioning

All the network gear and computing equipment will take care of the heating. That's the problem. Ensure that the ISP has the appropriate amount of air conditioning to handle the thermal output of the equipment in the room. Ask what the expansion plans are, both in capacity of the air conditioning units and the amount of new equipment that will be placed in the room.

Don't be timid—walk around the computing room to check for "hot spots," areas where the ventilation doesn't move the cooling air from the air conditioners. Check the environmental gauges for the room; you want to keep the temperature close to 68°F (20°C), with 50% or less humidity.

Ask about the fire suppression systems. Halon, which used to be the industry standard, was outlawed due to environmental reasons. Luckily, there are alternatives, such as FM-200 from Great Lakes Chemical, which extinguishes fire without water damage or damage to the ozone. Although the fire suppression system waits before dumping the gas (so that people can evacuate the room), FM-200 is also "breathable" at fire-suppressing levels, although you probably wouldn't want to do it on a regular basis.

For all your electronic equipment, you'll need power. Not just any power, but clean, consistent, non-interrupted power. Most computer rooms are on an uninterruptible power supply or two. Make sure the ISP maintains the battery banks. Redundancy through multiple uninterruptible power supplies is a plus, as are diesel generators. A UPS will generally only provide minutes, or at most a few hours, of uptime with 80% capacity. Any power outage past that timeframe and handling the number of hits per second will be the least of your concerns. If your uptime is absolutely essential, make sure the ISP has the diesel fuel onsite to power the generator.

Taking redundancy a step further, ask the ISP if they are drawing power from two different power grids. That way if one goes down, the second should pick up the slack.

Do yourself a favor, and when preparing to move into a co-location facility, provide the ISP with an accurate count of required amps. Often times the ISP will only provide 30–40 amps with the default package. Any additional power capacity will come with an additional monthly recurring charge.

Extended Support Services

To reduce your need to visit the co-location facility, you can rely on the ISP's 24/7 support. This might require the ISP to have physical access to your equipment for power cycling, tape rotation, or hardware swap-out. If you become intimate enough with your ISP, you can rely on it to be your remote hands.

Network Infrastructure

The network infrastructure the ISP is using is extremely important. It doesn't make sense to build a nice, scalable architecture that sits behind dual OC-3Cs to the Internet if your co-located equipment is connected to a 10Mbps Ethernet hub with 16 other people.

The ISP should be able to offer switched Ethernet, preferably 100Mbps. If the ISP has ATM OC-3, OC-12, or Gigabit Ethernet as an internal backbone, that's even better. You should be able to view a network diagram of the backbone of the co-location center.

Monitoring Network Equipment

Does the ISP allow for monitoring of your equipment? Can it monitor your vendor's equipment? Do you want the ISP monitoring your equipment? Can you configure the monitoring systems on your equipment to page the ISP, your internal IT staff, or both? There could be security considerations in allowing the ISP to monitor your equipment, so you might be relegated to monitoring your own equipment remotely.

Getting to Know the ISP

Bypass the marketing people and contact the ISP's technical support directly to get the detailed answers to the questions that are beyond the scope of the front desk. Make an appointment to physically inspect the data center. Look at its wiring center. Meet the technical people who will be caring for your servers and network equipment. Get personal with them; you'll be relying on them to be your remote hands. Their attention to you will reflect the level of attention your servers will get while you're gone. Remember, you and your ISP should have a symbiotic relationship; the ISP should like working with you and you should like working with it. If everybody does their job properly, you both win.

Customer Support

Large pipes do you no service if they are constantly filled. Although all other attributes of an ISP are important, the customer support people are critical for co-location. Response to service requests and knowledge of your products and operating systems is important. And not just during the day; because the Internet is global, it's important to note that it's always day somewhere.

World Peace and the Perfect ISP

Finding the right ISP, especially for the right price, is not a trivial task. One possible solution to the problem is to find two ISPs that fit the bill, and duplicate installations at each ISP. Using load-balancing hardware such as those from Foundry Networks, Nortel Networks, or Cisco Systems, you can reduce your risk while maximizing your uptime. Of course this might double your initial capital investment, but it will get you closer to 99.999% uptime.

Fair Access to Bandwidth

Class Based Queuing (CBQ) is a technique used to rate-limit bandwidth hogs. CBQ enabled systems and routers enforce bandwidth rate policies on Point-to-Point links. CBQ is often done on a per-hop basis, and negotiated on end-to-end traffic on a per-flow basis. CBQ is implemented in several vendor's routers and operating systems such as Solaris, FreeBSD (ALTQ), and Linux. CBQ is extremely helpful in guaranteeing fair access to available bandwidth when an ISP/co-location provider oversells its capacity.

DiffServ, defined in RFCs 2474 and 2475, is an IP QoS (Quality of Service) recommendation. DiffServ is backward-compatible with the IP ToS (Type of Service) bits, but is not yet widely available. DiffServ does not guarantee bandwidth reservation like RSVP does.

Extended Protocols and Services

You might need some things from your ISP that are above and beyond its "standard fare" for which you might, or might not, have to pay extra.

For example, multicast applications, such as mbone and mbone6 (the IPv6 version of mbone), need multicast capability to stream audio and video. If you're using them on your site and your ISP isn't configured to pass them, you're out of luck. Mbone requires that your ISP have a multicast router, separate from the network's other (production) routers—usually it's a workstation running special software (the mbone routing daemon "mrouted"—versions of this are available for many operating systems, including Windows NT, Solaris, and various UNIX variants).

The mbone network is a virtual network, existing on top of the Internet, which carries streamed multicast data between virtual "tunnels" cored through the Internet. A typical application for mbone would be a media outlet streaming live video or audio signals to hundreds or thousands of end users. Protocols required for this are IGMP, RSVP, and DVRMP. If you'll be using mbone, be sure that your ISP is prepared to route them.

Border Gateway Protocol (BGP4)

BGP is an EGP (exterior gateway protocol) originally defined in RFC 1105. Version 4 of BGP was originally defined in RFC 1654 and later updated in RFC 1771. The main driving force for BGP4 was the large number of networks advertised on the Internet. BGP4 includes a feature to aggregate multiple route advertisements into a single routing table entry. Sounds very similar and complementary to Classless Inter-Domain Routing (CIDR), doesn't it?

BGP4 differs from many other routing protocols in that it is a Path Vector Protocol, rather than a Distance Vector Protocol. DVP routing usually determines a route by the hop count (usually number of routers) and link speed. PVP chooses routes based on the number of Autonomous Systems that need to be traversed.

An Autonomous System is a network or group of networks that is controlled by a single administrative organization. The autonomous system allows administrators to control routing policy for the systems sharing routing information internally. Each Autonomous System is assigned a globally unique number known as an Autonomous System Number (ASN). Autonomous systems are often referred to as routing domains. Because there might be multiple routers in a single AS, and bandwidth is not taken into consideration in BGP4 routing, the path chosen might not always be the most optimal path. BGP4 allows for tweaking of parameters to override route selection through the use of the local-pref attribute.

Multiple connections to different upstream ISPs does not happen without BGP4. Load balancing traffic across multiple links to a single ISP with a single AS is far easier than load balancing across multiple ISPs; keep that in mind when configuring your routers. Modification of BGP4 parameters to affect traffic patterns should always be coordinated with your ISP(s).

IGMP

IGMP is Internet Group Management protocol as defined in RFC 2236. IGMP is used to manage what group memberships you are subscribed to for multicast traffic.

RSVP

RSVP (Resource Reservation Protocol) is another protocol related to multicasting and multimedia. It reserves a requested amount of resources along a path to make sure that multicasting traffic gets through. Ordinarily, the Internet makes a best-effort at delivering data; however, in the eyes of the Internet all data is created equal. RSVP augments this with traffic and service request specifications which allow some data to be more equal than others. This is done by enabling the allocation of bandwidth, stating maximum allowable delays, and packet loss rates.

RSVP sits at Layer 4 in the OSI model and works in conjunction with IP routing protocols and access control. RSVP attempts to guarantee a particular level of data transmission by reserving bandwidth. It does this through the use of traffic queues, timers, and filters. ATM was designed from the ground up to support QoS natively, however packet-based networks such as Ethernet and Token-Ring do not.

To compensate for this deficiency there is a relatively new IETF draft protocol called the Common Open Policy Service (COPS) protocol. To help enforce QoS over the overall connection COPS exchanges policy information between network resources such as servers and routers. The servers act as policy decision points (PDPs); network administrators can define what classes of traffic have specific priorities. The routers act as policy enforcement points (PEPs), prioritizing or rate limiting the traffic as it is tagged by RSVP. Prioritization of traffic on routers is nothing new; network administrators have often used traffic priority queues on their routers to enhance the perceived performance of interactive traffic such as TELNET over noninteractive traffic like FTP. RSVP basically prioritizes traffic in a temporary and dynamic manner.

RSVP is also responsible for describing the tunneling of multicast packets across non-RSVP connection points. If your ISP doesn't support RSVP, obviously that prevents you from using it. RSVP has been designed to run over both IPv4 and IPv6. RSVP was originally defined in RFC2205 and then later updated in RFC2750. COPS and its usage with RSVP is defined in RFC2748 and RFC2749 respectively. There are several other RFCs discussing RSVP over IPv4 tunneling, and RSVP over IPSec. Feel free to search for RSVP at http://www.rfc-editor.org/.

DVMRP

DVMRP (Distance Vector Multicast Routing Protocol) is the protocol that the mbone router uses. (The mbone router is typically a workstation running mrouted.) It is basically for forwarding packets within a single autonomous system. It also describes how to tunnel packets in an nonmulticasting environment.

Multiple Points of Presence

If you absolutely have to be up 24/7, you might want your ISP to provide multiple Points of Presence. In the event that one site is hit by a bomb or buried beneath a flood, the second (or third, or fourth) Point of Presence will take over your data traffic. This, of course, requires extra work on the part of your ISP to provide a mesh of interconnectivity in its backbone. Otherwise, a POP is just a convenient connection point.

Provisioning a WAN

Provisioning is the actual ordering of the leased-line circuits from the telecommunications company. The circuit is terminated at your site and your selected ISP's nearby Point of Presence (POP). The POPs feed back into the core of the ISP's network. ISPs often bundle the provisioning of the leased-line circuits with the setup of your dedicated Internet connection.

There are several advantages to allowing the ISP to provision the leased-line circuit for you:

- The ISP "owns" the circuit, and if there are problems, it's generally staffed to talk directly to the telco provider to resolve the trouble.
- ISPs usually have partnerships with ILEC/CLECs, and as such most likely have reduced rates due to volume agreements.
- The pricing, ordering, scheduling, and trouble resolution is handled for you by the ISP.

If you already have experience with ordering circuits from your telecommunications company, then you might be able to realize some savings. Provisioning the circuit yourself allows you the flexibility of shopping for a bandwidth provider that meets your criteria. Of course, you will have additional responsibilities, such as placing trouble tickets if there is a problem with the circuit, and a separate telecomm bill from your Internet service.

Various bandwidth delivery options are discussed extensively in Chapter 2, "Understanding WAN Bandwidth Delivery."

Customer Premises Equipment

The leased-line circuit does not magically make your network connected to the Internet. Rather, a class of equipment known as customer premises equipment (CPE) is used to interconnect the leased-line circuits with your LAN.

The CPE usually consists of a channel service unit/data service unit (CSU/DSU), and a router. CPE can be purchased outright or leased through your ISP. Most ISPs offer some sort of managed circuit services similar to those listed here:

- **The ISP provides the CSU/DSU and router**—All CPE is owned, maintained, and configured by the ISP. You do not have any control over the configuration of the equipment; all administrative changes go through your ISP's tech support.
- **The ISP sells you the CSU/DSU and router**—All CPE is owned and maintained by your company. The CPE is configured and managed by the ISP on your behalf. You have administrative control over the configuration through your ISP's tech support.
- **You purchase and maintain the CSU/DSU and router**—You have complete administrative control over the CPE, and generally the ISP has no administrative access. Your in-house IT staff is responsible for making required changes when notified by the ISP.

The most important part of the CPE from an enterprise prospective is the router. This piece of equipment is your gateway to the Internet, and the first bastion of defense to keep your data and your users safe. As such, the configuration on the router might require occasional adjustments as features are requested or security exploits become known. It is important that your IT staff be capable of managing the configuration of the router, or that your ISP is not only capable, but tasked to do so.

Managed Services

ISPs have recently started including value-added services in their repertoire of offerings. As more providers enter the bandwidth market, the profit in selling high-speed connectivity to the Internet starts to diminish. Not many people imagined how quickly the falling prices of leased-line circuits coupled with deployment of newer technologies such as DSL and cable modems would drive bandwidth into nearly a commodity market.

The only avenue ISPs have to maintain profitability is to staff up and offer services along with bandwidth. Those services are more important than the connection itself now. Without security, a connection to the Internet is only a high-speed conduit for intruders to gain access to your network and disrupt business.

Managing Your Router

Managing your router could be as mundane as monitoring your WAN interface to ensure you have the right amount of Internet connectivity for your business, or as frantic as the daily application filters to keep out new exploits and Distributed Denial of Service attacks.

Additionally there might be connectivity changes with IP address block assignments, routing topology changes, upstream hardware replacement, and so on.

Managing Your Firewall

Managing the firewall includes validating the current ruleset, applying fixes to the host operating system or firewall software as they become available. The firewall logs must also be monitored for attacks, exploits, and other abnormal activity.

Managing VPN Connectivity

Managing the VPN is nearly the same laborset as with managing the firewall. The additional requirements depend on the type of user authentication being used. Most VPN products use X.509 certificates or RSA digital keys to authenticate users. Maintaining a Public Key Infrastructure (PKI) for authentication of VPN users is yet another layer of administrative overhead.

Some VPN products can authenticate against RADIUS, ACE, or Windows NT servers. This allows you to authenticate against an existing infrastructure, rather than having to manage a separate subset of your userbase.

As is almost always the case, software implementations will not outperform hardware implementations. A hardware-based VPN, while possibly less upgradeable, will be significantly faster than any software-only VPN solution. The tradeoffs between software and hardware based solutions should be compared and matched to your requirements. Software-based solutions are easier to upgrade, and therefore provide product longevity and flexibility as a trade-off against raw speed and simultaneous connection capacity. Conversely hardware-based solutions offer much greater capacity and lower latency, thus greater throughput in a single installation.

When the new National Institute of Standards and Technology (NIST) Advanced Encryption Standard (AES) becomes the new Federal Information Processing Standard (FIPS) in mid 2001, you will not have to forklift-upgrade your VPN equipment to be compliant if it is software-based.

This is not to scare people into thinking current hardware-based VPN solutions will be obsolete in 2001. First, until someone can prove that Triple-DES (3DES) has a significant design flaw or backdoor, while not the fastest, it is currently considered the most secure and most analyzed of the encryption algorithms available today. 3DES-based VPNs will not disappear simply because AES is available. Second, many hardware-based VPNs have a software component that *is* upgradeable, and will therefore be able to use the AES algorithms in software but without the benefit of hardware acceleration.

To completely muddy the obvious choices, many software implementations have support for hardware-based accelerators. Software-only implementations such as CheckPoint Software's VPN-1 and OpenBSD's native IPSec implementation support hardware DES encryption accelerators. Chances are we will see hardware accelerators of the AES winner, and those software products will have new versions to take advantage of them.

Offering Proxy Services

Proxies are generally thought of to reduce traffic by caching information locally. Although this is true, and an effective method of reducing WAN traffic, proxies can also be used to filter.

Filtering proxies are numerous in the industry now. Useful proxy products have add-on services and reporting features such as the following:

- **Automatic or manual filtering database updates**—New Web and ftp sites are available every day, and a filter is only as good as its database of access lists.
- **Easy access to customize the filtering ruleset**—The flexibility of being able to restrict access to sports, entertainment, and financial Web sites during business hours while allowing them during lunch and after hours.
- **Reports showing workstation/URL use as productive and unproductive**—Allows managers and network administrators to adjust the WAN bandwidth to the true needs of the business.

Many commercial products, such as W3Thermo from W3Control, allow you to analyze your firewall and proxy logs to determine what your Internet use is, and when you might need to increase your connection speed.

Domain Name Registration

Many ISPs will, as part of their setup fee, offer to register and administrate a domain name on your company's behalf. Registration is normally a fairly painless procedure, but unless you have the in-house staff, it might not be a bad idea to allow your ISP technical control of your domain name.

During the registration process, there are normally three named contacts for the domain name, one each for administration, technical aspects, and billing purposes. The technical administrator has the ability to add, change, or remove DNS servers for the domain name. If your upstream ISP needs to change DNS servers for any reason, it would be convenient to allow them to do so.

If you have the internal staff to support domain administration, then it certainly is more secure to have it handled by internal staff.

DNS Mail Exchanger Records

Another service the ISP generally offers is backup Mail Exchanger (MX) records. In the event that your Internet connection goes down, mail can be spooled on the ISP's mail servers by configuring both the authoritative DNS servers and the ISP's mail servers appropriately.

6

CONSULTING, CONSULTANTS, AND CONTRACTORS

One chops the wood, the other does the grunting.
—Proverb

Consultants, Contractors, and Projects

The term *consultant* is used to signify a person whose knowledge you rely upon to make decisions. If you're playing baseball and you ask Pete Rose "Should I steal second?" that's consulting. You're asking questions about a specific area of knowledge. Consultants are often given specific tasks to complete, and normally in a short period of time. Examples of this would be assessing the IT capabilities of a firm you are acquiring, reviewing a network design to suggest improvements, performing a security audit, or helping you find the correct development platform for your e-commerce strategy. The consultant's main job is educational, and his deliverable product is knowledge usually in the form of a recommendation report.

A *contractor*, on the other hand, is a person hired on a more protracted time scale to perform a multiplicity of tasks. A contractor can be hired to do a specific project, such as "install this Web server," or to fill a specific role, "we need a project manager to get our e-commerce rollout back on schedule." Whether the contractor is hired for a specific project or hired to supplement existing staff, his objectives and deliverables are usually different than a consultant.

A contractor might manage numerous "consultants," because project leading is one of a contractor's main purposes. Also, contractors typically are expected to provide, or to be able to provide, hardware resources as well as bodies.

In short, you might hire a consultant to design an Internet connection scheme for your company and then give that plan to a contractor to build.

Can You Do It All Yourself?

Depending on the size of your operation, you'll be called upon to perform more or less of the actual connecting to the Internet and security design. The realistic success of doing it yourself depends on the complexity of the task. For the times you can't do it yourself because of lack of either time or expertise, the telephone book (and especially the Web) is filled with IT consultants. These range from huge corporations (sometimes called "Body Shops" because of their ability to produce warm bodies quickly) to small one-, two-, or three-person outfits. The size of the shop depends on the needs of the job. You might be able to get a better price and possibly even better attention out of a one-person consulting shop than out of a huge IT body shop. If the job is going to require a dozen people working ludicrous hours, you'll have to go with an outfit that can provide the resources you need.

You can contract someone to do something as simple as set up Windows NT on half a dozen workstations or as complicated as rewiring your entire building and installing a router core, firewalls, servers, racks, and so on. If it can be done, you can hire a consultant to do it.

From the Inside

When you're on the inside looking out there are some things you need to consider. After all, you might have little or no experience working with consultants and contractors, and they might have years of working with clients.

Before You Hire a Consultant

Before you hire a consultant, you should have done at least two things. First, determine what you need done. Determining the appropriate e-commerce development platform for your needs, or performing a due diligence evaluation of a potential partner's IT capabilities, are excellent uses of a consultant. Asking a consultant to sit at the phones of your help desk and add user accounts is probably not the most judicious use of your budget. Any task that requires a great deal of research and a report or recommendation as a deliverable is best suited for a consultant; tedious, simple tasks can usually be farmed out to a temp agency that specializes in providing low- to mid-level people quickly.

If you're going to ask for a proposal and the job isn't too large, you usually don't need to give the consultant anything in writing. You can often schedule a meeting with the consultant and discuss what needs to be done, if necessary take the consultant on a tour of your site, and then ask for a proposal. Otherwise you might need to detail the task in the form of a Request for Proposal. An example of what RFPs include is discussed later in this chapter.

The second thing you should do is research the prospective consultants. It's possible that your company even has a policy that contracts valued at more than a certain amount must be sent out to bid and you need to get quotes from a number of different vendors. Even if that's not the policy, it's a good idea. Consultant prices can vary with what the market will bear. After you find someone you like working with, you can stick with them, but in the early stages, it can pay to do some research. After you've established a working relationship with a consultant, it's always in your best interest to occasionally keep getting competitive bids to ensure that you keep your budget intact.

What Can You Expect From a Consultant?

When a consultant comes into your place of business, you should expect her to be up-to-date on current technology. If she says something weird during the interview (like "Macintoshes and PCs won't work together on the same subnet") press her on it and find out what she means. You're going to be spending money on this. Don't hire a screwball. In fact, never hire a consultant who knows less than you do in her field of expertise.

Before You Hire a Contractor

Hiring a contractor is very similar to hiring a consultant; before you hire a contractor, you should have done at least two things. First, determine what you need done. "Installing the Web server" is a goal, but it is not a detailed description of what you need done. When looking to hire contractors, detail the project as explicitly as possible. Your goal of having a Web server installed might be expressed as the following:

- Unpack and assemble the Web server
- Verify that the hardware is working to specification
- Install the operating system (Linux, Solaris, OpenBSD, Windows NT, etc.) and all the appropriate patches
- Configure the server and operating system to work within the network environment (internal, DMZ, co-located, etc.)
- Install the required Web server software (Apache, IIS, iPlanet, etc.) and related patches
- Install required supporting utilities such as Perl, Python, PHP, Java, log analysis software, etc.
- Work closely with the developers to get the appropriate data on the server from the development machines
- Stage the configuration in a lab environment to ensure proper functionality and performance

- Migrate the staged configuration to the production environment
- Document and work with the existing staff on operations procedures.

Contractors have skill levels that match their bill rates. You can find a contractor in the low- to mid-level skill set to do the tedious, simple but time-consuming tasks that are overwhelming your staff. You can also find a contractor to manage or implement the design delivered to you by your consultant.

The second thing to do is interview the contractor just like you would a normal employee. If you are using a contractor to manage or implement a design conceived by a consultant (i.e. someone else), it may be useful to have the consultant who developed the plans interview the contractor as well to make sure they feel confident that the person you are hiring understands what must be done.

What Can You Expect from a Contractor

When hiring a contractor, especially for staff supplementation purposes, it's no different than hiring a permanent employee. The contractor should have all the appropriate skills and qualifications necessary to perform the task you're hiring him for. He should be able to integrate with your existing team. The main difference is that you don't pay benefits, vacation, or taxes for a contractor. And when the job he was hired for is completed, he leaves—there is no need to find an easy way to let them go.

When hiring a contractor to do a project, especially a project that is beyond the scope of your staff's experience levels, you set the same expectations as those of a consultant. The project contractor should be up-to-date on current technology and be an expert in his field of focus. If you are hiring the contractor to manage the project, expose the contractor to your team to determine if they will work well together.

The same axioms for hiring a consultant apply to project contractors. Ideally, you want someone who is organized to the point of alphabetizing his neckties and who can keep track of details and respond to your questions and requests on-the-fly.

What Tasks Should You Farm Out?

There are two types of tasks to farm out to outside labor: the very difficult and the very dull. Consultants spend all day reading exciting articles about new technology and doing server installs, so there are a lot of things they can do more quickly than you can. At the same time, there's no reason you should have to unpack, set up, and configure 200 workstations for your new summer rollout. You make too much money for that. Have the contractor send over some drones.

Questions You Should Ask Your Hired Help

So what do you say when you have a contractor sitting in a chair on the other side of your desk? Well, first of all, you explain the project and ask for a proposal; that's a given. But how do you distinguish between a good contractor and a bad one? A bad contractor can still turn in a good proposal; he could be very capable but woefully undermanned or overburdened with labor, or he could be very good at making proposals but not so good at following through. The foreman could be the type of person who takes a lot of vacation days. He might only work from 9 to 5 and be absolutely unreachable afterward. He might use substandard equipment. It's better to find out all these things before you invest your time and energy into working with a contractor.

Who Else Have You Contracted For?

When you ask this question, you don't just want names, you want phone numbers and email contacts as well. And don't be afraid to call those numbers and ask candid questions to find out how each reference feels about that contractor.

Now there's nothing inherently wrong with being a small contractor, or a contractor who is just starting out after some years working in the industry. In such a case, you're taking a gamble and the consultant realizes this. Your price with a start-up company will probably be less than with an established contractor. Some of the potential benefits are that the contractor wants to do a really good job so he can use *you* as a reference in the future and you'll get good value for the work. Some of the potential downsides are the company could go belly-up before your job is done and the company might not be capable of providing the manpower or expertise you need. You need to be sure your contractor is capable of completing the job before you take the company on. One strategy is to break your work down into smaller segments and make separate contracts for, say, doing the wiring, then installing the routers, and then connecting to the ISP. If the contractor bails on you, it's a smaller subset of the whole that needs to be fixed by someone else.

What Is Your Main Area of Expertise?

Whether it's security or Cisco routers, there's probably something they do best; let them tell you about it and make it work to your advantage.

Have You Ever Taken on a Project This Big?

Remember that pivotal scene from *Flight of the Phoenix* when the plane crash survivors have been struggling for weeks in the desert to build an airplane out of the wreckage under the direction of the stern German airplane engineer only to discover that he engineers *model airplanes*? The looks on their faces, disastrous as they are, are amusing because you're not them. And you don't want to be them. You don't want to discover a third of the way into your multi-million dollar contract that your head consultant has never installed an operating system before and that this is his big break into IT.

How Many Employees Do You Have?

Is this a one-man shop or are there dozens of engineers, or hundreds even? Will you be seeing the same people day to day, or will the work be done by anonymous faces who work for six hours and then vanish, only to be replaced by someone else? Typically, you want the same people coming back day to day so they have some familiarity with the job, but you also want the best person for the job. You don't necessarily want the wiring guy configuring your router. Find out how many people will be involved with the project—your building manager is going to want to know anyway.

Will You Dedicate Resources to My Project or Share Them with Other Contracts?

There's nothing wrong with a contractor sharing individuals between multiple projects. In fact, most jobs are too small to warrant full-time participation by anybody on the contractor's staff, so the guys working on your network Wednesday might be working somewhere else installing printers the next afternoon and back to your place Friday morning. That's fine for a lot of things. But if your project is big enough or lengthy enough, you might want to insist that they dedicate full-time people to it.

How Do I Contact You or the Project Leader 24/7?

A contractor good enough to get your business is good enough to give you a pager number where someone can always be reached in the event of an emergency. They might charge a premium for paging the site manager at 2:24 a.m., but it's better to pay the premium than be without access.

What Other Projects Are on Your Calendar?

You definitely don't want to discover that your project is running overtime and your contractor has obligations to another client to start work before your project is finished. The contractor, at the same time, doesn't want to be out of work for a month in between projects. Working together and staying on schedule will be beneficial to you both. The best way to do this is through regularly scheduled meetings. Have a well-thought-out list in the beginning and make sure you stick to it. A good contractor will take delays into consideration. Make sure you ask about this when looking at the time table.

Bonding and Insurance

You don't want to go out of business, and neither does the contractor. Carrying insurance is one of the burdens of a litigious world. Never hire a consultant or contracting firm that doesn't carry insurance. Here are industry standards for dealing with contracting firms and insurance:

- Workers Compensation Insurance. All employers need to carry this, even the self-employed ones.
- Professional Liability, also known as Errors and Omissions. Usually $1,000,000 is acceptable. Any professional should know better than to ever type `rm -fr /` without a note signed in triplicate, but the fact is accidents do happen.
- General Liability in the amount of $1,000,000. Spilling soda on your shiny new ultra-mega hyper-cube Web server will warrant an expensive cleanup.

Be prepared to ask the contracting company to produce certificates to prove insurance coverage.

The Request For Proposal

A Request For Proposal (RFP) is a document outlining the requirements, goals, and objectives that a client wants to achieve. Although you are not asking for the consultant's hand in marriage, you are asking for a commitment. The RFP is the document that tries to ensure that both sides can live together successfully.

The proposal document provided by the contractor will closely mirror the RFP, except it will have the contractor's answers filled in. The following sections deal with some of the more salient parts of the RFP and Proposal.

Agreeing Parties

The agreeing parties are those entities between which the proposal is written. Although the technicians in your IT department might agree with the specific contractor, the agreement will normally take place between corporate entities, or at least the business units. Hopefully the responsible individuals within the corporate entities are people within your department. Usually your sourcing and procurement department will be involved as well.

Stated Objectives

Stated objectives are the answers to "What do you require?" spelled out in excruciating detail. This tends to be an easy if not tedious process if you have both the knowledge and time to detail those objectives. If you are unable due to time or expertise constraints, you can hire a consultant to help you define not only your objectives, but the deliverables and requirements.

Deliverables

Deliverables are those items delivered to you by the contractor to meet your stated objectives. Although an objective might be to have a corporate Web presence, the deliverables might be as follows:

- Install and configure the ultra-mega hyper-cube for HTTP and Java Servlet 2.2 application framework.
- Install and configure superior hypo-cube for firewall and corporate Internet connectivity.
- Harden both Web server and firewall.
- Document configuration and institute change management procedure.
- Test firewall and Web server in production environment.
- Perform vulnerability analysis and report any potential threats with the current security policy and applications necessary for Web application framework.
- Document disaster recovery procedures for Web and firewall devices.
- Train internal staff on new system.
- Transition responsibilities to trained personnel.

The deliverables detail what will be delivered, produced, and documented to reach the stated objectives. Documentation is critical to this process; it allows both you and the contractor to maintain a clear communication of the status of the project.

Scope of Services

The scope of services is used to try to set and manage expectations for both parties. The scope of services will delineate responsibilities between the agreeing parties. For example, it might be the responsibility of the contractor to recommend the appropriate hardware for the Web server and firewall, but it might be your company sourcing department's responsibility to procure the equipment.

Besides defining responsibilities, the scope of services is where you lay out things such as business locations that work will be performed in, technologies that will be used, the possible necessity of development, any expected data manipulation, and so on.

Risks

In the RFP, you identify any risks, their potential impact on you or the project, and a mitigation plan to keep the project moving forward. Risks might be as simple as delays caused by being shipped the wrong memory for your ultra-mega hyper-cube Web application server, or it might be more serious such as a known exploit on your selected software platform. Knowing about such risks beforehand is 90% of the battle. Properly mitigating the risks should they occur is the other 90%.

Requirements

In the requirements section, list fundamental requirements your business has. Is your business a union shop, so that you cannot move equipment around without enlisting facility's help? Do you require Classified clearance? Do you have a "crunch time" during which your business is busier than all other times?

Coordinators

As mentioned earlier, if it's 2:24 a.m. and the satellite network is down, you must know who the responsible parties are on each side so you can restore service. Coordinators should also include information on financial controllers to help resolve billing issues.

Issues and Change Management

Every project has issues that can hinder progress on the project. The initial steps in effectively dealing with these issues are to identify them, document them, and then work toward their proper resolution.

To best do this, use a structured change management process. It should be the primary vehicle for managing scope and ensuring that the client is delivered the work that is of most value within the time and cost constraints. It is imperative that potential changes are identified early, their impact documented carefully, and that the changes are agreed upon by both the client and the consultant.

Changes are broadly defined as work activities or work products not originally planned for or defined in the original scope of work or Project Proposal. More specifically, changes include the following:

- Any scope items not listed in the Scope of Work or Project Proposal
- Provision for or development of deliverables not included in the Project Proposal
- Any rework of completed activities or accepted deliverables
- Investigative work to determine the impact of major changes

Issue Management

To ensure that project issues are identified and resolved quickly, you must first identify issues. When the project begins, start identifying any issues that could hinder the ability to meet the objectives of the project.

When an issue is first identified, document it as completely as possible. Try to include the following information in the documentation, because it will help to track issues in discussions with the contractor:

- Unique issue number
- Description of the issue
- Date the issue was logged
- Description of the resolution
- Schedule resolution date
- Date the issue was resolved

If you have help desk software, that might be the best place to track issues. If not, there are several issue-management packages available on the Internet that are Web-based and can easily be installed to help tracking. If all else fails, a manually written log and a photocopier will keep everyone on the same page.

Whatever the common repository, you should continuously monitor and control the progress of the issue. This is most easily achieved by making the issues part of the weekly status report and discussing them at any project status meetings.

Change Management—Controlling Indecision

The Change Control Process is a crucial mechanism that can affect the success of a project. To manage change properly, you and the contractor need to agree to use a change control process that will identify, record, and assess impact, thus allowing you to approve or reject changes. It will save both you and the contractor numerous headaches by clearly defining change requests. To make the appropriate decisions on the change requests, information such as cost and schedule impacts must be determined and clearly stated. Make sure the contractor does not proceed without prior authorization and approval from you or your decision-making body. For example, if your contract calls for Mondo Brand Network Cable #23 and during the course of production, Mondo Brand releases a souped up version of its cable that costs 40% more, you don't want your contractor switching to it without letting you know first. And you can be assured that some things in your specifications will be obsolete by the time they're to be installed and not everything you asked for might be available any longer.

Here are some common steps in a formal change management process:

- **Identify a change**—When you identify a needed change in requirements or objectives, formally state that you will be filing a change request form.

- **Initiate the change request**—After a change has been identified, use a change management form to file the requested change. The details of the change are explicitly described in this process.

- **Impact Analysis**—The impact of the requested change must be analyzed and evaluated. Small changes such as "move the server from the top of the rack to the bottom" don't require much effort, or even a formal change request. However, switching network vendors, operating systems, development platforms, services supported, and so on all involve a potentially non-trivial amount of work.

It might require several days or more for the contractor to properly analyze and evaluate that change and incorporate the changes into the design. Make sure you are aware of this, and make sure that you authorize and approve any extended time needed to properly complete the impact analysis. The impact analysis should show any schedule and cost impacts to the project as a direct result of the change.

During the impact analysis, both you and the consultant should be in communication to provide feedback to one another in an attempt to limit the scope of the impact of the change.

After a change is fully analyzed and approved, you need to coordinate with the consultant on both work breakdown and schedules that need to be updated and replanned. The change management process should be tracked as part of the issue management process outlined previously.

Timeline and Costs

At this point you have already done quite a bit of work breaking down the project into meta-categories. Those same categories make it easier to determine an overall timeline and cost for each segment of your project. You can put an estimated number of people hours to each stage of the project, and arrive at a direct cost using the bill rate of the contractor. Some contractors or consultants provide fixed cost for a project or project segment, but that is the exception rather than the norm. When you do request a fixed-cost project, be sure to anticipate significant limitations of scope or changes from contractors so they can bound their costs. Any changes will then most likely come at a premium price.

Additional Costs

In the additional costs section, outline any anticipated additional costs not related specifically to the project. These include travel expenses such as mileage, tolls, parking, train or plane tickets, hotels, and so on.

If you have a number of outlying campus buildings that the contractor must visit to complete the project, your additional costs might quickly add up.

Other potential costs might be outlined in the Risks section and then detailed in the Additional Costs section. Risks involving large capital expenditures, such as having to replace core network components such as routers or ATM switches, may shelve the project or call for an alternate design. Others, such as the need to upgrade the software version on your router to support IPSec, may be able to be accommodated from a discretionary expense budget.

Defining a Statement of Work

A Statement of Work (SoW) is a document detailing the work to be performed by each party. This document can be derived almost directly from the RFP by including the Stated Objectives, Deliverables, and Scope of Services.

If you are writing a SoW only, use the descriptions of those sections of the RFP as a guideline.

Segment the Project into Stages

If the project is of any substantial size, your best insurance in making the project a success is to segment the project into smaller milestones. This will allow you to keep track of progress and makes for a cleaner takeover if, for some reason, the contractor is unable to complete the job. The method you use to segment the project is your own choice, but you should make it follow logical boundaries. For example, you might want to break it down into the following metacategories that can fit any specific project:

- Information Collection
- Analysis and Evaluation
- Recommendation
- Implementation
- Acceptance and Transition

Breaking it down as such allows you to terminate, postpone, or complete any stage of the process as necessary. This also allows you the flexibility to use the contractor to work on Stages 1 through 3, but allow your internal staff and facilities to carry out implementation and testing. That way you use the experts to get the right answer and a good design, but your internal staff gets and keeps a working knowledge of the new environment.

Information Collection

The purpose of this stage is to gain an understanding of your environment, its key components, and your objectives. This stage includes the following:

- Understanding the business
- Understanding the goals and vision
- Actually collecting the data
- Understanding the roles and expectations of both parties
- Evaluating the current state of environment as it relates to the preceeding bulleted items
- Developing a draft of a high-level project plan

Deliverables for this stage are documentation of all the findings, a high-level risk analysis and mitigation plan, and a high-level project plan.

It's a lot of grunt work, and you might already have the beginnings of the documentation necessary for your environment. Unfortunately most often with understaffed, overworked IT departments, the creation of documentation is the first thing to be cut from the schedule.

Analysis and Evaluation

The purpose of this stage is to analyze and evaluate the different solutions using information collected in Stage 1. The analysis of the data collected in Stage 1 is used to help formulate a recommendation on how to achieve the stated objectives. The development of this recommendation is an iterative process that depends both on the accuracy of the data collected and feedback from you. High-level tasks for this stage include the following:

- Evaluating the areas of need
- Creating a gap analysis
- Creating an impact analysis
- Identifying high-level potential solutions to incorporate into design
- Evaluating products to address both the gaps and the needs
- Creating a high-level migration plan
- Developing a recommended high-level design based on evaluations

Deliverables for Stage 2 are a recommended high-level design, documentation describing product evaluation results, a refined risk analysis, and the most important—a detailed project plan.

Recommendation

The purpose of this stage is to discuss and refine recommendations from the consultant. Feedback is an integral part of ensuring that what is recommended will not only meet your stated needs, but also your unstated needs. Let's face it, not every requirement is going to make it into the RFP. Not every dependency will be collected and documented in Stage 1. Constant communication between you and the consultant is the only way to make sure everyone is on the same page. Be sure to review the data collected and presented in the deliverables. Confirm that the consultant's interpretations of your needs match reality. Cooperate on determining responsibilities; the more internal staff you can involve in the project the more likely they will take full ownership of the completed result.

Implementation

The purpose of this stage is to roll out the design you and the contractor agreed to in the Recommendation stage. This can be a large and time-consuming task; the bulk of your work will take place here. Implementation can be segmented out into different responsibilities for different parties, including yourself and multiple vendors. For example, if your facilities department normally runs cabling, you can take advantage of that. There are many internal and external structured cabling contractors available that could be better suited to the task than the IT consulting company that's installing your Web servers. And at the same time, you wouldn't ask CableCo to design the network router core.

In the implementation stage, all the real IT work happens. High-level tasks include the following:

- Architecting a working design
- Ordering equipment and software
- Staging and piloting the solution
- Evaluating the results of the pilot project, and comparing to the expected outcome from design documents

- Reviewing the results with the consultant and revising the architecture as necessary to achieve the expected results
- Transitioning the final results of the pilot environment to production status
- Documenting the workflow and production environment

Deliverables for Stage 4 include an actual implemented, and hopefully fully functional, solution; a document comparing actual outcome to the proposed expected outcome and architecture; and supporting documentation.

Acceptance and Transition

The purpose of this stage is to ensure that all project deliverables have been met to your satisfaction. This requires that you sit with the consultant and review the original stated objectives and compare them with the results. If there is a gap between what you asked for and what you received, this is the time to discover it. Hopefully most gaps of any significance will have been caught and mitigated during the Implementation stage.

Acceptance involves qualifying the finished project with an Acceptance Test Plan. The Acceptance Test Plan is a guideline that is used to ensure that the finished product does indeed meet your stated objectives, and performs within expected parameters.

Transition includes not only the move from pilot project to full production roll-out, but the training of your internal IT staff to handle the day-to-day operations. A well planned transition will have your operations staff trained prior to production roll-out. This is made easier if you are able to allocate resources to be involved with the project from the start. After all operational responsibilities have been transitioned to your IT staff and your requirements have been met in the Acceptance Test plan, the project can then be considered successful.

7

DESIGN
CONSIDERATIONS

Exhilaration is that feeling you get just after a great idea hits you, and just
before you realize what is wrong with it.

—Anonymous

Before Building Your Network

There are two ways to build your network. One is to design it on paper, with
meticulous planning, attention to detail, and weeks of meetings with vendors and other IT staffers. The second is to start with what seems reasonable and run with it. Carefully planning your network, however tedious,
will reward you in the end. Design considerations range from physical (will
this room always be a storage room or will it get turned into office space in
eight months after the company goes public?) to theoretical (how long will it
be before you need to double the amount of available bandwidth?). Some
networking difficulties cannot be anticipated, but others can. When designing your network, the decisions you make will affect your ability to do your
job in the months and years to come. A well-designed network is an adapt-
able one.

Getting Your Service from the Wall Through Hall

Cabling has long been the bane of telecommunications and this hasn't changed much since the introduction of the telegraph. The question of where to hang the wires exists in conjunction with where should the wires terminate? Rest assured that any place in the building that *can* serve as office space *might* serve as office space. Also, places that could never hold a person might at some time in the future hold a printer or some other networked device. If you have the luxury of planning your wiring before a building has been constructed, plan on as much wiring as you can afford—it gets significantly more expensive to add a wiredrop after the walls have gone up. Another thing you can do is have cable pulls installed in the wiring trays which will allow you to later add wiring less expensively.

If you're adding networking wires to an existing building, you're looking at spending some time in the plenum with a broom handle and some string.

Things you'll need to take into consideration:

- **Wiring plan**—Work with your vendors to plan how best to get network access to your users—will you subnet by floors? If so, you might require a router on each floor. How will you keep this secure? Do you have or need closet space?
- **The telco's dangling wire**—What are you going to do with the service your telephone company brings into the building? Will you be prepared to continue when they leave?
- **Wiring contractors**—Where do you find one? How much do you pay them? What can you expect them to do?

Terminating the Telecom Demarcation

The *demarcation* is the point at which the telco stops and your network begins. Everything outside the demarcation is their problem; everything inside it is yours. You shouldn't have anything to do with the demarcation termination other than pointing to a spot on the wall and saying "put it here, next to the router."

Typically, the telco will bring fiber to your building and then convert it. Most likely, the demarcation ends in an RJ48C connector, which looks a lot like an ordinary RJ45 connector. The telco should provide you with the proper cable for connecting it to your Customer Premises Equipment (CPE).

The only popular variation from this scheme is a DS-3 connection, which uses BNC-terminated coax.

Wiring Contractors

In the days when networking was a lonelier occupation, the system administrator (the guy who used to be in charge of the sliderules a couple of years before) usually ran his own wire.

But in today's specialized world, the complexity of wiring has gone beyond a length of coax dragged through the ceiling terminated at each end with a 50-ohm resister. These days it's best to leave your wiring to a wiring contractor. They're in the phone book under telecomm.

As with any other consultants, get bids from at least three vendors and tour the premises with them; make sure you have outlined your goals and needs very specifically.

Configuring Clients for a New Connection

After you have a connection and computers that want to access it, you'll need to configure those client machines to access your network. Simply plugging them in won't do.

Proxy Configuration

You should run an internal proxy server because it provides several benefits:

- Caching proxy servers cache static content and thus reduce the overall bandwidth requirement for bandwidth-hungry applications such as HTTP and FTP.

- For caching proxy servers, locally cached content is returned immediately, thus the perceived performance of your network is improved. This is an inexpensive win for you and your users.

- By using proxy servers, your clients are not making direct contact with the outside world, therefore TCP/IP exploits are not likely to affect the clients. It is important to keep your proxy and firewall servers patched, however.

- Using proxy servers allows you to report or filter Internet usage. You can then filter unproductive sites from access, or take appropriate action on people abusing Net privileges.

Installing a proxy server means that you will want to configure your clients to use it. To reduce the administrative burden of configuring clients, there are several "automatic" means with which you can configure and reconfigure your browser clients.

Proxy AutoConfiguration Script

The first example is to create a proxy AutoConfiguration script. The proxy AutoConfiguration script works with Internet Explorer 4.0x, 5.x, and Netscape Navigator, so it's an easy choice to make for cross platform shops where IE doesn't exist or that are largely Netscape based.

In this sample proxy AutoConfiguration script, a function is defined that determines for each URL what proxy to use. This function does the following checks:

- If the URL is a single hostname, it assumes it is an internal host, and therefore directly reachable without having to go through the proxy. The `isPlainHostName` command is used to check to see if the host name is fully qualified.

- If the URL is located within the local company domain, then it assumes it is directly reachable without need of using the proxy. This assumes you have named your local DNS domain differently from your externally visible domain. Your external servers could be on a DMZ, or at a co-location facility, in which case it is useful to differentiate between internal and external. The dnsDomainIs command is used to check the domain part of the URL.
- Some URLs might not be entered as a symbolic DNS domain, so you might need to check for IP networks. The isInNet command allows you to do this.

After you have applied the appropriate logic, you can return the value DIRECT for "no proxying," or you can define any or all proxy server and port settings.

In the following example, the URL is checked for nonqualified hosts, internal DNS domains, or the local network address range, and the script allows any of those conditions to be directly connected. If the URL is external, all HTTP and FTP requests go through the proxy server located at www-proxy.yourdomain.com:3128:

```
//
// JavaScript for auto-client proxy configuration,

function FindProxyForURL(url, host)
{
    if (isPlainHostName(host) ||
        dnsDomainIs(host, "internal.yourdomain.com") ||
        isInNet(host, "192.168.71.0", "255.255.255.0"))
        return "DIRECT";
    else
        return "PROXY www-proxy.yourdomain.com:3128;";
}
```

More complex examples and JavaScript syntax can be found both at Netscape's and Microsoft's technical knowledge base sites.

Internet Explorer Administration Kit

The Internet Explorer Administration Kit is a toolkit that allows an extensive amount of browser customization. You can configure which components get installed, custom icons, browser favorites, and other browser settings.

Additionally, these changes can be made post installation, by supplying the appropriate information during the install.

For Internet Explorer 4.0x, select Properties, Connection, and then Automatic Configuration. In the dialog box, enter the URL of the Proxy AutoConfiguration script.

For Internet Explorer 5.x, during the installation process, you have the option of enabling automatic configuration of proxies. By selecting Automatic Detect Configuration Settings, you enable Web Proxy AutoDiscovery (WPAD). WPAD works by one of two methods, DHCP or DNS. Each of these two methods is described in the next section.

Alternatively, you enable automatic configuration and manually enter the IEAK .ins URL, or the Proxy AutoConfigure script URL.

Configuring the Client for Automatic Configuration

If you have enabled Web Proxy AutoDiscovery, there are two methods to automatically configure the clients. Remember, WPAD works only for Internet Explorer 5.x or newer. If you have an older version of Internet Explorer, or a mixed IE and Netscape install base, you are better off manually configuring to use a Proxy AutoConfiguration script.

The first option is to disseminate the information in a push format using DHCP. With DHCP, whenever a client boots up, it requests a lease or a renewal of an existing lease of an IP address and the associated information.

The WPAD associated information is added by creating an option field with an identifier of 252. This option field is a string containing the URL pointing to the IEAK .ins or Proxy AutoConfiguration .pac file.

In Windows NT, you can add this to the DHCP server by going to the DHCP Options Menu and clicking Defaults. In the Options Class dialog box, click New. In the Add Option Type dialog, use the following values for each field:

- Name = WPAD
- Data Type = String
- Identifier = 252
- Comment = Web Proxy AutoDetection for yourdomain.com

The Internet Software Consortium's (ISC) reference implementation of DHCP is one of the most popular DHCP servers on non-Microsoft platforms. To enable WPAD via the ISC dhcpd, place the following line in the /etc/dhcpd.conf file:

```
option option-252 "http://www-internal.domain.com/proxy.pac"
```

The second option is to distribute the information via DNS. This is done by placing a CNAME record in DNS for the current domain. The CNAME of wpad should point to a Web server that serves the URL in this format:

```
http://wpad.yourdomain.com/wpad.dat
```

The wpad.dat file must either be the .ins or .pac script, or a redirection that points the browser client to the script.

IP Addressing

Your computers can be addressed in two ways: manually or server-based. Server-based configuration can be accomplished either by static or dynamic IP addressing.

On a network of any size, manual IP addressing is not a viable option; it's time consuming and extremely labor-intensive to change the clients. Server-based IP addressing, whether static or dynamic, is the obvious solution.

Server-based IP addressing is advantageous for several reasons:

■ It allows you to make changes to your network and have those changes automatically propagated to the clients.

■ Moves, adds, and changes can more easily be accommodated.

■ Duplicate IP addresses happen much less frequently with a server-based solution.

Anything that can save maintenance and speed implementation of changes should certainly be considered.

The Bootstrap Protocol, known as BOOTP, has been the most common server-based client configuration protocol. BOOTP assigns IP addresses from a table matching MAC addresses to IP addresses and other possible client information. Although dynamic versions of BOOTP exist, BOOTP was basically a server-based manual configuration method. If the MAC to IP address mapping did not exist in the BOOTP table, then no IP address would be handed out.

BOOTP has been largely replaced by Dynamic Host Configuration Protocol, DHCP. DHCP was directly derived from BOOTP, and it runs on the same UDP ports as BOOTP. The main drive for DHCP was to allow dynamic assignment of IP addresses from predefined pools, or scopes. Before the Internet was popular, sites that had more machines than available IP addresses could use DHCP to dynamically assign IP addresses for a limited lease time. So, people who only checked email once or twice a day would not necessarily need to keep that IP address all the time. Since then, most companies use RFC 1918 private addresses if they do not own a block of publicly accessible IP addresses.

Also, don't let the Dynamic part of DHCP fool you; DHCP can hand out static IP addresses. There are two ways to assign static IP addresses with DHCP: Assign an IP address to a MAC address, or assign the lease for exceptionally long periods of time, such as one year. If you explicitly assign an IP address to a MAC address, that IP will never be handed out to any other network node. The better method to handle static IP address assignment is to map the MAC address to the IP.

Microsoft's client operating systems support server-based configuration through DHCP. Microsoft's server operating systems, Windows NT, and Windows 2000 support DHCP server services. The default DHCP client in Microsoft's operating systems does not work with BOOTP. And, Microsoft's DHCP server cannot service BOOTP requests. This might not be of concern to you, however, most network equipment has used BOOTP rather than DHCP when configuring from the server.

The ISC dhcpd server can handle both BOOTP and DHCP requests. As a matter of fact, the ISC dhcpd does one better than that. The ISC dhcpd can tailor the reply differently depending on criteria from the client. So, HP printers might receive different information than Nortel Network switches. And, Windows PCs can get their WINS server information, whereas Macintosh computer don't need to be bothered with useless info they cannot use.

Internet Software

For your clients to usefully access the network, they'll need some type of Internet software such as Web browsers, email, groupware, collaborative computing suites, FTP, and Telnet clients. In the case of many popular operating systems (such as Microsoft's Windows operating systems), much of this is built in but can be supplanted by better versions. (Microsoft's command-line FTP option, for example, can be replaced by something such as Ipswitch's WS_FTP.) It's best to pick your Internet apps based on ease of support, so install those and disallow others. It's a support nightmare to have 400 users using Internet Explorer, 75 using Netscape Navigator, and 6 using Foobrowse. Making your Internet software part of your default disk image allows you to repair problems by re-imaging the drive rather than troubleshooting.

Standard Build Process

After you have a hundred or a thousand workstations, you need to figure out how to get software to all of them. Ideally, you want each machine to be identical. This will never be the case, however, because obsolete machines are phased out and new ones rolled in at the rate of about 25% a year and you'll always have some computers that require different drivers than others.

Let the Computers Do the Work: Ghost, Drive Image Pro

Applications such as Ghost and Drive Image Pro enable a computer on the network to pull down a multicast image with no more enticement than a boot disk. Software updates can also be pulled or pushed down on a large scale to keep updates simple. In conjunction, multiple images can exist on the network for different machine models, departments, or even individuals.

Sysprep: the Microsoft Way

For building Windows 2000 and Windows NT 4.0 image installations, Sysprep is the standard suggested Microsoft system build tool.

Cloning workstations will only get you so much. Sure, it duplicates your software, but it duplicates everything exactly. This is fine for your copy of Office, but it's not good for things that need to be unique, such as the SID and NetBIOS name.

Sysprep generates SIDs (Secure Identifiers) and works with third-party disk-cloning utilities such as Norton's Ghost and Drive Image. It will also set things such as the local admin password.

Sysprep comes on the Windows 2000 CD and can be found in the `\Support\Tools\Deploy.cab` folder.

The Windows NT 4.0 version can be found on the resource kit.

Sysprep prepares a drive to be imaged and does not perform the imaging itself. For that, you'll need a third-party utility such as Ghost or Drive Image. Sysprep pops up a Mini-Setup Wizard, which you can use to customize the images, and things such as the computer name, domain name, and so on.

Drive Image Pro even comes with a wizard for answering Sysprep questions.

Determining IP Architecture

Determining IP Architecture for your internal LAN is beyond the scope of this book. There are far too many variables, such as whether to use a RFC 1918 private address range or an assigned IP address range rented from the ISP or directly assigned by ARIN. Other variables include subnetting to accommodate internal network structure.

One easy tip to mention, however, is that if you decide to use RFC 1918 private addressing, make sure you do not have duplicate network addresses for multiple locations. You should set up an internal ARIN-like registry to keep track of used network ranges. Allocations should only be made after ensuring that it will not conflict with existing numbering infrastructure. Pre-allocate ranges so that perhaps WAN links only use 192.168.0.0/16, and internal networks use 172.16.0.0/12, whereas lab networks use 10.0.0.0/8, and so on.

Multi-Protocol Network Requirements

There is essentially one protocol on the Internet today: IPv4. IPv6 is currently in the experimentation stage, but is not yet considered production ready. Many development protocol efforts are progressing at a rapid clip, and IPv6 will eventually supplant IPv4. On the long road of that transition, however, IPv6 and IPv4 will live side by side. Actually, IPv4 will eventually live inside IPv6 because there are provisions for tunneling IPv4 in IPv6 address spaces. Because almost no ISP will route anything other than IP, where does this leave other networking protocols such as your existing IPX-based NetWare LAN?

Tunneling of Protocols Within IP

NetWare versions prior to NetWare 5 used IPX as the base protocol. IPX is LAN efficient; however, IPX is not as good as IP on WANs. The accompanying protocol of SAP, Service Advertising Protocol, is also extremely noisy for larger NetWare installations. In NetWare 4,

Novell made available a product known as NetWare/IP, which allowed IP to be the base protocol for clients and servers. The NetWare Core Protocol (NCP), which is the base of all NetWare networking, was essentially encapsulated in IP. SAP was replaced with a DNS lookup of NetWare services in a subdomain. NetWare/IP allowed you to gateway-IPX—only services through IP-only networks.

NetWare/IP was not the only option you had when needing to connect to remote NetWare installations. Novell NetWare natively has the ability to tunnel IPX through IP tunnels. There are many options available for you to establish IP tunnels that enable you to tunnel IPX across WAN links and the Internet to other locations. NetWare and Linux are two examples of network operating systems which natively support IP tunneling.

Tunneling IPv6 in IPv4

Curiosity has the best of you, and you would like to deploy IPv6. Since the Internet isn't yet 100% IPv6 friendly, what can be done to advance your knowledge? There is currently an IETF draft standard that outlines a mechanism known as *6to4*, which allows IPv6 networks to connect to each other through an IPv4 backbone. The IETF draft can be found at
`http://www.ietf.org/internet-drafts/draft-ietf-ngtrans-6to4-07.txt`.

In summary, you must have at least one globally unique IPv4 address. Globally unique means that by definition the IPv4 address must not be an RFC1918 private address. IANA has allocated a single IPv6 Top Level Aggregator (TLA). The TLA of 0x0002, along with the IPv6 Format Prefix 001, is expressed as `2002::/16` in IPv6 syntax. The IPv4 address is then concatenated to the IPv6 address providing you with a unique IPv6 48-bit prefix.

As an example, suppose our 6to4 gateway IP address is 63.69.110.75. The first step is to convert this IP address to hex; the result is 3f45:6e48. Concatenating this value to the IANA allocated TLA and Format Prefix gives us a unique IPv6 address: `2002:3f45:6e48::/48`.

Additional examples and documentation can be found with the various IPv6 implementations. Microsoft Research has a technology preview implementation of IPv6 for Windows 2000, which can be found at `http://www.research.microsoft.com/msripv6/`. Documentation for configuring 6to4 can be found on that site. FreeBSD 4.1 and OpenBSD v2.7 both have full IPv6 stacks integrated into the kernel as well as all the appropriate userland tools to setup 6to4.

The last step, connecting to sites through the 6bone needs to be done through gateways that have both 6to4 routers and a connection to the 6bone. One such site is Freenet6 (`www.freenet6.net`). Their web site contains forms for automating the setup process of connecting to the 6bone through their site.

Availability, Capacity, and Reliability

In designing an Internet connection eventually you will have to deal with certain issues pertaining to robustness. *Availability* is the measurement of what percentage of the time a particular service is functioning for your intended audience. Availability is strictly dependent on the reliability of each component in the path between your audience and your service offering. For example, if you offer patient records to authorized doctors in any hospital, you want the highest availability possible. Consider that the traffic needs to come to you through your ISP, through your WAN connection, through your router, through your firewall, through your DMZ LAN, to your server. Outlined here is a quick list of components at your service delivery point alone that can cause an interruption of service:

- **ISP**—Any problems that affect your ISP's network affect the flow of traffic to your site. Unfortunately you normally do not have any control over the configuration of your ISP's internal network. Of immediate importance is the router connecting your site, the cable connecting the CSU/DSU to the router, and the cable connecting the CSU/DSU to the demarcation point.

- **Provider's Network**—Often drawn as an amorphous blob, there are occasionally bit-errors, equipment failures, accidental disconnects, billing mistakes, etc. that all affect the availability of your bandwidth delivery.

- **Local Customer Premises Equipment**—The demarcation point is connected to your CSU/DSU, which is connected to your router's serial interface. Your router has a router configuration, which must be maintained. Most routers connect to LANs via an Ethernet interface, which is plugged into an Ethernet switch.

- **Firewall**—Your firewall is composed of individual components: power supply, mother board, disk controller, disk drives, keyboard, video controller, network interface cards. All of this is controlled by an extremely complex piece of software known as the operating system. On top of that is another extremely complex piece of software, the firewall.

- **DMZ Server**—Your DMZ server is likewise composed of similar hardware and software components. Additionally, there is a server service, such as a Web server, that is providing data, possibly provided from application servers and database servers.

Each of the hardware components can be have their reliability calculated in advance by examining the meantime between failure information provided by the manufacturer. Unfortunately calculating the reliability of operating systems, and applications running on top of the operating system, is much more difficult. In the real world those services can really only be monitored.

As you can see, there are a significant number of potential failure points. The risk of failure at each of those points can be compensated by redundant technologies. RAID for storage, duplexing disk controllers, redundant power supplies, clustering technologies, fail-over capability in firewalls and routers, and multiple ISP providers are examples. Unfortunately the highly available technologies introduce a significant amount of administrative overhead as well as capital expenditure for components.

Reliability can be improved upon by removing risk. Sounds simple, but you will soon realize that 100% reliability is nearly impossible to obtain, even purchasing "quality components." So if each component of your information path is by definition not 100% reliable, then how do you achieve high availability? Redundancy. Simply put, you design multiple paths to the same service, or multiple components offering the same service. Additionally you can make those components distributed; then if one component fails your service offerings are not impacted.

Capacity is simply the ability to pass information, whether it is measured in bits per second, hits per second, or transactions per second.

Bandwidth, Latency, and Throughput

Bandwidth, as you remember from Chapter 2, "Understanding WAN Bandwidth Delivery," is the raw speed at which bits are transmitted on a physical medium. *Latency* is the delay that is added to the transmission and receipt of the data. Latency can be introduced anywhere along the transmission path of the data. Normally, latency is introduced by LAN switches, routers, packet inspection by firewalls, the transmission onto the transport medium itself, congestion, and client and server use and activity.

Throughput is the actual measure of the amount of data that can be sent and received in a given time period. Throughput is affected by both the raw bandwidth available and the latency introduced along the way.

It is important to note that the more latency is introduced, the slower the perceived response, despite the availability of raw bandwidth. If you have a slow router and firewall with a large, unoptimized rulebase, you might be unable to properly use the full capacity of a high-speed WAN connection. Latency is the bane of network designers and administrators.

Backup Circuits

Backup circuits are generally circuits that provide secondary paths for data to travel over. They might be lower bandwidth, or circuits that are not always established (see "On-Demand Circuits" next).

Backup circuits should be considered when a connection provides access to a critical resource. For example, if you are hosting your own Web server farm, rather than hosting it at a co-location facility, you might want to have multiple paths from multiple ISPs coming into your server farm.

A cost/benefit analysis will easily tell you if you should be implementing backup circuits to resources.

On-Demand Circuits

The most common example of bandwidth on demand is ISDN. Most ISDN devices only establish a circuit using one B channel. If the traffic fills the circuit for any sustained period of time, the second B channel is brought up and traffic distributed across both. After the use drops below the defined threshold, the second circuit is torn down.

Remote Access Policy

Remote access is a common point of headbutting between system administrators and users. Users want the freedom to work from home or the road and administrators are continuously paranoid that intruders will breach the walls and make off with the data.

Remember that it has been estimated that 80% of all information theft occurs not from intruders, but from the inside. When you extend the workplace to remote office locations such as branch offices with less security, or employee homes, there is a much larger chance of sensitive information being leaked.

When sensitive data is made available to employees on their home systems, or to traveling users and their mobile systems, it is desirable to potentially use software to ensure that sensitive information remains confidential. For example, providing hard drive encrypting software for all internal documents might help keep the curious out. Unfortunately, whenever editing documents, most applications create temporary files. Those temporary files can be undeleted, and thus the information retrieved. And, there is no good method for automatically and remotely ensuring configuration and compliance with policy.

Doing Away with Dialups

Dialup remote access can be a security problem because you normally don't firewall or filter access from your RAS servers and the rest of your internal network. Providing a remote access infrastructure can be expensive, not just in budget, but in maintenance. There is administrative overhead in managing a large number of modem banks, or ISDN Primary Rate Interfaces. Additionally, if you offer national or international access to your RAS services through a toll-free number, your phone bills will become quite large, as your remote user population will tend to stay on longer.

In the past, many employees considered their company to also be their ISP. The company would make available banks of modems so that users could connect from home, supposedly to do work. The employees would take advantage of that situation by using the work connection to access the Internet, further driving up costs and tying up resources.

A more cost-effective means of remote access is through the Virtual Private Network (VPN). By making your remote access services available through a VPN, you leverage existing infrastructure: your connection to the Internet. This removes the company from the ISP role that many employees hold it to.

Additionally, using VPN provides the users the opportunity to access the internal network at speeds above the analog modem's 56Kbps and ISDN's 128Kbps. With the proliferation of commercial ISPs today providing xDSL services, cable modems, or some other such high-speed Internet access service, the employee will be able to get more work done with a faster connection.

Wherever your network is headed, you *don't* want to be providing anybody with dialups unless it's absolutely necessary.

8

ASSESSING YOUR
SECURITY NEEDS

"Any medium powerful enough to extend man's reach is powerful enough to
topple his world. To get the medium's magic to work for one's aims rather
than against them is to attain literacy."

> —Alan Kay, "Computer Software", Scientific American,
> September 1984

Build an Adaptable Infrastructure

Proper architecture design is difficult. You won't get the right design on the
first try. That's why, when designing a network, you first select a prototype,
look at it on paper, and consider all the implications apparent there. For
example, "How will we get our network connection across the street? Is
there conduit running beneath our two buildings? Is the closet where we
want to put the hubs made completely secure? Or is it also used to house
the copy machine?"

Another place to spot design flaws early is in other people's networks. Your
vendors should be able to provide you with a list of other clients who have
installed their equipment or services. Take a day and visit them. Ask "What
have been your main problems and successes with this equipment or service? What do you wish you had done in its implementation that you didn't?"

Incremental design changes will develop through each iteration of your
design phase. Embrace the challenge because it will give you a chance to

show off all the wonderful things you learned in the first half of this book. If everything is designed properly and implemented well, people will start calling you guru. Your confidence will improve and your stocks will split. Design or implement poorly, and your management and userbase will hunt you down like torch-bearing peasants marching on Frankenstein's castle.

The Tao of Security: Simplicity

Effective security is best achieved through multiple layers of simple to understand and implement policies. Simplicity is the key. The more complex a security gateway's rules are, the more likely you are to misconfigure it.

Quoting Deng Ming-Dao from "Farmer, Day 244" of his book *365 Tao*:

> Those of us who live in the cities would be hard pressed to equal the farmer in simplicity. Simplicity, after all, is what Tao most celebrates. Who needs to know all the digits of pi? Who needs to engineer a new monetary policy? Who needs to strive for political office? None of these things is necessary to be a human being. Give up unnecessary things.

With apologies to Mr. Ming-Dao, this could easily be converted to an IT/Security mantra:

> Those of us who live in the IT departments would be hard pressed to equal the user in simplicity. Simplicity, after all is what Tao most celebrates. Who needs to know all the services users want to access? Who needs to engineer a new security policy? Who needs to strive for management office? None of these things is necessary to be secure. Give up unnecessary services.

Service Assessment

Depending on your paranoia level, and the ignorance level of your upper management, you will take different stances on what your users will be able to access. Many IT managers take the stance that their internal users have the freedom to access any service available on the Internet. This certainly simplifies your security policy, and will reduce the amount of future modifications necessary to support the newest whiz-bang business-critical service offered by Datek Online and ESPN.

It will also be very likely that your users will grumble about your firewall. The desire to access all their sensitive data from any computer on the Internet with little or no hassle might conflict with your desire to keep it safe from intruders. Sometimes a firm hand is necessary.

Many organizations will take a more restrictive approach. The userbase will have access to only basic services such as HTTP/HTTPS, FTP, and email on standard well-known ports. Additional services, such as DNS, which are necessary to support these protocols are also permitted. Many organizations do not see the value of Napster, Gnutella, Telnet, AOL Instant Messenger, Real Media, and Java streaming stock tickers. By allowing specific services and denying everything else, you can increase your security, increase your available bandwidth by eliminating non-business related traffic, increase your administrative load, and frustrate your users in a single policy decision.

Allowing your users unrestricted access to Internet services is the easiest stance to take, and because it simplifies the security policy, it will be used as the basis for the first example. Allowing specific services and denying everything else will be illustrated in packet filter routers. You should be able to easily see how quickly the complexity of security policies increases.

Which method is right for your organization? That is something you will need to decide with management and your organizational policies and procedures. Most academic and research related organizations will opt for the more open and simpler security policy. Most businesses, especially those in the financial districts, will opt for the more controlling security policy.

Serving the World

Deciding what services to offer the world will be easy. Whatever the objectives are by connecting your organization to the Internet will almost directly dictate what your security policies will be. If you are hosting DNS and email, then those are the services to allow in through your security gateways. DNS and email are pretty much considered mandatory. Additional services you might be offering include Web, News, and FTP.

If you are allowing Web traffic generated dynamically from a database, you will allow the Web traffic through, but not open access to your database ports. Common sense reigns securely here. Things get more complex if you are serving streaming media, or networked Java applications that must open network ports back to your servers. Most streaming media servers, such as Real Network's Real Server and Apple's QuickTime Streaming Server provide tech documents specifically for supporting streaming media through firewalls. There might be instances where those servers cannot sit behind a firewall and might need to be on the unprotected side of the DMZ. In those instances your only protection is to harden the box as discussed later.

The only other major service you might be offering to the world at large is Virtual Private Network (VPN) access to your internal network for traveling users, remote office locations, telecommuters, or business partners. By allowing VPN into your network, you reduce, or eliminate, the costs associated with dedicated leased lines between locations. You can also eliminate analog modem or digital ISDN-based dial-up remote access servers.

Many users will lean toward implementing Microsoft's Point-to-Point Tunneling Protocol (PPTP) because it is already built into all modern Microsoft operating systems and does not add additional expense. However, you shouldn't use PPTP, not because the recent revision of the specification has any inherent problems, but rather Microsoft's implementation is not secure. Look into an IPSec-based VPN. IPSec is an industry standard authentication and encryption protocol suite. IPSec implementations are available for cross-platform solutions for Microsoft Windows operating systems, Mac OS, and most UNIXes. Recent operating system releases of Windows 2000, Solaris 8, OpenBSD, FreeBSD, and some Linux distributions (SuSe to name one) include native IPSec support.

For More Information

For more information on PPTP version 1 and PPTP version 2, check out Bruce Schneier's whitepapers, which can be found at http://www.counterpane.com/pptp.html. Bruce Schneier is the author of *Applied Cryptography* (John Wiley & Sons, ISBN 0471117099, $54.95 list) and inventor of the blowfish and twofish encryption algorithms.

IPSec is a large and complex suite of protocols. There are three primary components of IPSec that you are most likely to encounter when deploying IPSec based VPNs: IKE, ESP, and AH.

IKE, or Internet Key Exchange protocol, is responsible for setting up IPSec ESP and AH connections. Automated key exchange between two parties is an extremely complex procedure. There are myriad parameters necessary to establish identity, encryption algorithms, keys, and connection lifetimes. And although the Tao of security is simplicity, many parts of IPSec seem to fly in the face of that philosophy. This explains why many vendors do not implement all options of the IPSec protocol suite, to reduce the complexity of their products and the chance that you might misconfigure it. IKE, defined in RFC 2409, combines the following protocols:

- **ISAKMP, or the Internet Security Association and Key Management Protocol (RFC 2408)**—ISAKMP is often used interchangeably with IKE by vendors.
- **IPSec DOI for ISAKMP, the IPSec Domain of Interpretation for ISAKMP, RFC 2407**—IKE was developed over years of constant arguing in the IETF working groups. IPSec DOI for ISAKMP endeavors to fill in the details that are missing from the ISAKMP specification.
- **Oakley key determination protocol (RFC 2412)**—Oakley uses the Diffie-Hellman protocol to create keys for IPSec Security Associations (SAs).

IPSec AH is the Authentication Header as defined in RFC 2402. IPSec AH is IP protocol 51 and is neither TCP or UDP, thus there are no ports associated with AH. The job of AH is to authenticate the IP packet so that you can ensure the integrity of the packet has not been compromised between security gateways. The authentication data is actually generated by using a 96-bit Message Digest Algorithm (MD5) or Secure Hash Algorithm (SHA) over the payload and immutable IP header information. The IP Time To Live (TTL) field is decremented for each router hop, and thus is not authenticated. For most implementations of IPSec, AH is not necessary, and it is unlikely you will use it when deploying a VPN. The one large exception to this is IPv6. IPv6 implementations are required to include IPSec AH and ESP.

IPSec ESP is the Encapsulated Security Payload as defined in RFC 2406. ESP includes both data privacy in the form of encryption, and data integrity in the form of authentication. Like AH, ESP is IP protocol 50 and is neither TCP or UDP and therefore has no concept of ports. ESP can be combined with AH if so desired for additional authentication. However, because simplicity is key for security, there is normally no need to make things more complex than necessary. Currently in the real world if you are using different vendor's implementations of IPSec, the more options you use, the more likely there might be an interoperability problem with the configuration.

ESP has the option to choose from many encryption algorithms, including none (Null encryption), DES, and 3DES. There is little use in using ESP with both Null and DES encryption algorithms. Both are insecure when trying to hide data, and even worse, DES gives the illusion of being safe. 3DES is the de facto standard for IPSec secure interoperability between different vendor implementations. When an AES candidate is selected, most vendors will implement the winning algorithm.

For More Information on IPSec

The description of IPSec here does not even scratch the surface with the various complexities and nuances of the IPSec protocol suite. For more details, you would need to read the following RFCs:

Overview RFCs

- 2401 Security Architecture for the Internet Protocol
- 2411 IP Security Document Roadmap

Basic protocol RFCs

- 2402 IP Authentication Header
- 2406 IP Encapsulating Security Payload (ESP)

Key management RFCs

- 2367 PF_KEY Key Management API, Version 2
- 2407 The Internet IP Security Domain of Interpretation for ISAKMP
- 2408 Internet Security Association and Key Management Protocol (ISAKMP)
- 2409 The Internet Key Exchange (IKE)
- 2412 The OAKLEY Key Determination Protocol
- 2528 Internet X.509 Public Key Infrastructure

Details of various components and technologies used

- 2085 HMAC-MD5 IP Authentication with Replay Prevention
- 2104 HMAC: Keyed-Hashing for Message Authentication
- 2202 Test Cases for HMAC-MD5 and HMAC-SHA-1
- 2207 RSVP Extensions for IPSEC Data Flows
- 2403 The Use of HMAC-MD5-96 within ESP and AH
- 2404 The Use of HMAC-SHA-1-96 within ESP and AH
- 2405 The ESP DES-CBC Cipher Algorithm With Explicit IV
- 2410 The NULL Encryption Algorithm and Its Use With IPsec
- 2451 The ESP CBC-Mode Cipher Algorithms
- 2521 ICMP Security Failures Messages

(continued)

Older RFCs which might be referenced

- 1321 The MD5 Message-Digest Algorithm
- 1828 IP Authentication using Keyed MD5
- 1829 The ESP DES-CBC Transform
- 1851 The ESP Triple DES Transform
- 1852 IP Authentication using Keyed SHA

RFCs for secure DNS service, which IPsec might use

- 2137 Secure Domain Name System Dynamic Update
- 2230 Key Exchange Delegation Record for the DNS
- 2535 Domain Name System Security Extensions
- 2536 DSA KEYs and SIGs in the Domain Name System (DNS)
- 2537 RSA/MD5 KEYs and SIGs in the Domain Name System (DNS)
- 2538 Storing Certificates in the Domain Name System (DNS)
- 2539 Storage of Diffie-Hellman Keys in the Domain Name System (DNS)

RFCs labeled "Experimental"

- 2521 ICMP Security Failures Messages
- 2522 Photuris: Session-Key Management Protocol
- 2523 Photuris: Extended Schemes and Attributes

Related RFCs

- 1750 Randomness Recommendations for Security
- 1918 Address Allocation for Private Internets
- 1984 IAB and IESG Statement on Cryptographic Technology and the Internet
- 2144 The CAST-128 Encryption Algorithm

This list of RFCs comes from FreeS/WAN's documentation for its implementation of Linux at
`http://www.freeswan.org/freeswan_trees/freeswan-1.5/doc/RFCs.html`.

Services Allowed from the Internet

As previously discussed, you have a choice of allowing generally unrestricted access to services from the Internet or to identify those services your users need and allow those only.

If you decide to allow unrestricted access, you can still block certain services by blocking the servers they rely on. A perfect example of this is AOL Instant Messenger. By dropping all traffic destined for the AOL Instant Messenger servers, you effectively disable that service. Because of their multiple numbers of database servers, services such as Napster and Gnutella, unfortunately, cannot be stopped by packet filtering or even dropping traffic to all the catalog servers `*.napster.com`. The only way to truly stop Napster-type traffic is with content-inspection type of firewalls/proxies. Examples of such content-inspection systems are the new 3.5.x version of IP Filter (not yet available at publication time), and a commercial package called PacketHound by Palisade Systems, Inc. Commercial Firewalls are likely to get content-inspection plugins as well.

If you are providing specific services and denying all others, be prepared to revisit and modify your rulebase often. It is inevitable that someone will rise from the ranks of userland with a business-critical service he needs to access, most likely at 4:30 p.m. on the Friday before a long weekend. Those services might be one-offs, such as "I need SQL*net access to this vendor's public database," or vague and all-encompassing such as "The new SOAP application using BXXP as the transport protocol isn't working. Can you find out why?"

The point here is to be careful about where, and when, you add rules to allow services. A misplaced or misconfigured rule can render useless the rules that follow it.

With all the warnings out of the way, be prepared to do some footwork and tweaking of the rulebase to support the services you want to enable for your users. Make a list of the supported services you want your users to access from the Internet (see Table 8.1). Additionally, poll the users and managers in the various departments to gather application requirements.

Table 8.1   Example Applications and the Protocol/Ports Used

Application	Service	Protocol	Port
World Wide Web	HTTP	TCP	80
Secure WWW	HTTPS	TCP	443
Electronic Mail	SMTP	TCP	25
	IMAP4	TCP	143
	POP3	TCP	110
Name Resolution	DNS	UDP	53
	DNS	TCP	53
File Transfer	FTP	TCP	20, 21
Terminal Emulation	TELNET	TCP	23
Encrypted Telnet	SSH	TCP	22
Usenet News	NNTP	TCP	119
Time Synchronization	NTP	TCP	123
Virtual Private Network	IPSec	ESP	N/A
	IPSec	AH	N/A
	IKE	UDP	500
Streaming Media	RTSP	TCP	554
	RTP	UDP	6970-7170

Identifying the Internet applications your users need will dictate your initial outbound security policy. Most Internet Application services have specific, well-known protocol and port definitions that allows the client software to connect to the servers providing those services. The problematic services are those that remote procedure call (RPC) and portmapping services.

Portmapped services attach themselves to a randomly available unprivileged port and then register with a port mapping service. Clients wanting to use those portmapped services first contact the portmap service and request the port of the service they are seeking. The client will then initiate a connection to the service running on the port as returned by the portmapper. Examples are the Microsoft Exchange server message retrieval and address book services. Each start/stop of the service, including reboots, causes the services to usually bind to a different port. This makes portmapped services extremely difficult to securely support with packet filter routers and most firewalls.

Similar problems arise with distributed network-aware programming such as Java's Remote Method Invocation (RMI) and CORBA's Internet Inter-Orb-Protocol (IIOP).

Even if you are able to get your packet filter router or firewall to support such services, they will be passing over the Internet in the clear. This is not the wisest course for mission critical distributed applications. The best method is to investigate encrypted tunneling of the RMI/IIOP calls (such as HTTPS), or to use a VPN.

The Special Case of FTP

In Chapter 1, "TCP/IP and Related Protocols," you learned about various common TCP/IP services. Among those services, FTP seemed much more complicated than the rest. FTP is the bane of many a network administrator's existence to properly support. FTP servers are often the focal point of automated script kiddie attacks. This is unfortunate because many FTP servers at one point or another have had root-compromise exploits. Offering secure publicly available FTP servers requires a lot of effort on the part of the administrator. Many believe the designers of the FTP protocol must have been on the same hallucinogens that inspired the duck-billed platypus.

From a firewall/packet filtering perspective, there are two major problems with FTP. Those problems are, of course, different depending on whether you are supporting outgoing client connections or incoming server connections.

For Outbound Client Connections

The problem for outbound client connections is that there are two types of FTP transfer modes, active and passive. Remember that for Active FTP, the PORT command causes the FTP server to initiate a data connection back to the client on port 20. In Passive FTP, the PASV command causes the FTP server to reply with an available port for the client to open a connection to. The passive server-supplied available port is *unprivileged*, meaning that it is always greater than 1,023, but less than 65,536.

That is a very large range to open up for TCP connections to any FTP server. To support passive FTP using a packet filter router or firewall without state table support, you must essentially allow any unprivileged TCP traffic out of your network. This is almost certainly not what you want.

You can avoid this problem by only supporting Active FTP sessions to the outside world. The main problem with this is that most FTP transfers are now done with Web browsers as the clients. Most Web browsing clients today default to passive FTP, so this might confuse your users when FTP doesn't work through their Web browsers.

A better way of handling this is to set up an internal proxy. By setting up an internal proxy, all clients establish connections to the proxy first, and the proxy opens the FTP connection on behalf of the client. That way, you can support passive FTP; just restrict the permit rule to the IP address of the proxy server. Microsoft's Proxy Server and Squid (found at `http://squid.nlanr.net`) are two popular proxy products.

The downside to this is that all the clients must be configured to use the proxy. Client configuration can be mitigated by server-side and automatic proxy configuration. Recent versions of Internet Explorer and Netscape Communicator both support automatic proxy configuration, either through scripts, or DNS tricks.

The best way to handle FTP is to not rely on packet filter on a router, but to use a firewall that has FTP support.

For Inbound Server Connections

The same support conundrum exists for offering the service of an inbound FTP server, except, of course, to make things easier the problem is exactly opposite that of supporting the outbound client.

Handling the Active FTP transfer mode for an inbound FTP server is significantly easier than supporting passive FTP sessions. Inbound connections go to port 21 of your FTP server, and you must only permit port 20 traffic back out from your FTP server.

Passive FTP transfers are more difficult because the client will be initiating a connection to an unprivileged TCP port on your FTP server. On most packet filtering routers and firewalls without specific passive FTP state table support, you have no other option than to allow any unprivileged TCP traffic to your FTP server. This will open your server up to additional attacks, and is generally not the best approach.

A better, but still inefficient workaround, is to configure your FTP server to use a predetermined range of ports to assign for passive FTP transfers. Using a known small window of PASV ports, you can shrink the packet filter/firewall range of open port addresses from 1,024—65,535 to say 15,000—15,500.

Rules, Rulesets, and Rulebases

Generically, a rule is a set of criteria to match against a packet's properties, and an action to take should the criteria and properties match. The criteria might be as vague and all encompassing as "all packets," or it might be as specific as "any inbound fragmented TCP packet arriving on interface eth0, with the IP source routing option and TCP flag FIN set, destined for port 143 on host 192.168.7.25 originating from network 172.16.30.0/24."

The table of actions of a rule generally are composed of one of the possibilities shown in Table 8.2.

Table 8.2   Generic Firewall Rule Actions

Action	Action Description
accept	Accept the packet, and pass or forward it on to its final destination.
drop	Drop the packet on the floor. Do not pass go. Do not even acknowledge the fact the packet ever existed. Don't let the sending machine know the packet has been discarded. What packet?
reject	Do not accept the packet, but alert the sending machine that the packet has been rejected. This is normally done for TCP by sending a packet with the reset (RST) flag set. For UDP, because it has no concept of state, an ICMP is returned with the type destination port unreachable.
Action Modifiers	**Modifier Description**
log	Log the action applied to the packet and all pertinent information. This could be date/time, source/destination IP addresses, source/destination ports, rule number that triggered the action, and the action itself. Some log modifiers allow you to log part or all the packet itself for later inspection.
map	Rewrite the packet address and possibly port information. This is normally used to do Network Address Translation (NAT), or Network Address Port Translation (otherwise known as IP Masquerading).
redirect	Redirect the packet to reroute it from one IP address and port to another. This is useful for implementing transparent proxies.

Rule Order

In most firewalls, the packets are inspected and matched against the rules in the rulebase in a sequential order. This means that the packet is compared to the first rule, and then the second rule, and then the third rule, and so on until a match is made. After the packet is matched to a rule, no additional actions or comparisons of the packet to the rulebase are made. One notable exception to this rule is the IP Filter firewall that is native to OpenBSD, FreeBSD, and NetBSD but also available for Linux and several other UNIX systems. IP Filter normally processes packets in rule groups, and maintains status of the last matching rule. You have the flexibility in IP Filter to stop the process of matching further rules by using a special command in the rule. However, unless configured differently, the decision to drop or pass the packet is not made until the last rule in the group has been compared to the packet.

To better illustrate the difference, take the following sample rulebase:

```
block all inbound traffic
pass all inbound traffic
```

For most firewalls, including CheckPoint's FireWall-1 and native Linux ipchains firewalling, the first rule to match applies to the packet. In the sample rulebase, an incoming packet matches rule #1. The packet is then immediately dropped by rule #1, and no further comparison takes place.

IP Filter, and firewalls like it, apply the action on the status of last matching rule. In the sample rulebase, the incoming packet matches rule #1. At this point, IP Filter sets the state for that packet to "matched rule #1, drop packet," but continues to compare the packet to the remaining rules in the ruleset group. The incoming packet in the example also matches rule #2, so the state of the packet is now "matched rule #2, pass packet." Because there is no rule #3, the packet is actually passed rather than blocked by IP Filter.

If you want to make IP Filter act more like other firewalls, you can apply the `quick` modifier to an individual rule. The `quick` modifier halts the packet comparison process of a ruleset on a match. The following IP Filter rules then mimic the actions of ipchains and FireWall-1:

```
block in quick all
pass in all
```

Significantly more detail of differences between firewall implementations will be discussed in Chapter 10, "Implementing Security."

Performance-Tuning Your Firewall

Knowing what traffic is passing through your firewall and how your firewall applies rulesets in a rulebase will help you tune your firewall for performance. For example, you can increase the performance of a firewall that processes a packet on the first matching rule by moving your most commonly matched rules to the beginning. In effect, this causes the firewall to do less work per packet. Firewall performance tuning should only be attempted after you have a working rulebase, and special attention should be made to the order. Do not misconfigure your firewall by placing accept rules before rules that would otherwise deny those packets. The importance of ordering rules in a rulebase is illustrated better in the examples in the following sections.

Remote Administration of Firewalls and DMZ Servers

There are many mentions of Secure Shell (SSH) in this and the remaining chapters of the book. SSH is a suite of applications that includes the `ssh` program, which replaces `rlogin` and `telnet`, and `scp`, which replaces `rcp` and `ftp`. Also included is `sshd`, which is the server side of the package. SSH encrypts all traffic (including passwords) to effectively eliminate eavesdropping, connection hijacking, and other network-level attacks. Additionally, SSH provides many secure tunneling capabilities. There are several implementations of the SSH suite and protocols. SSH is available in many implementations and formats:

- SSH is a commercial product from SSH Communications Security (`http://www.ssh.com/`) supporting the Windows Win32 platforms (Windows 9x/NT/2000), Linux, and several UNIX flavors including MacOS X.

- F-Secure SSH is another commercial implementation for cross-platform environments available from F-Secure Corporation. F-Secure SSH supports Windows Win32 platforms (Windows9x/NT/2000), Macintosh, and most major UNIX platforms. F-Secure SSH can be found at `http://www.datafellows.com/products/ssh/`

- OpenSSH is a free implementation maintained by the OpenBSD team at `www.openssh.com`. It supports SSH protocol versions 1.3, 1.5, and 2.0. It runs on many versions of UNIX and UNIX variants. Versions for other platforms can also be found there.

- NiftyTelnet is a free software implementation of SSH available for MacOS. It includes support for `scp` and SSH protocol version 1.5. NiftyTelnet can be found at `http://www.lysator.liu.se/~jonasw/freeware/niftyssh/`.

- MindTerm is a 100% pure Java implementation of SSH 1.5 from MindBright, an IT Consulting company in Sweden. MindTerm runs on just about any platform that has a recent Java Runtime Environment. It can be executed on the command line or launched from within a browser. MindTerm can be found at `http://www.mindbright.se/mindterm/`.

With the various commercial and free implementations of SSH available, there is no reason not to install it on your servers. Unless you are using hardwired serial consoles to manage your servers, it would be otherwise irresponsible for an administrator to not be using SSH for remote administration.

Managing your Windows NT/2000 servers securely is slightly more difficult because of the primary "ease of use" feature: the GUI. There are a plethora of "remote desktop" utility programs available. The main difficulty you will have is in ensuring the security of the product, and gauging the time-to-fix from the vendor for any exposed exploits.

Windows NT 4.0 has a Terminal Server Edition, which allows remote clients to "natively" control desktop sessions. Unfortunately the release of both service packs and hotfixes from Microsoft are delayed weeks to months behind the normal Windows NT 4.0 releases. The additional risk assumed during the delayed release window for intruders to take advantage of known exploits is high enough that you should not consider this option.

pcAnywhere from Network Associates is a commonly implemented remote control utility. It allows network traffic to be encrypted (through the Microsoft Crypto API), and file transfer so you can also replace FTP.

Obviously you will have to evaluate your current remote management strategy and ensure that it makes sense to control your DMZ servers or remote servers at the colocation facility. Criteria to compare include the following:

- File transfer capabilities. Transfer of files both to and from the remote server. Compression of files is useful, especially over lower bandwidth links. Delta file transfer will only transmit the changes to files, which can save time and bandwidth as well.

- Data encryption. Encrypting the data over the wire is important, otherwise intruders may be able to sniff account, password, or other critical information. Strong encryption of 3DES, TwoFish, Rijndael, Serpent, or CAST is preferred.

- Configurability. Security through obscurity isn't security at all. But it certainly may help keep out the script kiddies. Look for the ability to reconfigure the listening ports for the remote administration service.

Many intruders use a remote administration tool known as Back Orifice 2000, found at `http://www.bo2k.com/`. It is normal for management, and most administrators, to feel uneasy at using a tool created by a group of hackers known as the Cult of the Dead Cow. However the tool is quite flexible, easy on resources, and open source. Utilizing a plug-in architecture, it can easily be expanded to support additional encryption technologies or authentication methods for example. Since the source is available, it can easily be audited and patched for discovered vulnerabilities.

Turning Security Policy into Security

The following section illustrates taking a simplistic set of security policies, formulating it into a security architecture, and then explaining what that means in terms of ruleset implementation.

Security Policy

For this example, the simplest useful policy is used. You can be completely secure by allowing nothing to pass and dropping all inbound traffic, but then there wouldn't be much sense in connecting to the Internet:

- Provide internal users with unrestricted access to Internet resources.
- Allow access to the Company-hosted Web Server, DNS server, and email server.
- Deny everything else.

Notice how this doesn't imply anything about the architecture of the Internet connection. Selecting a working architecture will be discussed shortly.

Default Stance

The default stance is your policy on what action is taken for a packet that doesn't match any of the previously defined rules. Normally, for securing a site, the default policy will be to DROP the packet.

Security Architecture

Defining a security architecture is the process of converting security policies into technical implementation. The security architecture is where you decide the following:

- Whether you are hosting your servers on one, or many, demilitarized zone (DMZ) LANs or being dangerous and hosting them on your internal network
- Whether you are using just a packet filtering router or a firewall in conjunction with the router, and so on

The first part of the security policy is to allow any internal network traffic outbound to the Internet. This really doesn't impact any security architecture you might choose.

Hosting Web, DNS, and email services on-site will provide intruders a handhold to access your internal network resources. To protect both your servers and your internal resources, choose to host them on a DMZ. The security gateway, whether a packet filtering router or a firewall, will then be the first line of defense against intruders attacking your servers.

Next, a dedicated firewall system is deployed that connects the internal network to the unprotected network on the router. Additionally, there is a single DMZ segment on which the Web server, DNS server, and mail server will reside. The DMZ is a protected network segment that allows access from both the Internet and the internal network. However, because Internet users will be accessing those servers, the servers can't be trusted. Making the assumption that the servers could be compromised at any time helps define another policy: Any connections initiated from those servers to the internal network will be refused.

Because DNS provides host, server, resource, and internal organizational information, you should use a split DNS. The split DNS provides a minimal subset of the necessary information for external users to contact and interact with the DMZ protected servers. An internal DNS server on the internal network will carry the full zone information. This qualifies as security through obscurity, but there is no real need to give intruders a map of your network to focus their attacks on.

The mail server will be configured as a queuing mail-hub. This allows internal hosts to relay mail out to the Internet, and it allows the internal mail server to periodically poll the DMZ mail server for queued email. The mail server will not allow unauthorized relaying, the act of forwarding email destined for another domain through your server. This is not only courteous, but helps reduce spam and email abuse. Speaking of which, the mail-hub will also be configured to reject email coming from sites in the Mail Abuse Prevention System (MAPS) Realtime Blackhole List (RBL). The MAPS RBL contains sites that have been used to relay spam and have refused to take any action against preventing the spammers from relaying through their sites.

Administration of all the boxes will be provided by Secure Shell. As previously discussed, SSH provides both secure terminal emulation and secure file transfer capabilities replacing rsh, rlogin, telnet, and ftp. There's no point in passing your account and passwords in the clear (see Figure 8.1).

Security Architecture to Rulebase

The next step is to take our modified security policy and security architecture and convert them into rulesets that make up our firewall rulebase. This step is generally firewall agnostic and doesn't depend on any special features such as stateful inspection or built-in support for specific application services such as FTP. The actual implementation of these generic rules for a specific firewall is where the details of such joy will fall out.

Start Free and Clear

First and foremost flush all existing rules, and reset all existing firewall properties. This ensures that there are no existing holes, gaps, misconfigurations, or surprises that you weren't expecting.

Remember simplicity: It is better for your firewall to err conservatively and block needed traffic than it is to allow unwanted traffic. Starting with a clean slate by blocking all traffic assures that you at least start out secure with the goal of remaining that way.

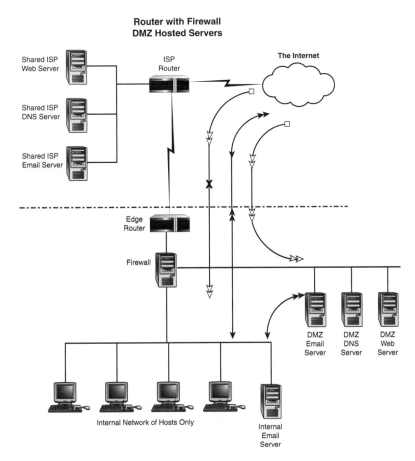

Figure 8.1   Internet connection with packet filter router, firewall, and DMZ hosted servers.

Allow Internal Network Traffic Outbound to the Internet

Allow all internal network traffic outbound to the Internet. This rule becomes more complex the more non-contiguous internal networks you need to represent. Because the point of having a DMZ is to host servers that are not trusted, you must ensure that the internal users are not normally accessing the DMZ servers directly. To accomplish this, allow all internal network traffic to any destination except the DMZ. Most all firewalls have the negation operator that allows you to express this rule easily.

Protect the Firewall

Drop all traffic destined for the firewall itself. You don't want people succeeding in sending traffic to the firewall proper. This won't hide the firewall from intruders, but it will generally deny packets and responses directly accessing the firewall. There is a way to hide the firewall, but it's specific to a firewall implementation. Here is where rule order starts to become important, as this rule must go prior to the Allow Outbound rule. If the order were to be reversed, internal hosts could access the firewall.

Allow Only Internal Admin Access to the Firewall

The firewall needs to be managed, however it should be managed only by the firewall administrators. Administrative access should be restricted to which machines the administrators use and types of network traffic required to access and to manage the firewall. For example, UNIX-based firewalls should allow access only by encrypted SSH sessions. Commercial firewalls such as Checkpoint's FireWall-1 have specific firewall administrative ports (256, 257, and 258) that are accessed via encrypted sessions through their management console. This rule must go prior to the drop everything destined for the firewall rule or even administrative traffic will be dropped.

Default Policy of Drop Everything

The default stance of *that which is not explicitly allowed should be denied* needs to be implemented. In addition to dropping all other packets, a useful diagnostic method enables logging of the dropped packets. This provides you with the means to troubleshoot firewall issues, and to audit the attempted intrusions. This rule generally goes last.

Drop Traffic You Do Not Want Logged

Broadcasts, Multicasts, and other traffic your firewall sees but you do not want logged should have a rule defined that drops or rejects the traffic, but does not log. This prevents excessive, unnecessary logging that would otherwise clutter up your logfiles. Reviewing your logfiles will be difficult enough without having to wade through page after page of NetBIOS, RIP, OSPF, or DHCP requests. This rule needs to be ordered prior to the protect the firewall rule.

Services Provided to the Internet

You need to allow Internet users access to the servers and services that you are providing to the Internet. This includes DNS name lookups, Web (HTTP/HTTPS), and mail (SMTP):

- Allow DNS name lookups (UDP/53) from any network, but allow the internal networks to the DMZ name server only. The internal users should be using the internal DNS servers. If your ISP is acting as a secondary for your external DNS name server, you would need to add an additional rule allowing DNS zone transfers (TCP/53) between the ISP's name server and the DMZ name server.

- HTTP (TCP/80), and HTTPS (TCP/443) if necessary, access from anywhere to the DMZ Web server will be allowed. To enable HTTP/HTTPS access from the internal network, this rule must be before the allow-outbound-to-everywhere-but-the-DMZ rule.

- SMTP (TCP/25) access from anywhere to the DMZ mail server will be allowed. To enable SMTP access from the internal mail server, this rule must also be before the allow-outbound-to-everywhere-but-the-DMZ rule.

Drop DMZ Initiated Traffic

The servers on the DMZ should never initiate a connection to the internal network. If this occurs, there is a good chance that one of your servers has been compromised. The rule that governs this activity should deny and log the occurrence. If you have the ability to trigger an alert, that certainly is timely and valuable information to have.

Additional Rules

If you want to block additional services, such as ICQ or AOL's Instant Messenger, rather than block the ports, block the destination hosts. AIM can use Telnet, HTTP, SMTP, or HTTP Proxies to access the AIM servers:

- Block all TCP traffic to `login.oscar.aol.com`
- Block all TCP traffic to `toc.oscar.aol.com`

Change Management

Comments in a comments field or in the firewall startup script are necessary forms of documentation that allows organizations to better manage and maintain the integrity of their firewall rulebases. The following information, at a minimum, should be logged with a rulebase change:

- Name of admin modifying the rule
- Date/time change implemented
- Reason for the rule change

Be sure to log your changes; this advice can't be stressed enough. You will appreciate it when there are problems, which there will be. Even better, have your firewall rulebase or script under revision control. This could be something as simple as a backup copy of the file with the date in the filename to Revision Control System (RCS) or Source Code Control System (SCCS) enabled archives.

Harden All Your Servers

As briefly discussed in Chapter 3, "Security Concepts," hardening is about minimizing risk and increasing robustness. Hardening refers to the process of disabling unnecessary services, ensuring all security patches have been applied, and paying careful attention to file system permissions. Hardening a server that is Internet accessible includes, but is not necessarily limited to, the following tasks:

- Reducing the number of network services that are running and accessible to the Internet.
- Removing unnecessary software and features, which reduces the overall complexity of the system. This includes removing additional protocols such as IPX, AppleTalk, NetBIOS, DLC, LAT, and DecNET.

- Removing software that allows access to internal system information, such as SNMP.
- Removing insecure remote control software, such as X Window or the ADMIN$ share for remote Windows NT administration.
- Applying all known security updates and service packs. Oftentimes, security exploits in necessary software such as DNS are resolved in a simple configuration change or security patch.
- Enabling traffic filters if available. Windows NT and most UNIX systems have built-in or freely available software that allows more control of the kinds and sources of IP traffic that are accepted.
- Removing unnecessary accounts on the system. Rename existing administrative or root accounts to something unique and hard to guess.
- Removing unnecessary and overly generous file permissions for both accounts and the file system.

The details of such tasks are operating system specific, not only to vendor but to version. An overall guide to hardening several flavors of operating systems can be found at the following URL: http://advice.networkice.com/Advice/OS/default.htm

Microsoft Windows NT and 2000 operating systems have a well-known source of information to help you harden your servers. Although these documents are IIS specific, many of the steps to harden your server that do not include IIS are extremely useful. Visit http://www.microsoft.com/technet/security/iischk.asp for Windows NT 4.0, and visit http://www.microsoft.com/technet/security/iis5chk.asp for Windows 2000 information.

Drop Source Routed Traffic

Normally, an IP packet leaves the client with only the source and destination addresses. All routing decisions are made by routers on the way. There is an IP option that allows you to specify what routes to take, which are specified from the sending machine. Thus, it is source routed rather than router routed.

You might ask yourself, why the sending node would want to specify routing information rather than let the network routers make those decisions. Well, it's useful for performing network diagnostics. Traceroute can be used to specify source-routed traffic, and traceroute is useful. Unfortunately source-routed traffic can also be used to override packet filter routers and firewall rulebases.

There are actually two forms of source-routed traffic: Strict Source Routed and Loose Source Routed. The differences aren't that important, because all the source routed traffic needs to be dropped. Dropping source-routed traffic should be done on the edge routers, and any capable security gateways.

Drop Directed Broadcast Traffic

IP networks normally have two reserved IP addresses, the network address which is the host portion of the IP address filled with all zeros, and the broadcast address, which is the host portion of the IP address filled with all ones.

If an ICMP echo reply, easily generated by a ping, is sent to either the network or broadcast address, each node on that network would respond. This originally was used to determine the status of network nodes; however, more recently, this is used to create denial of service attacks.

A simple denial of service attack is to send an ICMP echo request to the broadcast address of a network of hosts with a spoofed address. All the hosts on that subnet respond with an echo reply to the spoofed address. Each ping is multiplied by the number of hosts on the subnet, which generates instant traffic.

Now imagine a user on a 56Kbps dialup modem sending spoofed ICMP echo requests to a subnet of 100 hosts. Those 100 hosts generate 100 ICMP echo replies that are sent to the IP address in the spoofed packets. That is 53Kbps × 100 or 5,300Kbps. That is three times the size of a T1, all generated from a dialup user.

This type of attack, and others like it, can be defeated by disabling directed broadcasts on the edge routers and servers exposed to the Internet. Further information can be found in RFC 2267, Network Ingress Filtering: Defeating Denial of Service Attacks Which Employ IP Source Address Spoofing.

Lock Down Your DNS Servers

DNS servers are often the focus of root-compromise exploits. To reduce the probability that you will be a target, there are some simple configuration options to consider for your DNS server:

- Run the newest stable release of the name server. All prior versions of both BIND and Microsoft's DNS server have vulnerabilities. If you are using the Internet Software Consortium's version of BIND, which is used on almost every installation of UNIX, make sure you are using 8.2.2pl5 or newer. For Microsoft Windows NT, make sure your DNS server is running *at least* Service Pack 4. Service Pack 6a is now available.

- Restrict zone transfers to known secondary servers. This reduces additional information that can be gathered by potential intruders. The important thing to keep in mind here is to not allow zone transfers from the secondary servers. There is no point locking down the primary servers if the intruders can just do a zone transfer from a secondary server.

- Do not use dynamic updates on external DNS servers. None of your Internet accessible servers should be using dynamic IP addresses. Therefore there is no need for dynamic updates. It should be obvious why it is a security risk allowing intruders to send dynamic updates to your DNS server.

- If possible, restrict the queries that the DNS server will do recursive queries for. There is no reason your DNS servers should do recursive DNS queries for anyone other than your internal network hosts. Create an access control list (ACL) to restrict queries to internal hosts.

Disable Relaying and Other Information Features on Your SMTP Server

As previously discussed, it is bad netiquette to allow email relaying through your mail server. Many mail servers have built-in support to reject email coming from sites in the Mail Abuse Prevention System (MAPS) Realtime Blackhole List (RBL) or similar lists. To prevent abuse of your mail server and other people's resources, block mail relaying and spam.

Sample Prototype Designs

The following sections describe some common basic example security and WAN architectures. Because this section is about assessing your security needs, the WAN architecture is de-emphasized in favor of concentrating on securing the connection to your ISP from the router on back.

Earlier in the chapter, an example of a packet filter router coupled with a firewall and protected DMZ network was used. Here, additional designs are discussed to round out the picture. Please keep in mind that these prototype designs are not the end-all, be-all in secure network designs. Rather, they are meant to illustrate how the various components interact and should be used as a basis for more complex designs.

Packet Filter Router Only

For locations on an absolute no-money budget, the best (and least) you should do is use the native packet filtering capabilities of your router to protect your internal network.

In this configuration it is expected that there are no internal servers. Services such as DNS, email, and Web are hosted by your ISP. All your hosts are on an internal network behind the router connecting you to the Internet.

Although this configuration is economical in the sense that it requires no additional startup equipment, and no additional staff to support the equipment that is owned by the ISP, it will increase your monthly cost from the ISP.

Additionally, it provides a thin veneer of security. The packet filter is better than nothing, but you are not protected the way that you could be with a real firewall, DMZ, and intermediate relay hosts and proxies.

A logical network diagram outlining a typical packet filtering router connection to the Internet is shown in Figure 8.2.

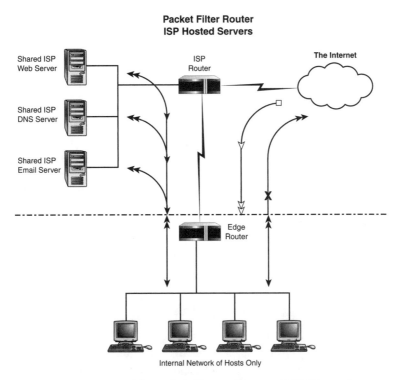

**Packet Filter Router
ISP Hosted Servers**

Figure 8.2   Internet connection with packet filter router and ISP hosted servers.

Because no services for your company are hosted on your internal network, your job of taking security policies and converting them to packet filters is simplified. Table 8.3 lists the service, and the English equivalent of the policy filter.

Table 8.3   Packet Filter Router Security Policy

Service	Security Policy
DNS	For your internal hosts, permit outbound UDP/53 traffic to your ISP DNS server and permit inbound replies to clients from your ISP DNS server with a source port of UDP/53.
HTTP/HTTPS	For your internal hosts, permit outbound TCP/80 and TCP/443 traffic to any Web server from your internal networks and permit inbound replies to clients with the ACK bit set.

Table 8.3 Continued

Service	Security Policy
SMTP	For your internal hosts, permit outbound TCP/25 traffic to your ISP SMTP server from your internal networks and permit inbound replies to clients from the ISP SMTP server with the ACK bit set.
POP3	For your internal hosts, permit outbound TCP/110 traffic to your ISP mail server from your internal networks and permit inbound replies to clients with the ACK bit set.
IMAP4	For your internal hosts, permit outbound TCP/143 traffic to the ISP mail server from your internal networks and permit inbound replies to clients with the ACK bit set.
FTP	As previously discussed, consider using a transparent or application proxy to handle your FTP requirements. For such a configuration, permit outbound TCP/21 and TCP ports greater than 1,023 traffic to any FTP server from your internal networks and permit inbound replies to your proxy server and either TCP/20 or with the ACK bit set.
ICMP	For your internal hosts, permit outbound echo request from your internal networks and permit inbound echo reply, destination unreachable, and time exceeded messages.

Packet Filter Router with a DMZ

The first step in migrating from the reliance on your ISP's services is to bring your more critical, but low bandwidth services in house. Servers that handle DNS and email are the most logical choices. If your Web site is low traffic enough, or your bandwidth is expansive enough, then moving that on-site will make sense as well.

In this configuration, it is expected that you will be hosting some or all of the most critical services and servers. Services such as DNS, email, and Web will be hosted on-site rather than by your ISP or in a co-location facility. Rather than locate those servers on the internal network, they are placed on a perimeter network demilitarized zone (DMZ). Because the servers will be accessed by the general populous of the Internet, it would be unwise to place them on an internal network where a compromised server could do an amazing amount of disruption to your IT environment. All your client hosts remain on an internal network behind the router connecting you to the Internet.

The primary advantage of hosting your own servers is that you now have greater control over them. You are not sharing resources with 100 other companies or individuals, some of which might be higher-profile targets for attacks. You are in complete control, which includes responsibility for applying security patches, updates, fixes, and capacity planing and management. Ultimately you are in control of your own response-time on maintaining and managing your servers.

Any servers that are accessed directly by clients on the Internet should be placed on the DMZ. All traffic from the DMZ should be considered untrusted. Even though you have control over the servers, you should assume the likelihood that they are already compromised and build your security policy accordingly.

A logical network diagram outlining a typical packet filtering router connection to the Internet is shown in Figure 8.3.

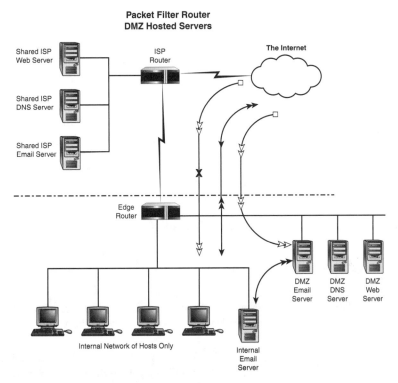

Figure 8.3   Internet connection with packet filter router and DMZ hosted servers.

Because some or all your provided services for your company are hosted on your DMZ network, your job of taking security policies and converting them to packet filters is simplified somewhat. For all intents and purposes, you consider your DMZ the Internet when building policies for your internal network. You will also restrict traffic to the DMZ network except for the services you are offering. A packet filter router is still not as flexible or capable as a firewall, and it is a single layer of security. As mentioned before, you want to layer your security so that if one component is compromised you are still protected.

Most people might think to just migrate the existing ISP's mail server functionality to a mail server on the DMZ. That functionality might include SMTP, POP3, and IMAP4 protocols.

However, this example is aiming for both simplicity and security. Giving the potential intruders more services to target for exploits cannot help your cause. Therefore make a relatively simple architectural change: Configure the mail server as a queuing mail hub relay, which is essentially a front-end drop box to an internal mail server.

Incoming mail from the Internet gets queued up for the internal mail server on the DMZ mail server. The DMZ mail server runs SMTP only, and never tries to deliver queued email to the internal mail server. The internal mail server is configured to periodically poll the DMZ mail server for queued email using the SMTP ETRN command. The internal mail server runs the normal client mail access protocols such as IMAP4 and POP3 in addition to the SMTP service.

How does this change help? SMTP connections from the Internet terminate at the DMZ mail server. The only communication through the packet filter router is initiated from the internal mail server to the DMZ mail server. No clients, internal or external, talk to the DMZ mail server. All internal clients send (SMTP) and receive (IMAP4/POP3) email internally. There is no need to add additional filtering rules. As an added benefit, if the router were to fail, it would not interfere with the normal internal email operations of the business.

Although you certainly could just migrate the ISP mail server functionality to a single box on the DMZ, you shouldn't. If that is absolutely your only option, you can use the previous sample security policies for IMAP4 and POP3 as examples to build your own configuration.

Table 8.4 lists the service, and the English equivalent of the policy filter.

Table 8.4   Packet Filter Router and DMZ Security Policy

Service	Security Policy
DNS	For recursive queries by your DMZ name server, permit outbound UDP/53 query traffic from your DMZ name server and permit inbound reply UDP/53 traffic to your DMZ name server.
	For clients on the Internet, permit inbound query UDP/53 traffic to your DMZ name server and permit outbound reply UDP/53 traffic from your DMZ name server.
	For your internal hosts, permit outbound query UDP/53 traffic from your internal networks to your DMZ name server and permit inbound reply UDP/53 traffic from your DMZ name server to your internal networks.
	For secondary name servers that do not reside on the DMZ, you must permit inbound TCP/53 traffic to DMZ name servers from known secondary name servers, and you must permit outbound TCP/53 traffic to known secondary name servers from your DMZ name server.
HTTP/HTTPS	For clients on the Internet, permit inbound TCP/80 and TCP/443 traffic to your DMZ Web server and permit outbound replies from your Web server with the ACK bit set.

Table 8.4   Continued

Service	Security Policy
	For your internal hosts, permit outbound TCP/80 and TCP/443 traffic to any Web server from your internal networks and permit inbound replies to clients with the ACK bit set.
SMTP	For delivering email from your DMZ mail server, permit outbound TCP/25 traffic from your DMZ mail server and permit inbound replies to your DMZ mail server with the ACK bit set.
	For receiving email from the Internet, permit inbound TCP/25 traffic to your DMZ mail server and permit outbound replies from your DMZ mail server with the ACK bit set.
	For your internal mail server, permit outbound TCP/25 traffic to your DMZ mail server from your internal mail server and permit inbound replies to your internal mail server from the DMZ mail server with the ACK bit set.
FTP	As previously discussed, consider using a transparent or application proxy to handle your FTP requirements. For such a configuration, permit outbound traffic on TCP/21 and TCP ports greater than 1,023 to any FTP server from your internal networks and permit inbound replies to your proxy server and either TCP/20 or with the ACK bit set.
SSH	For your internal administrative hosts, permit TCP/22 to your DMZ network and allow outbound replies from the DMZ network to your internal administrative hosts with the ACK bit set.
ICMP	For your DMZ servers, permit inbound destination unreachable, time exceeded, and fragmentation needed messages.
	For your internal hosts, permit outbound echo request from your internal networks and permit inbound echo reply, destination unreachable, and time exceeded messages.

Router/Firewall and DMZ Revisited with VPN

In keeping with the previous example (Packet Filter Router with a DMZ), this section notes the differences in the architecture and rulebase necessary to accommodate an IPSec based VPN.

The architecture is modified slightly to accommodate the VPN. Many people call the termination point of a number of road-warrior or remote branch connections a server. Although the concept is fine, the terminology does not match the common use of IPSec lingo. In IPSec, there is no client and there is no server. There are only peers. Peers can initiate connections or receive them, but the act of initiating a connection does not make a node a client or server.

So, what do you call the IPSec peer that is the terminus of all those connections? The commonly used term is *security gateway*, often abbreviated SG.

Many commercial firewalls include the capability to be an IPSec security gateway. Although this is convenient in terms of hardware and licensing, having your firewall and VPN terminus on the same machine is not optimal. Encryption is CPU intensive. 3DES encryption is not the most efficient encryption algorithm, although it is the interoperability-standard for IPSec. High CPU use on your firewall leaves fewer cycles to evaluate packets and rules. Placing a dedicated security gateway in the DMZ is a more efficient, and more secure, design. Think simplicity and security in layers.

Although there are configurations of security gateways that use a single interface, the most common and secure is multiple interfaces. Normally one interface will receive encrypted sessions, and the rest will receive unencrypted traffic. This design lends itself to placing the security gateway in parallel with the firewall.

A more secure configuration, as used in this example, is to have a secondary DMZ connected to the firewall. The unencrypted traffic will be on the second DMZ. This gives you the added flexibility of controlling what traffic enters and leaves your internal network to VPN connected hosts and remote locations (see Figure 8.4).

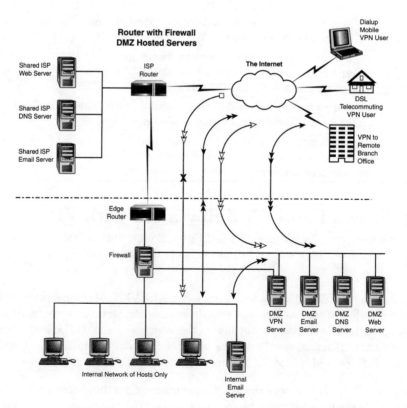

Figure 8.4 Internet connection with packet filter router, firewall, and DMZ hosted servers and remote access via VPN.

The security policy will be amended as follows: All VPN-connected hosts will have full access to the internal networks. Again, you can decide to limit traffic to certain subnets, servers, and the types of traffic into and out of the VPN through the firewall.

To support the VPN and the new policy, three rules are added to the rulebase. The first rule allows IPSec IKE traffic from the Internet to reach the security gateway on the DMZ. IKE, as you remember, is UDP/500 traffic both source and destination. This rule is placed before the Drop DMZ Initiated Traffic and Allow Outbound except to DMZ rules. Now that you have remote clients able to exchange keys for the IPSec Security Association (SA) pairs, you can let through ESP, IP protocol 50, from the Internet to the security gateway on the DMZ. This rule is placed after the IKE rule, but before the Drop DMZ Initiated Traffic and Allow Outbound except to DMZ rules.

The third rule allows internal networks to the security gateway interface on the second DMZ. This allows internal traffic to reach the security gateway and be encrypted to its final destination. This rule should go between the allow IPSec ESP rule and the drop everything rule.

There you have it: instant remote accessibility with security. Now the only thing left is to actually implement it, and validate that it works as advertised. Those topics are covered in Chapters 10, "Implementing Security," and 11, "Testing and Validation."

9

GETTING CONNECTED

Albert Einstein, when asked to describe radio, replied: "You see, wire telegraph is a kind of a very, very long cat. You pull his tail in New York and his
head is meowing in Los Angeles. Do you understand this? And radio operates
exactly the same way: You send signals here, they receive them there. The
only difference is that there is no cat."

Equipment Selection

In selecting your Customer Premises Equipment (CPE), you're outlining the
capabilities of your Internet connection. You're also determining what type
of media you'll be using inside and outside. There are two parts to your CPE
that you are normally involved with: a CSU/DSU and a router.

Router Selection

If you are leasing the router from your ISP, you may not have much of a
choice in what router you get. You'll just be handed one based upon your
LAN technology and what your ISP uses. If purchasing for yourself, the possibilities are numerous. Although any router from any reputable manufacturer will most likely work as well as any other, your ISP might have a
preference, or at least a recommendation. There are certainly advantages to
taking the ISP's advice on things like this. If, for example, your ISP is
stuffed to the gills with Cisco certified engineers, it doesn't make much sense
to buy a 3Com if you're planning to call your ISP for help configuring it.

If you're getting no advice from anyone, you'll at the very least want a router that's easily configurable. These days telnetting to a router to configure it is falling by the wayside in favor of Web-configurable routers. Additional features to look for are packet filtering and firewall capabilities.

LAN/WAN Interface Requirements

When you buy a router, make sure it will accept the media you're using. Typically, this means Ethernet, although it could also be Fast Ethernet, Token Ring, FDDI, or ATM. How many different interfaces will you need? Routers have at least one connection for the "outside" world, (a WAN connection) and one for the "inside" network, (a LAN connection). Routers come in other flavors as well. They all have different uses:

- **1 WAN, 1 LAN**—Useful for small/branch offices. No onsite equipment exposed to Internet.
- **1 WAN, 2 LAN**—Useful for locations requiring onsite equipment that will be accessed by outside interests or Internet users.
- **2 WAN, 1 LAN**—Useful for aggregate bandwidth, bandwidth-on-demand, multi-homed redundant connections.
- **2 WAN, 2 LAN**—Useful for aggregate bandwidth, bandwidth-on-demand, multi-homed redundant connections with locations requiring onsite equipment that will be accessed by outside interests or Internet users.
- **Multiple WAN, 1 LAN**—Useful for hub router locations for private networks aggregating to a data center.
- **Multiple WAN, Multiple LAN**—Useful for hub router to aggregate remote locations to data center, which also is connecting many local area networks.

In the last two cases, it is better to have multiple routers: a "core" router used to do the aggregation and routing between LANs and WANs, and an "edge" router, or routers, responsible for connecting the data center to the Internet.

Figure 9.1 shows ISDN with an Integrated NT-1 interface—thus a "U" interface.

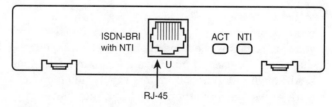

Figure 9.1   A LAN/WAN interface, ISDN with NT-1.

Figure 9.2 shows CSU/DSU for Fractional T1/E1 with a RJ48C connector. This looks the same on an AT&T Paradyne CSU/DSU, too.

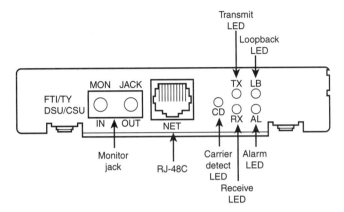

Figure 9.2   An RJ48C connector for connecting a fractional T1 to your LAN.

Software Suite Selection

The software suite you select for your router is actually more important than the physical router itself. Generally, there are several feature sets available from most router manufacturers. The availability of these feature sets will obviously depend on the model (and price) of the router.

As an example, Cisco provides a matrix showing what features are available on what routers on their Web site at:

```
http://www.cisco.com/univercd/cc/td/doc/pcat/io11v2.htm
```

The following are some popular combinations:

- **IP**—Basic IP and IP routing protocols such as RIP, RIP2, OSPF, and BGP4. Usually includes access control for packet filtering. Supports most bandwidth delivery methods, ISDN, Fractional T1/E1, and Frame Relay.
- **IP+**—Usually includes additional IP features such as ToS or QoS prioritization, Voice over IP, or Frame Relay. Supports additional bandwidth delivery methods, SMDS, ATM, and so on.
- **IP+/FireWall**—Includes a stateful inspection capable firewall software.

As an example, Cisco's IOS Firewall has stateful inspection (called Context Based Access Control in Cisco parlance) for a large number of "tricky" client application protocols that would be extremely difficult to support with just pure access control lists. These include, CU-SeeMe (only the White Pine version), FTP, H.323 (such as NetMeeting, ProShare), HTTP (Java blocking), Java, Microsoft NetShow, UNIX R-commands (such as rlogin, rexec, and rsh), RealAudio, RPC (Sun RPC, not DCE RPC), Microsoft RPC, SMTP, SQL*Net, StreamWorks, TFTP, and VDOLive.

Nortel Network's offering has embedded CheckPoint's FireWall-1 product into the routing software. Starting in 2001, the BaySecure FireWall-1 product will be replaced with Nortel's own Contivity-based integrated Firewall/VPN technology that Nortel originally acquired from Shasta technologies. The software is capable of the full stateful inspection capabilities that FireWall-1 inspection module is normally capable of. Authenticating users must still be relegated to the RADIUS or SecurID type of dedicated servers:

- **Corporate**—Multiple common LAN protocols, such as IPX and AppleTalk, in addition to the normal IP+ feature-set. This often includes appropriate routing protocols such as IPX RIP and NLSP. Generally supports additional LAN technologies, such as ATM and FDDI.

- **Corporate/Firewall**—All the features of Corporate plus Firewall capabilities. The firewall capabilities generally do not extend to the non-IP protocols.

- **Enterprise**—Includes all the features of the Corporate feature set, plus high-end capabilities. Also provides additional protocol support, such as DECnet, LAT, SNA, XNS, and so on. High availability in the form of Virtual Router Redundancy Protocol (or Cisco's Hot Standby Router Protocol).

- **Enterprise/Firewall**—All the features of Enterprise plus firewall capabilities.

CSU/DSU Selection

Often your CSU/DSU choice will also be dictated by your ISP. Buy what the ISP recommends and what it has experience supporting. If your ISP has no suggestions, your major deciding factor for the device besides price is generally whether it should be external or integrated. External CSU/DSUs are often available in either a standard 19-inch rack format or a small modem-sized unit.

Pros of an Internal CSU/DSU

Integrated CSU/DSUs are usually less expensive, but tied to one vendor. Integrated CSU/DSUs are usually less complicated, because they rely on integrated components of the host platform. No additional cables are necessary.

Cons of an Internal CSU/DSU

There is no choice in vendor. It might not have the feature sets necessary for some of your application solutions—for example, inverse-MUXing multiple T1 lines into a single aggregate link, or channelizing into individual links to different remote locations. If the hardware fails, it might damage the router.

Staging the Hardware

Staging the hardware involves setting it up in stages. It would be crazy to install a device like this and plug your network into it with fingers crossed before testing it out first.

Setting Up the Hardware: Out of the Box and Onto the Wall

The first stage in setting up the hardware is taking it out of the box, and making sure it's all there and undamaged. It might sound a bit pedantic, but making sure all the bits and pieces are there before going very far is an important step.

The next step involves making sure it all works: Attach it to the rack (if external) and plug it in to see if all the lights light up.

The next few steps involve some simple configuration, or configuration review if the ISP pre-configured it for you, and some simple diagnostics. It is best to do this in an isolated environment, making sure the equipment does what it's supposed to first, and then seeing how it interacts with your production environment. Whether this isolated environment is a separate lab network you've built to simulate the production network, or it's the old "in-place, just not connected" environment, you'll be glad when you find out the default Ethernet interface was configured with the accounting server's IP address. The cardinal rule of troubleshooting is to try one thing at a time to isolate the root cause. Otherwise you'll find yourself sacrificing chickens under a full moon to appease the IT spirits and keep your servers from crashing.

After you've identified that you have a complete, fully functional piece of equipment, the next step is to configure it and check to make sure nothing weird is happening. For example, does it configure according to the directions? Are you getting error messages? If the ISP preconfigured the router for you, check to make sure the ISP has configured it to specifications. Did they use the agreed upon IP address range? Renumbering your internal network can involve a tremendous amount of effort. Are you using Network Address Translation?

Connect and Configure the CSU/DSU

Select parameters that match your circuit. You can find these circuit parameters in Chapter 2, "Understanding WAN Bandwidth Delivery."

B8ZS

B8ZS, Bipolar with 8-zero substitution, encodes a string of eight consecutive 0s into a series of 1s, 0s, and a specific pair of bipolar violations. B8ZS does not reduce your overall bandwidth, and thus is required for all "clear channel" 64Kbps transmission rates.

Extended Superframe (ESF)

ESF has error correction in the form of Cyclic Redundancy Check (CRC6 specifically, the 6-bit version, CRC32 in TCP/IP is normally 32 bit). Additionally, Extended Superframe allocates 4Kbps of the overhead as a facility data link. The facility data link gives the phone company the capability to interrogate the customer premise equipment for error statistics and line performance to aid in predicting and preventing line outages.

56 or 64 Clear Channel

Clear channel is any signal encoding that does not require bit stuffing, so all eight bits per channel are available for data payload.

Internal or External Clocking

Remembering that the bandwidth being delivered to your door is synchronous in nature, there must be something to synchronize to. The clocking source for the signal needs to be agreed upon, and it's almost always going to be the bandwidth provider's equipment.

You will almost always be using external, or "line" in Cisco parlance, and synchronizing to the clock on the circuit being fed to your facilities.

You would use internal clocking over line or external if you were providing the source on both ends of the circuit, perhaps building a custom point to multi-point feed using a channelized DS3 to feed multiple locations. If you are configuring your router on your own, ask the bandwidth provider if it is providing a clock source on the circuit that you can sync to.

Connect and Configure the Router

Plug in the CSU/DSU to the router if external. Configure it if it's internal and connect the cable to the leased line.

Many routers supplied by ISPs will be plug-n-play ready—preconfigured with circuit information, IP address information, netmask, and routing.

Cisco routers, for example, come with an application called *config maker*. It includes a built-in tutorial for building WAN configurations and Virtual Private Networks, as seen in Figure 9.3.

Run your setup isolated from the rest of the network in the event that it has problems. Of course, this doesn't just apply to ISP-supplied network equipment. This applies to firewalls, DMZ servers, and so on. It's always better to build and test in an isolated environment. If for some reason some traffic in your production network were to cause excessive logging, some subtle problems in the configuration might get lost in the noise. There will be plenty of opportunity for problem solving after you connect your staged WAN environment to your production network.

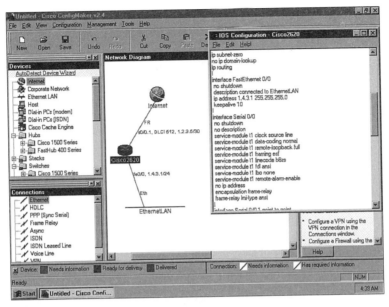

Figure 9.3   Simple WAN Configuration using Cisco's ConfigMaker.

Burn In

After you've verified the router configuration and removed any sources of error messages, it's time to plug it all in, turn it all on, and crank the volume up to 11. That's right, start the firewalls, servers, and the whole tamale. Then wait. Allow a burn-in time of at least five days. Most hardware failures happen in the first 100 hours of operation. There are some obvious tests, such as making sure it can pass IP traffic by pinging DNS servers, remote router interfaces, and the like. But if a piece of electronic equipment fails, it's usually in the first few days of use. Better find out now that the people in receiving didn't have a bad day at work.

During the burn-in period, you should attach non-critical test devices. This allows you to get a baseline for response time, and because no one else is using the link, you don't have to fight for bandwidth. Run some security tests on your environment to make sure there are no obvious holes. Try to Telnet to your router, or use SNMP tools to retrieve information. Port scan your installation to make sure there are no additional services open and available. At this point, it might be useful to allow a security consulting firm to assess and audit your connection.

During the staging process, be sure to communicate with your ISP. Let them know when you are connecting the equipment and that you are planning to run some tests, including a security audit. They might have automated facilities in place to monitor for port scans and other intrusive network traffic. Keeping them in the loop will make your relationship last longer.

10

IMPLEMENTING
SECURITY

When alerted to an intrusion by tinkling glass or otherwise, 1) calm yourself, 2) identify the intruder, and 3) if hostile, kill him.

—G. Gordon Liddy's *Forbes* column on personal security

Setting Proper Expectations

This chapter gives you a starting point for building a secure Internet connection. General security could easily cover an entire book. Specific topics in security, such as Public Key Infrastructure (PKI), IP Security for IPv4 and IPv6 (IPSec), Virtual Private Networks (VPNs), or a specific vendor's firewall implementation could all be (and indeed are) volumes all their own.

The goal here is to provide the absolute basics necessary to secure your Internet connection. Additional reading will be required depending on the equipment you purchase and the infrastructure you build. Additional effort on your part will be required. Security is a constant effort; the only thing guaranteed is that you won't be 100% secure 100% of the time.

You will need to spend some time with your internal security policies. You'll be using resources such as Chapter 8, "Assessing Your Security Needs," and RFC 2196: The Site Security Handbook. You should now have a good handle on the threat model as well as an idea of what you're protecting and whom you are protecting it from. Properly defining your threat model and internal security policies gives you a framework within which you can begin to build and maintain your organization's integrity.

> **A Basic Security Primer**
>
> These books can help you a great deal in designing and implementing your security:
>
> *Firewalls and Internet Security: Repelling the Wily Hacker* byBill Cheswick and Steve Bellovin. Published by Addison Wesley. ISBN 0-201-63357-4
>
> *Building Internet Firewalls* by D. Brent Chapman and Elizabeth Zwicky. Published by O'Reilly Books. ISBN 1-56592-124-0
>
> *Practical Internet & UNIX Security* by Simson Garfinkel and Gene Spafford. Published by O'Reilly Books. ISBN 1-56592-148-8

Hardening Systems

Hardening a server is a tedious process, however it is relatively easy to do, and incurs no additional software or hardware expense. First you must harden the base operating system. Then you must take similar precautions for any services you intend to run on the box. It does not help to harden the base OS and leave gaping holes in the Web or Database server installations. Remember *every product you install has the potential to allow intruders to gain access to your server*. A firewall will not stop an intruder from attacking the shopping cart application running on your Web server.

Windows NT 4.0

Windows NT 4.0 has been the workhorse for Microsoft for years now. And although its more feature-rich replacement is now available, there are many reasons Windows NT 4.0 might still be deployed. The current dearth of firewall applications for Windows 2000 is one such reason. As such, hardening guidelines for the elderly flagship product are discussed first. Many options apply to Windows 2000 as well, so reading through is still worthwhile.

Hardening Installation Guidelines

When installing Windows NT 4.0 Server, try to follow these guidelines as closely as possible. Some of these changes might remove a needed functionality that your application requires. If this is the case, you will have to work harder to protect the server.

Do install on NTFS partitions, not FAT. NTFS provides additional control via access control lists (ACLs). Do not install to FAT and then, after installation,convert to NTFS, because this will not apply the default ACLs.

Do install as a standalone server and do not install as a domain controller. There is no conceivable need to have a firewall or DMZ Web, mail, or DNS server participate in a domain.

Do not install any extra software that is not needed. By default the Windows NT installation includes many accessibility support tools, accessories, multimedia applications and themes, and communication applications. The more software you install, the more that can possibly be exploited. Follow the Tao of Security: simplicity, starting with installation.

Do not install Internet Information Server (IIS) v2.0 that comes with Windows NT, even if this server is to be a Web server. Upgrading earlier versions of IIS does not remove unused files, files that can still be exploited in the newer IIS installation. Until the upgrade process removes old files, it is often better to uninstall IIS and install the new version rather than upgrade in-place.

Do not install other networking protocols other thanTCP/IP. Additional protocols cause additional problems. NetBEUI is not useful outside of a workgroup, andIPX is often not handled properly by firewalls. One of the biggest and most common security problems is allowing IPX to run over NetBEUI. This can let intruders through your firewall to desktop machines.

Do not add additional services, unless of course this is to be a DNS server. Web servers, mail servers, and firewalls generally should not run DNS. The only possible service to add would beSimple Network Management Protocol (SNMP), for remote monitoring of the firewall and DMZ services. Be certain to block those ports externally, and change the read and write community strings from the defaults. SNMP can easily give away more information than you intend if you leave that service accessible from the Internet.

Do not install WINS. If you need to have NetBIOS resolution outside of DNS, use the LMHOSTS file.

Do not do DHCP relaying. In general, there is no need for DMZ servers to relay anything (unless of course it is a mail server acting as a smart hub for internal hosts.)

Do not enable IP Forwarding, unless this server will be the firewall. A firewall is not achieving its potential if it never forwards IP traffic.

Do use a nonexistent workgroup. There is no reason for a firewall or DMZ server to participate in domain or workgroup activities.

Do not install Internet Explorer 5 or 5.5; they provide way more additional functionality than you need on the average server. Remember that any additional functionality can be exploited in non-obvious ways. IE 5 and 5.5 are not a single program, but a collection of reusable components. That means that any program on your system can reuse that functionality. Don't give intruders additional tools to attack you with. If you need to update IE on your Windows NT 4 firewall or DMZ server, install IE 4.01 service pack 2. IE 4.01 SP1 comes on the Windows NT Option Pack CD, but IE 4.01 SP2 is available for download.

Do install the most recent service pack and hotfixes appropriate to your platform and installation. As of publication, Service Pack 6a was available along with several additional hotfixes.

Do remove unnecessary services installed automatically during the install process. These services include the following:

- Remote Procedure Call (RPC)
- NetBIOS
- Computer browser

These additional services can be removed, but might impact the functionality of the server. You should check with your software's requirements, or better yet, perform a lab install and test the configuration before deploying in a production environment. These services can be removed by choosing Control Panel, Network, Services.

- **Workstation**—Impacts services such as at.
- **Server**—Might impact some servers performance.

Do unbind WINS from TCP/IP. Choose Control Panel, Network, Bindings. Select All Protocols from the drop-down menu. Click WINS Client (TCP/IP) and Disable/Remove.

Do ensure the following services aredisabled:

- **Alerter**—A notification service to deliver messages to users of certain administrative events.
- **ClipBook**—Allows clipbook contents to be seen by remote clipbooks.
- **DHCP Client**—Allows the network settings to be configured by remote means.
- **Messenger**—Sends and receives messages send by administrators or the alerter service.
- **NetBIOS Interface**
- **Net Logon**—provides pass-through (workstation) or authentication and domain security database synchronization (server) to other machines in a domain.
- **Network DDE**—provides dynamic data exchange in a networked environment to remote machines.
- **Network DDE DSDM**—manages the shared database of DDE connections.
- **TCP/IP NetBIOS Helper**—NetBIOS over TCP/IP provides name-to-IP address mapping.

Although convenient for remote server administration, it is best to not add additional services including remote management services, such as telnetd and FTP. Neither provides encryption, so accounts, passwords, and other information can be gleaned via the network. If these services must be enabled, be sure to take precautions, such as allowing only access through the firewall from the internal network, and applying IP security filters on the servers running the services.

Do enable IP security filters on the DMZ servers. Firewalls have their own IP filtering and do not need or require native Windows NT IP filters. Choose Control Panel, Network, Protocols, TCP/IP Protocol, Properties, Advanced. Check Enable Security, and then select Configure. Add the inbound ports you want to accept, as shown in Figure 10.1.

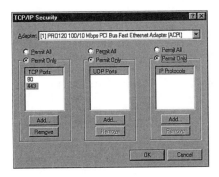

Figure 10.1   Windows NT 4.0 TCP/IP Security Filter configuration dialog.

Do remove the right for users to allowaccess to the server from the network; force console access only.

Do assign individual admin accounts if you have multiple admin accounts. This helps the auditing process.

Do rename theAdministrator account to another name.

Do create a dummy Administrator account with no privileges. As intruders try to compromise this account, they will be logged in the audit logs.

Do reduce the number of groups that have access to the server to only those necessary for operation and administration of the server. You should be able to reduce the groups down to Administrators and Power Users.

Do enable more secure system policies. Use User Manager to modify the Account, User Rights, and Audit system policies:

- Account policies control user password and lockout settings.Passwords should expire according to the timeframe set by corporate policy. Minimum password length should be at least 9 characters while remembering 24 previous passwords.Account lockout should occur after 3 bad logon attempts. The counter can be reset after 30 minutes.
- All User Rights should have the Everyone group removed. Remove all groups and users from Access This Computer From the Network, and limit the users and groups that can Log on Locally. Make sure to pay special attention to Manage Auditing and Security Log.
- Turn onauditing of success and failure of at least these events: Logon and Logoff, Security Policy Changes, and Restart, Shutdown, and System.

Do enable the blank screen saver with a low inactivity timer, say five minutes. Enable password protection on the screen saver.

Do run the SYSKEY utility to enhance the security of your Security Accounts Manager (SAM) database. The SYSKEY utility became available with Service Pack 3, so after you've applied Service Pack 6a or newer SYSKEY will be available.

Do remove the OS/2 and POSIX subsystems. This can be done by running the C2SECURITY tool from the Windows NT Resource Kit, or manually by editing the following Registry keys.

Remove this key which will remove all subordinate keys pertaining to the OS/2 subsystem:

```
HKEY_LOCAL_MACHINE\SOFTWARE
\Microsoft\OS/2 Subsystem for NT
```

Remove the Os2LibPath value from the Environment key:

```
HKEY_LOCAL_MACHINE\SYSTEM
\CurrentControlSet\Control\Session Manager\Environment
Os2LibPath
```

Remove the Optional, POSIX, and OS/2 keys from the Session Manager SubSystem key:

```
HKEY_LOCAL_MACHINE\SYSTEM
\CurrentControlSet\Control\Session Manager\SubSystems
```

After the Registry changes, you must manually remove the %WINNT%\system32\os2 directory and any subdirectories.

Registry Modification Guidelines

There are some functions and features of Windows NT that are controlled solely through Registry settings. Take care in modifying the Registry, as you can easily cripple your system. The following various Registry changes make Windows NT have a more secure default stance.

Set this key to 1 to clear the last used username from the login dialog box:

```
HKEY_LOCAL_MACHINE\SOFTWARE
\Microsoft\Windows NT\CurrentVersion\Winlogin
DontDisplayLastUserName
```

Set this key to 1 to restrict anonymous connections from listing account names:

```
HKEY_LOCAL_MACHINE\SYSTEM
\CurrentControlSet\Control\Lsa
RestrictAnonymous
```

Create the following key to restrict network access to the Registry, so Registry modifications must be made from the local system. Service Pack 3 or higher needs to be installed for this Registry entry to work.

```
HKEY_LOCAL_MACHINE\SYSTEM
\CurrentControlSet\Control\SecurePipeServers\winreg
```

Set the following key to 1 to disable the creation of 8.3 names for compatibility on NTFS partitions. The 8.3 names are normally only used by Win16 applications so this should not be a concern. Additionally it provides a slight performance gain by reducing the overhead of generating and writing the 8.3 name.

```
HKEY_LOCAL_MACHINE\SYSTEM
\CurrentControlSet\Control\FileSystem
NtfsDisable8dot3NameCreation
```

Set to 0 to disable the automatic sharing of administrative shares (ADMIN$, C$, and so on). Make sure you delete the shares manually using the net share /d command.

```
HKEY_LOCAL_MACHINE\SYSTEM
\CurrentControlSet\Services\LanmanServer\Parameters
AutoShareServer
```

Set the Application, Security, and System keys to 1 to prevent Guest and null sessions (sessions with no username or password authentication) from viewing the event logs specific to that log:

```
HKEY_LOCAL_MACHINE\SYSTEM
\CurrentControlSet\Services\Eventlog\Application
\CurrentControlSet\Services\Eventlog\Security
\CurrentControlSet\Services\Eventlog\System
RestrictGuestAccess
```

Set this key to 0 to prevent any caching of user credentials (credentials of the last 10 users to interactively logon to the system are normally cached locally by Windows NT):

```
HKEY_LOCAL_MACHINE\SOFTWARE
\Microsoft\Windows NT\CurrentVersion\Winlogon
CachedLogonsCount
```

Commonly attacked Registry keys should have their access restricted via ACLs. The following Registry keys at the very least should be protected by providing read-only access to Everyone, and Full-Control to Administrators and SYSTEM only. Creator Owner should be given Full-Owner control:

```
HKEY_LOCAL_MACHINE\SOFTWARE
\Microsoft\Windows\CurrentVersion\Run

HKEY_LOCAL_MACHINE\SOFTWARE
\Microsoft\Windows\CurrentVersion\RunOnce
```

```
HKEY_LOCAL_MACHINE\SOFTWARE
\Microsoft\Windows\CurrentVersion\RunOnceEx

HKEY_LOCAL_MACHINE\SOFTWARE
\Microsoft\Windows NT\CurrentVersion\AeDebug

HKEY_LOCAL_MACHINE\SOFTWARE
\Microsoft\Windows NT\CurrentVersion\WinLogon
```

Windows 2000 Server

At the time of publication, Windows 2000 is the current flagship server product from Microsoft. Windows 2000 is a much larger, more complex product than Windows NT 4.0, and as such will take more time to fully analyze its default security stance and guard against any weaknesses. These guidelines should be taken as a snapshot in time, and might not always be correct. There are several living documents published by Microsoft in its Technet library that should be referenced for up-to-date information.

Hardening Installation Guidelines

Do install on NTFS partitions, not FAT. NTFS provides additional control via access control lists (ACLs). Do not install to FAT and thenconvert to NTFS, because this will not apply the default ACLs.

Do try to reduce the number of Windows 2000 components you are installing. Windows 2000 offers many more features by default than Windows NT 4, many of which you do not want to offer the denizens of the Internet. By default, the Windows 2000 installation includes many accessories, utilities, multimedia applications and themes, and communication applications. It might be tempting to just install the default software selections; however, take the time to determine what needs to be installed, and what should not be. The more software you install, the more that can possibly be exploited.

For most firewall and DMZ server builds there will be no need for Terminal Services, Remote Installation Services, Networking Services, or File and Print Services. Do select only the components and services necessary for the server's specific purpose. For example, ensure that FTP support in the IIS server is not being loaded if this server is to serve HTTP pages only. If you will not be serving streaming media there isn't any need to load Windows Media Services.

Do not load Certificate Services; that should be an internal-only service, as the CA (Certificate Authorities) private key should be kept secret, and you generally aren't offering Certificate enrollment to various Internet users. As a general rule, corporate Certificate Authorities are kept in a tightly controlled and secure environment on an isolated internal network.

If you need system monitoring, install SNMP from Management and Monitoring Tools but be sure to change the read and write community strings.

When configuring the Network Settings, select Custom settings to manually configure the networking components. Do remove File and Printer Sharing for Microsoft Networks. If this server is going to be a Web or SMTP mail relay, disable Client for Microsoft Networks by unchecking it, but leave it installed. Apparently the RPC Locator Service used to perform authentication is only available with the Microsoft Networking Client installed. Without this service installed, you will be unable to start the IIS or SMTP services.

Then select IP Protocol Properties. Do not use DHCP to configure the IP address and DNS information automatically. After you have manually configured the network settings, click the Advanced button and make the following changes:

- Select the DNS tab. Uncheck Register This Connection's Addresses in DNS.
- Select the WINS tab; disable WINS by removing any WINS addresses. If you must enter NetBIOS names, use the LMHOSTS entry. Disable NetBIOS over TCP/IP by selecting Disable NetBIOS over TCP/IP.
- Select the Options tab to configure any TCP/IP filtering as described in the previous Windows NT 4 section.

Do not install into a domain or Active Directory structure. Do install into a nonexistent workgroup. There is no conceivable need to have a firewall or DMZ Web, mail, or DNS server participate in a domain.

After Windows 2000 finishes the install and reboots, you might notice some additional errors in the Event Log. At the time of publication, this affected Windows 2000 both with and without Service Pack 1. The most common is Event ID 31 or 36 relating to the Windows Management Instrumentation (WMI) ADAP service being unable to load a performance library. You might be able to resolve this problem by executing the following commands:

```
winmgmt /clearadap
winmgmt /resyncperf -p processID
```

processID is the process ID of the running WINMGMT process from the task list. If this does not solve the problem for you, you can either ignore the error (not the best habit to get into), or disable the performance counter by setting the following Registry value to 0x0:

```
HKEY_LOCAL_MACHINE\SYSTEM
\CurrentControlSet\Services\Spooler\performance
WbemAdapStatus
```

This turns off the performance counter.

Finally, if you continue to receive errors in the Application Event Viewer, you can disable individual performance counters. Using theExCtrlst utility found in the Windows 2000 resource kit (or downloaded from ftp://ft.microsoft.com/reskit/win2000/exctrlst.zip) you can disable individual performance counters such as Spooler, RAS, perfnet, perfdisk, perfmon, and so on.

Windows 2000 Does Policies Right

If hardening Windows NT 4.0 seemed a little haphazard, you're right. There is no easy way to define and apply all Registry, file system, network, and user/group policy changes. Even worse, there is no easy way to audit your changes to ensure that the policy changes have not been undone by intruders, installed software, or applied Service Packs.

With the release of Windows 2000, Microsoft introduced a wonderful set of snap-in tools for the Microsoft Management Console (MMC). The Security Templates Tool allows you to select, review, and even define custom security policy templates. The Security Configuration and Analysis Tool allows you to not only apply all those policies in one simple action, but it allows you to audit those changes to see what has changed.

By default, the Security Templates Tool and Security Configuration and Analysis Tool are not visible in the MMC. Add those two snap-ins to manage your server's policies and settings.

There are many bundled security templates, including High Security for Workstations as defined in the template HISECWS.INF. Additionally, Microsoft has made available a High Security Template targeted for Web servers. The security template includes most of the policy and Registry changes you made previously for Windows NT 4.0. The HISECWEB.INF security template is available from Microsoft at http://download.microsoft.com/download/win2000srv/SCM/ 1.0/NT5/EN-US/hisecweb.exe. Copy the downloaded file to %WINDIR%\security\templates and you will be able to use it in the Security Templates Tool.

Take the time to browse through and read the individual templates using the Security Templates Tool or manually using a text editor such as WordPad. Read through the suggested changes to determine if they make sense for the deployment of your particular application. You can use the Security Templates Tool to develop your own security template using an existing template as a basis (see Figure 10.2). After you have a template that meets your needs, the next step is to do an analysis of how this will affect the server.

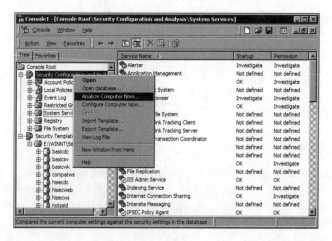

Figure 10.2 Auditing the state of the server's security policies and settings using the Analyze Computer Now menu of the Security Configuration and Analysis Tool.

Use the Security Configuration and Analysis Tool to load your template, right-click Security Configuration and Analysis Tool, and select Analyze Computer Now. The findings will be displayed in the right-hand pane showing you the template setting, the current server setting, and any inconsistencies. Review Findings and if necessary adjust your template.

After you have tweaked the security template to include all the appropriate permissions, policies, Registry settings, and restrictions, right-click Security Configuration and Analysis Tool and select Configure Computer Now. Sit back and watch the magic.

A nice command-line equivalent of the Security Configuration and Analysis Tool is available. SECEDIT can be used from the command-line to analyze, configure, refresh, and validate the server's current policy against your known template. This is convenient, because it can be run from a Telnet session, not that you should be managing a server with an unencrypted remote session.

Secure or Disable telnetd Service

Be sure to disable the telnetd service. If you must allow Telnet into the box, be sure to restrict Telnet users to authenticated users of the TelnetClients group. Just create the TelnetClients group, add the users you want to grant Telnet access to, and the telnetd service automatically restricts Telnet access to TelnetClients group members.

Lock Down Your DNS Server

Restrict zone transfers to only authorized servers. Use the DNS Manager to modify the zone properties (see Figure 10.3). On the Notify tab, check the option Only Allow Access From Secondaries Included on Notify List. Be sure to protect primary zones as well as secondaries.

Figure 10.3 Lock down the DNS server by restricting DNS Zone Transfers.

Unfortunately the built-in DNS servers that come with Windows NT and 2000 do not have controls to restrict query requests. If you want to use this feature, you can use the ISC BIND

(Internet Software Consortium Berkeley Internet Name Daemon) reference implementation that is used in most UNIX installations. You lose the integrated GUI administrative features, but you will have all the granularity and control available in the BIND implementation. The source code and binary packages can be found at the ISC site at http://www.isc.org/products/BIND/.

Application-Specific Hardening

Application-specific servers that reside on the firewall will need to run additional services that you are offering to the Internet population. Because there are numerous applications and an incredible combination of ways that those applications can be configured, it is well beyond the scope of this book to attempt to cover configuration of even those common applications such as HTTP, FTP, and SMTP. If you do nothing else, however, remove the sample applications installed by default with IIS and the various components. Sample applications and directories are listed in Table 10.1.

Table 10.1   IIS Sample Application Install Locations

Application	Installed Directory
IIS	\inetpub\iissamples
IIS SDK	\inetpub\iissamples\sdk
Admin Scripts	\inetpub\AdminScripts
Data Access	\Program Files\Common Files\System\msadc\Samples

There are living documents that provide an excellent starting point for properly configuring the more common DMZ server application services:

Microsoft Windows NT 4.0 and IIS 4.0: http://www.microsoft.com/technet/security/iischk.asp

Microsoft Windows 2000 Server and IIS 5.0:
http://www.microsoft.com/technet/security/iis5chk.asp

Microsoft SQL Server http://www.microsoft.com/technet/SQL/Technote/secure.asp and http://www.sqlsecurity.com/faq.asp

UNIX/Linux Systems

It has been said that the wonderful thing about standards is there are so many to choose from. The same choice is available in the UNIX arena. There are two basic flavors, BSD derived and AT&T System V derived. BSD derived UNIX systems include OpenBSD, FreeBSD, NetBSD, BSDi, MacOS X, and SunOS 4. System V-derived UNIX systems include HP-UX and Solaris (SunOS 5). Other UNIX systems, such as AIX, provide commands that will act BSD-ish or System V-ish depending on how they were invoked. Linux is not derived from any UNIX, but depending on the distribution, borrows from both BSD and System V semantics. Actually,

Linux itself is just the operating system kernel and supporting drivers. Most Linux distributions use the GNU system (http://www.gnu.org), thus they are called GNU/Linux distributions. There are hundreds of available GNU/Linux distributions, but even the "top 5" are different in their default commands, startup scripts, filesystem layout, included utilities, and packaging systems.

What does this mean to you? Unlike Windows NT, including Windows 2000, it is a far more complex process to describe how to harden a UNIX/Linux server. This next section provides some common procedures that can be applied across UNIX versions and GNU/Linux distributions. Following that are some pointers to living documents on the Internet, which track available data and releases and go into a more detailed account of how to harden a server for a particular task.

Common Steps for Hardening UNIX/Linux Servers

The process of building a UNIX or GNU/Linux server for use as a firewall or DMZ server begins with installation. Eliminating points of attack, such as filling the filesystem, or removing unnecessary libraries and services, is equivalent to removing possible entry points for intruders.

Some common guidelines for configuring UNIX servers with a more secure default stance are available from CERT's Web site at
ftp://info.cert.org/pub/tech_tips/UNIX_configuration_guidelines.

Partition for Protection

Besides having separate partitions for the obvious such as SWAP and /tmp, you should protect against out-of-disk-space denial-of-service attacks. Intruders might try to create excessive generation of logging data or fill your file system with large files through FTP or mail spool. The best way to protect against this is to segment the filesystem hierarchy into separate physical partitions.

The root partition / can be small because it generally contains just the kernel—the necessary files, libraries, and configuration for booting in /bin, /sbin, /etc, and /lib. Access to the attached devices is provided through the /dev and /devices directories. Many GNU/Linux distributions store kernels and symbol data in the /boot directory, whereas kernel libraries are stored under /lib.

The /usr partition is normally where user-accessible applications are stored. Normally, /usr does not contain data or configuration files that change; therefore, an added security measure can be mounted as read-only.

The /var partition stores system logs and data services such as mail, Web, databases, printing, running services, package management, and so on. On a mail server, you might want to make /var/spool/mail, or /var/mail in Solaris, a separate partition, or even better, a separate disk array. If you only create one separate partition from /, /var is the one you should separate.

The /usr/local directory structure, and in Solaris the /opt directory, often contain locally installed optional software, configuration files, and data. /usr/local is normally not affected by operating system upgrades. Depending on how you use those directories, they too can be mounted as read-only.

These are suggestions and guidelines only, and are different from recommended settings for a system that contains user accounts, usually in /home.

Disable Extraneous inetd Services

inetd is the UNIX "Internet Super Server." It is a daemon process that is invoked at boot time and reads in a flat file configuration database normally found at /etc/inetd.conf. inetd listens for incoming connections on the defined IP ports. When a connection is initiated on a defined port, it invokes the configured program to service the request. After the connection is finished, the process invoked to service that request terminates. This was originally designed to lighten the load and resources required for systems.

There are a number of services enabled through inetd, and almost all of them should be disabled for building firewalls and DMZ servers. Besides normally disabling FTP, TFTP, Telnet, and the Berkeley r* commands, disable the following:

- **in.named**—BIND name services daemon. Except for your DNS servers, you should not be running DNS on your firewall or DMZ servers.
- **in.fingerd**—Finger daemon can be used to show user information and lists of users who are logged in. There is no reason to advertise that information to would-be intruders.
- **daytime**—Connections to this service display the date and time on the system in a string format. Getting the date and time of a system is useful for an intruder trying to implement replay attacks.
- **time**—Connections to this service return the time as a 32-bit value representing the number of seconds since midnight 1-Jan-1900. Do not provide intruders with your exact system time.
- **echo**—This is a diagnostic service that echoes incoming data back to the connecting machine.
- **discard**—This is a diagnostic service that does not echo (thus discarding) the incoming data stream back to the connecting machine.
- **chargen**—This is a diagnostic service that automatically generates a stream of characters sent to the connecting machine.
- **systat**—Connections to this service provide a list of all processes and their status.
- **netstat**—Connections to this service provide a list of current network connections and their status.

Install and Configure `tcp_wrappers`

Install and configure Wietse Venema's `tcp_wrappers` on both your firewall and DMZ servers. `tcp_wrappers` allows you to define access control to various services depending on a limited set of criteria, such as username, IP address, or DNS domain.

You might be asking why it's necessary to configure and install additional products when your firewall will be doing the same thing. And that's a valid question. The answer is to avoid single points of failure and to provide security in layers. Should one layer be pierced and bypassed, other layers will be standing guard behind the breach.

`tcp_wrappers` are lightweight, and extremely useful on internal servers as well, not just on firewalls and DMZ servers. Keep in mind that most information security breaches, intentional or accidental, happen internally. It's only the external defacements, massive distributed denial of service (DDoS) attacks, virus-du-jour, and stolen credit card databases that grab the press. That, and misplaced hard drives with highly sensitive nuclear information.

`tcp_wrappers` have two main files that allow access to the individually defined services. The following twofiles are checked for rules governing access to individual or wildcard services:

    /etc/hosts.allow

    /etc/hosts.deny

Like most firewalls, access is granted or denied on the first matching rule. The rules are checked in order first in `hosts.allow`, and then in `hosts.deny`.

Care should be taken using the KNOWN or UNKNOWN wildcards. ALL will always match whatever criteria you are testing. Read the `hosts_access` manual page included with `tcp_wrappers` for further details on syntax and rules setup.

`tcp_wrappers` is installed and configured by default on most GNU/Linux distributions and BSD releases. For those UNIX systems that do not have `tcp_wrappers` installed by default, they can be found at `ftp://ftp.porcupine.org/pub/security/index.html`. Retrieve the source, compile, and install the binaries on the servers.

Lock Down Your DNS Server

TheBerkeley Internet Name Daemon, or BIND, is the reference implementation of the name service providing DNS for the Internet. The Internet Software Consortium (ISC) is responsible for implementing and maintaining BIND. There are three basic versions of BIND: BIND 4, BIND 8, and recently BIND 9.

BIND 4 has been around forever, and has its share of exploits. Only very old versions of UNIX systems and GNU/Linux distributions came with BIND 4. Still, you'll be surprised how many installations still have the older BIND 4 running. You should upgrade to a newer version of

BIND. The unfortunate thing is that the file format defining the zones served by the server has changed. There are conversion scripts, but there is sure to be some hand editing.

BIND 8 is the current stable release, and offers many more features and better control and granularity in access control. The settings described later are discussed with BIND 8 in mind.

BIND 9 was released late in 2000. It offers many new features, such as IPv6 support, DNSSEC, full Dynamic DNS, incremental zone transfers, multiple views (internal, external, and so on) from a single server, and scalability improvements. If any of those features are important to your configuration, you should investigate using BIND 9; otherwise it's best left to the adventurous.

Although almost all UNIX systems and GNU/Linux distributions come with BIND as the name server, it is important you make sure you are at a recommended release. Before deploying a DNS server, internally, or on the DMZ, make sure it is at least version 8.2.2-P5. Any version prior to that has serious exploits. This warning should not be ignored. The Internet Software Consortium themselves have issued a statement that if you are running any version of BIND prior to 8.2.2-P5, you should assume your server has already been compromised. Check your UNIX system or GNU/Linux distribution. If the version of BIND is not at least 8.2.2-P5, check with your vendor for upgrades. If an upgrade is not available, you can compile a version of BIND yourself on a workstation and install the binaries on your server. The source code can be found at `http://www.isc.org/products/BIND/`.

First restrict zone transfers to specific secondary servers in your primary zones. The `acl` command allows you to define an access control list composed of blocks of addresses to be used with a named identifier. Using ACLs provides a self-documenting method of administrating the `named.conf` configuration file. In the following example, we define two ACLs comprising our externally visible DNS servers and the secondary servers at our ISP:

```
acl your-company-dns {
    172.16.30.12;
    172.16.30.24;
};
acl your-ISP-dns {
    199.177.202.10;
    204.95.224.200;
};
```

The following `allow-transfer` option directive placed in your `named.conf` file will default all defined zones to only allow transfers for the defined hosts:

```
options {
    allow-transfer {
        your-company-dns;
        your-ISP-dns;
    };
};
```

You can override the `allow-transfer` statement in the `options` directive by placing the
`allow-transfer` statement in the zone definition:

```
zone "yourdomain.com" {
  type master;
  file "db.yourdomain-com";
  allow-transfer { 172.16.30.12; 192.168.71.200; };
}
```

The default `allow-transfer` option will prevent zone transfers to hosts not specified in the
ACLs. However, should you want to restrict all zone transfers on your secondary servers, and
any secondary zones on your primary servers, use predefined match list `none`. This can be
accomplished with the following `allow-transfer` directive in your zone definitions:

```
zone "yourdomain.com" {
  type slave;
  file "db.yourdomain-com.s";
  masters { 192.168.71.1; };
  allow-transfer { none; };
};
```

Finally, because you will be allowing recursive queries through your servers, it's best to enable
access control lists for your internal networks. Using a nested, named `acl` with the `allow-query`
option in the zone definition, you can then restrict recursive queries to internal hosts only as
seen in the following example:

```
acl internal-net {
  192.168.71.0/24;
};

acl dmz-net {
  172.16.30.0/24;
};

acl trusted-hosts {
  localhost;
  internal-net;
  dmz-net;
};

zone "yourdomain.com" {
  type master;
  file "db.yourdomain-com"
  allow-query { trusted-hosts; };
};
```

Que's *Concise Guide to DNS and BIND* by Nicolai Langfeldt is a wonderful resource to further
grok BIND configuration and maintenance.

Tighten Sendmail Default Options

Send mail comes with just about every UNIX/Linux installation as the default mail transfer agent (MTA). As a result of being so widely installed, it has been estimated that sendmail handles a majority of the email on the Internet. Because it runs as suid root, sendmail exploits affect millions of machines.

sendmail version 8.11.0 is available at time of publication and supports new features such as STARTTLS and SMTP AUTH encryption. Upgrade to the newest version available if possible, but please make sure that you are running a version no later than version 8.9.3 because of security exploits.

To enable the Realtime Blackhole List feature, use the following in your sendmail.mc file:

```
FEATURE(rbl)dnl
```

Additionally, you might want todisable the SMTP VRFY and EXPN commands in sendmail. These commands are often used by intruders to gather information about your system:

```
define(`confPRIVACY_FLAGS', `novrfy,noexpn')dnl
```

There are several additional flags you can set to make sendmail have a more secure stance:

- **authwarnings**—Add X-Authentication-Warning header in messages on certain conditions that might indicate mail system spoof attempts.
- **needmailhelo**—Require that the sending site uses the SMTP HELO command first when connecting to send email.
- **needexpnhelo**—Require that the sending site uses the SMTP HELO command before allowing any EXPN usage.
- **needvrfyhelo**—Require that the sending site uses the SMTP HELO command before allowing any VRFY usage.
- **noreceipts**—Disable Delivery Status Notification (DSNs) of delivery and read receipts.
- **goaway**—Set all flags except restrictmailq and restrictqrun.
- **restrictmailq**—Prevent users from using the mailq command to view the contents of the mail queue.
- **restrictqrun**—Stop users from processing the queue.

Better than sendmail: Making Postfix Your MTA

According to its Web page, Postfix's goals are "to be fast, easy to administer, and secure, while at the same time being sendmail compatible enough to not upset existing users."

Postfix was primarily written by Wietse Venema of tcp_wrappers fame. Postfix was designed to be modular, thus Postfix is not a single executable like sendmail; rather, Postfix comprises a collection of specialized programs that perform specific tasks. All the programs except for the master control process oddly called master since it runs without root privilege. Because of the speed, ease of configuration (and thus less chance of misconfiguration), and security, it is recommended that you investigate replacing sendmail with Postfix. For those of you who do not dream in sendmail.cf syntax, Postfix will make email administration both easier and more secure.

Postfix is now distributed with most GNU/Linux and BSD releases, although it is not often installed by default. Usually it is a simple matter of installing it via your package management system, or in the BSD case, via the ports collection.

If you are using an operating system that does not distribute Postfix, despair not. You can download and compile the sources easily on a development workstation, and then install the binaries on your mail server. The sources, FAQs, and documentation can be found at `http://www.postfix.org/`

Linux-Specific Tasks

There are many GNU/Linux distributions out there. Each vendor has its own installation process, which usually changes between new versions of the vendor's distribution. The "forerunners" of GNU/Linux distributions are Red Hat, SuSE, TurboLinux, Mandrake, Caldera, Slackware, and Debian. That does not mean specifically that you should use any one of them, as the high number of distributions allows vendors to tailor their GNU/Linux distributions to specific tasks, such as embedded systems, routers, and firewalls. Take the time to carefully investigate the available distributions and determine which best fits your needs.

With that said, two of these general distributions stand out, but for different reasons. Red Hat, because it has had the most name recognition, and is usually the first to get any sort of corporate support in the way of commercial software or commercial technical service. Many vendors, such as Oracle, IBM, and Check Point, have released products for Red Hat-specific distributions. This does not mean that those software releases will not run on other GNU/Linux distributions, but rather if there is a problem, the vendor might not support your installation of its product on a non-Red Hat distribution.

Debian is the second distribution that deserves mention. First, not because it is entirely free, but because it is maintained by a nonprofit organization made up entirely of volunteers. These volunteers are highly motivated by quality and pride in their efforts to make Debian the most stable and completely 100% free distribution available. Debian has proven to be extremely stable and easy to manage and upgrade remotely. The upgrade process is by far the easiest of any of the GNU/Linux distributions. Debian installations can be upgraded without the need for reboots, replacing every installed package and running process excepting the kernel. Additionally, the Debian packaging system and its front ends allow extremely fine-grained control over which packages, utilities, libraries, and files exist on your system. Debian also is currently available on six different architectures, with over 3,900 included software packages to select from when installing.

For both Debian and Red Hat installations, you should choose custom installations, and select the individual packages you want on your system. There should be no need to install development packages, any of the new KDE or GNOME desktops, and certainly not X Window. Unfortunately, neither distribution yet has a minimal secure server or firewall predefined install-set.

During the installation process, you should choose to enable shadow password file support; choose to use MD5 hashes for the passwords rather than the normal crypt function. If you miss these options during the install, you can change them after installation. In Red Hat, use the `setup` utility. In Debian, you can use the `shadowconfig` utility to enable or disable shadow passwords. To enable MD5 hashes, you have to edit the appropriate files under `/etc/pam.d` to include `md5` on the password lines.

You should also enable ipchains support, even if this is an application server on the DMZ. ipchains provides additional layers of security and allows you to protect the server from traffic should the firewall fail for some reason. A sample ipchains configuration is discussed later in the chapter.

You should additionally read and monitor the security and errata/updates lists from your distribution vendor. With Debian, it is extremely easy to automatically install security updates using the apt-get utility. For Red Hat installations starting with the 6.0 release there is the up2date utility to retrieve updated packages for your release.

For those people who choose to install Red Hat Linux, there is a security-related project called Bastille Linux whose aim is not just to harden your Linux installation, but to educate the administrators on how to harden the system. Bastille Linux supports Red Hat and Mandrake Linux distributions, with project goals to become distribution, and UNIX flavor, agnostic. The Bastille Linux product is a set of scripts that ask a series of questions and then allow you to apply those modifications to your system. The questions describe what needs to be done, why it should be done, and why you might not want to do it. It is very educational, especially for those administrators just getting familiar with Linux. Bastille Linux can be found at `http://www.bastille-linux.org/`.

Another excellent source of information for administrators is the Linux Administrator's Security Guide. It covers an extremely wide array of topics related to Linux and security. You can find the Linux Administrator's Security Guide online at `http://www.securityportal.com/lasg/`.

Solaris-Specific Tasks

Solaris has four default install-sets: Core, End-User, Developer, and Entire Distribution. Installing any install-set higher than theCore installation will enable more services than are required for DMZ servers or firewalls. In reality, you can often remove a significant percentage of the default Core install-set, depending on your server's application requirements.

For Solaris-based servers, there are several excellent documents from Sun in its Blueprints Online archive at `http://www.sun.com/software/solutions/blueprints/online.html`. The following three papers are excellent starting points for building secure Solaris servers:

- "Solaris Operating Environment Minimization for Security: A Simple, Reproducible and Secure Application Installation Methodology" by Alex Noordergraaf and Keith Watson. Although this paper specifically covers the iPlanet Web server requirements, similar requirements are necessary for using Apache or other Web servers.
- "Solaris Operating Environment Security" by Alex Noordergraaf and Keith Watson. An overview of general security options on a Solaris server. This paper includes some specifics for the SPARC architecture; however, most of the material is applicable to Intel architectures as well.
- "Solaris Operating Environment Network Settings for Security" by Alex Noordergraaf and Keith Watson is another excellent paper on kernel tuning and application parameters that affect network security.

As a matter of fact, Sun's Blueprints Online is a wealth of whitepapers outlining Best Practices regarding Solaris Operating Environments, whether it is a DMZ Web server, firewall, or internal highly available database cluster.

Lance Spitzner also has an excellent Solaris hardening document detailing the hardening process for building a Check Point FireWall-1 firewall on several recent versions of Solaris (through version 8) for the Intel and SPARC platforms. The living document resides at `http://www.enteract.com/~lspitz/armoring.html`.

Finally, there is an equivalent to the Bastille-Linux hardening scripts for Solaris called TITAN. The TITAN project and documentation can be found at `http://www.fish.com/titan/`.

OpenBSD Specific Tasks

This section concentrates on OpenBSD 2.7, which is one of the three more famous BSD variants, the others being NetBSD and FreeBSD. Each variant has focused on a different problem: NetBSD is the most portable, FreeBSD has the best performance, and OpenBSD is the most secure.

One of the great strengths of OpenBSD is the highly secure default stance of a default install of OpenBSD. The OpenBSD Web site claims "three years without a remote hole in the default install, only one localhost hole in two years in the default install." Almost all services are disabled until the administrator has enough experience to properly configure them.

Two additional changes necessary for an OpenBSD box to become a firewall are to disable sendmail, and enable IP filter support. Both changes are made to the same file, /etc/rc.conf. To disable sendmail, change

```
sendmail_flags="-q30m"
```

to

```
sendmail_flags=NO
```

To enable IP filter support, you must change

```
ipfilter=NO
```

to

```
ipfilter=YES
```

Additionally, if you will be doing Network Address Translation (NAT), providing transparent proxying, or providing support for FTP, you must enable the ipnat option by setting ipnat=YES. Syntax for IP filters will be covered briefly later in the chapter.

Tweak Your Network Configurations for Security

To protect your WAN connection, firewall, and DMZ servers from common attacks, take these simple steps to disable certain TCP/IP features.

Drop Source-Routed Traffic

There are actually two forms of source-routed traffic: Strict Source Routed and Loose Source Routed. The differences aren't that important, because you want to drop all source-routed traffic. Traceroute is the most common command that uses source-routed traffic. This allows you to diagnose trouble spots in your network by specifying the route to take. Unfortunately, intruders can use source-routed traffic to try and bypass firewall rules and TCP/IP filters. Dropping source-routed traffic should be done on the edge routers, and any capable security gateways:

- For Cisco routers, issue the following global directive: `no ip source-route`
- For OpenBSD, use the following sysctl: `net.inet.ip.sourceroute=0`
- For FreeBSD, use the following two sysctls: `net.inet.ip.sourceroute=0`, `net.ip.accept_sourceroute=0`
- With Solaris, use the following command: `ndd -set /dev/ip ip_forward_src_routed 0`
- For Linux 2.2.x, use the following command:
  `echo 0 > /proc/sys/net/ipv4/conf/all/accept_source_route`

- With Windows NT/2000, make the following Registry change:

  ```
  HKEY_LOCAL_MACHINE\SYSTEM
  \CurrentControlSet\Services\Tcpip\Parameters
  DisableIPSourceRouting
  ```

  Create this value as a `REG_DWORD` and set it to 2.

Drop-Directed Broadcast Traffic

The Smurf Denial of Service attack, and others like it, can be defeated by disabling directed broadcasts on the edge routers and servers exposed to the Internet:

- With OpenBSD, use the following sysctl: `net.inet.ip.directed-broadcast=0`
- For Solaris, use the following command: `ndd -set /dev/ip ip_forward_directed_ broadcasts 0`

Ignore ICMP Echo Request Broadcast

The draft RFC `draft-vshah-ddos-smurf-00`, found at `http://www.ietf.org/internet-drafts/ draft-vshah-ddos-smurf-00.txt` states that if the network node is set to reply to an IP ICMP echo reply on a broadcast or multicast address, the node *must* check to make sure the source address is on a local network of the network node. If the source address is not local, the reply must be discarded. By changing the behavior to not respond to ICMP broadcasts, you ensure that those replies are always discarded:

- With Solaris, use the following command: `ndd -set /dev/ip ip_respond_to_echo_ broadcast 0`
- With Linux 2.2.x, use the following command: `echo 1 > /proc/sys/net/ipv4/icmp_echo_ ignore_broadcasts`

Linux has an additional control to disable ALL ICMP Echo Reply requests. Issuing the following command will make the Linux kernel ignore all ICMP Echo Requests: `echo 1 > /proc/sys/net/ipv4/icmp_echo_ignore_all`.

Ignore ICMP Redirect Messages

An intruder might try to redirect traffic from your servers to a different gateway, or a non-existent gateway. Additionally the intruder might try to inject bogus routes into your routing table. All these can be accomplished through the unassuming ICMP Redirect Message, and is a very effective denial of service attack. In addition to blocking ICMP Redirect messages at the firewall, if your OS supports it, add the additional layer of security of ignoring ICMP Redirect messages:

- With Solaris, use the following command: `ndd -set /dev/ip ip_ignore_redirect 1`
- With Linux 2.2.x, use the following command:
  `echo 0 > /proc/sys/net/ipv4/conf/all/accept_redirects`

Disable Sending of ICMP Redirect Messages

Only routers need to send ICMP Redirect messages. Because your DMZ servers and firewall are not routing any packets, there should be no reason to send them:

- For Solaris, use the following command: `ndd -set /dev/ip ip_send_redirects 0`
- For Linux 2.2.x, use the following command: `echo 0 > /proc/sys/net/ipv4/conf/all/send_redirects`

Time Stamp Request Broadcast

An ICMP timestamp request (ICMP type 13) allows a system to query another for the current time. The return value is the number of milliseconds since midnight. ICMP timestamp requests have been used to synchronize clocks between systems rather than using the rdate command because the precision is better. Individual timestamp requests are normal, but there is no need for a system to respond to a broadcast request. Finally, you should look into using NTP to keep time synchronized between servers because it is much better at keeping the time, and allows for authentication and peering of multiple time sources, which makes it much harder to spoof. This allows you to drop ICMP type 13 (timestamp request) and type 14 (timestamp reply):

- With Solaris, use the following command: `ndd -set /dev/ip ip_respond_to_timestamp_broadcast 0`

Remote Log Server

One of the many techniques intruders use to cover their presence is to wipe clean any logging facilities you might have enabled. This includes account logging, system messages, error logs, traffic logs, and so on.

One way to circumvent this problem is to log all your servers to a remote logging machine. The remote logging machine should only accept logging traffic from those servers. That way even if a server is compromised, you will still have the logs to perform the forensics analysis of what went on.

Configure the appropriate packet filter on your logging server to drop all traffic except UDP/514. The logs on your logging server can additionally be archived to media such as CD-R, WORM, or tape.

UNIX/Linux

UNIX has very strong centralized logging facilities. It is true that some applications use their own log files and do not use syslog. However the filesystem hierarchy is designed with support for a centralized location, /var/log. Additionally, most UNIX systems and GNU/Linux distributions come with an automated log rotation and management facility. The logs are automatically rotated based on criteria such as size or age, and can automatically be compressed, renamed, and even archived.

To further enhance the logging capabilities of your UNIX/Linux server, replace your normal syslogd with a more robust, configurable, and secure alternative known as syslog-ng. syslog-ng has several features over the normal syslogd, including the capability to filter messages on message content, not just facility.priority pairs. Using regular expressions, you could log hosts information to individual logs. syslog-ng might already come with your UNIX/Linux distribution, but if it does not, it can be found at `http://www.balabit.hu/products/syslog-ng/index.html`

Windows NT and 2000

There are several automated logging services built in to Windows NT and 2000. Most services use the EventLogs that everyone should be familiar with. If you are running any Internet services such as FTP, HTTP, SMTP, and so on, those are logged through a different facility. If you are tuning or troubleshooting your servers, you're sure to be using the Performance Monitor application. This application does not log to the Application log of the EventLog service, but rather to its own set of logs. Finally, one of the more important aspects of the system, scheduling of automated jobs, is logged through yet another service. Because there is no normal centralized logging service in Windows NT and 2000, each must be addressed individually.

The first thing to do is move all logs to a separate logging partition. It would be convenient, although not 100% necessary, to have this partition be a separate disk, so as to not impact performance for the data portion of the server. After a log partition has been created, the next step is to move the logs from their default locations. Why go through all this trouble? After all the logs are centrally located, it makes it easier for routine maintenance after your server is in production. You can provide automated backup and archiving of logs for later review and processing.

EventLogs

EventLogs are the default built-in Windows NT event logs that are viewed with the Event Viewer. EventLogs are the Windows NT/2000 equivalent to syslog. The EventLog service is divided into the Application Log, Security Log, and System Log. Most Windows NT/2000 applications, services, and system events are logged into the appropriate category. Each category is actually its own separate physical file that can be relocated. This task is accomplished by editing the following Registry key:

```
HKEY_LOCAL_MACHINE\SYSTEM
\CurrentControlSet\Services\Eventlog\Application
```

```
\CurrentControlSet\Services\Eventlog\Security
\CurrentControlSet\Services\Eventlog\System
File
```

Change the value of File to be the new directory of your log files partition. After editing that value, you must restart the server for the changes to take effect.

Internet Services

The services provided by the IIS infrastructure generate logs for each service: Web, FTP, and SMTP. The Internet Service logs are unique in that you can configure a time interval to rotate to a new log automatically. The log filename can be based on the specific time period.

To change the location of theselog files, edit the Web or FTP root properties and select the properties for the log file. In the Properties dialog box, you can set the new location to be your directory on the log files partition.

Performance Logs

The Performance logs are created by the Performance Monitor counters. The default location is %SystemDrive%\PerfLogs. They can be changed by editing the DefaultLogFileFolder value in the following Registry key:

```
HKEY_LOCAL_MACHINE\SYSTEM
\CurrentControlSet\Services\SysmonLog
DefaultLogFileFolder
```

Scheduler Logs

The Scheduler service is normally located at %SystemRoot%\SchedLgU.Txt. The scheduler service log contains all jobs scheduled and executed, as well as when it was started and stopped. The location of this file can be changed by editing the LogPath value in the Registry key:

```
HKEY_LOCAL_MACHINE\SOFTWARE
\Microsoft\SchedulingAgent
LogPath
```

Sample Packet Filter Router Only

The first example makes use of your Internet Service Provider's resources and has the following characteristics:

- DNS, Mail, and Web hosting for your organization is provided by the ISP.
- The only WAN connectivity equipment installed on-site will be a router connecting the wide area network to the local networking topology.
- The router will provide packet-level filtering for both outbound and inbound traffic.

The sample configuration includes packet filtering provided by the router. The packet filtering is expressed in Cisco IOS access-list syntax, since that is the most prominent router, and is easily understood. Assume that your ISP owns the 1.x.x.x address space, and because you are a large customer you have been extended the 1.4.3.x/24 CIDR network:

```
!
! Access List 111 controls Outbound traffic
!  applied to LAN interface as ip access-group 111 out
!
! First drop any spoofed internal traffic, you don't want
! to leak RFC 1918 private addresses to the world.
!
access-list 111 deny ip 10.0.0.0 0.255.255.255 any
access-list 111 deny ip 127.0.0.0 0.255.255.255 any
access-list 111 deny ip 172.16.0.0 0.31.255.255 any
access-list 111 deny ip 192.168.0.0 0.0.255.255 any
!
! Now allow ICMP echos for ping tests.
!
access-list 111 permit icmp 1.4.3.0 0.0.0.255 any echo
!
! Allow Internal hosts to query the ISP Name servers at 1.0.1.2
! and 1.0.2.2
!
access-list 111 permit udp 1.4.3.0 0.0.0.255 eq 53 host 1.0.1.2 eq 53
access-list 111 permit udp 1.4.3.0 0.0.0.255 eq 53 host 1.0.2.2 eq 53
!
! Allow Internal hosts to reach Web Servers on the Internet
!
access-list 111 permit tcp 1.4.3.0 0.0.0.255 any eq 80
access-list 111 permit tcp 1.4.3.0 0.0.0.255 any eq 443
!
! Allow Internal hosts to reach ISP mail server at 1.0.2.10
!
access-list 111 permit tcp 1.4.3.0 0.0.0.255 host 1.0.2.10 eq 25
access-list 111 permit tcp 1.4.3.0 0.0.0.255 host 1.0.2.10 eq 110
access-list 111 permit tcp 1.4.3.0 0.0.0.255 host 1.0.2.10 eq 143
!
! Allow Internal hosts to reach FTP servers on the Internet
!
access-list 111 permit tcp 1.4.3.0 0.0.0.255 any eq 21
!
! Finally, block everything else.
!
access-list 111 deny any any
!
!
! Access List 110 controls Inbound traffic
!  applied to WAN interface as ip access-group 110 in
```

```
!
! First drop RFC 1918 private network traffic, and any spoofed
! internal traffic and localhost traffic.
!
access-list 110 deny ip 10.0.0.0 0.255.255.255 any
access-list 110 deny ip 127.0.0.0 0.255.255.255 any
access-list 110 deny ip 172.16.0.0 0.31.255.255 any
access-list 110 deny ip 192.168.0.0 0.0.255.255 any
access-list 110 deny ip 1.4.3.0 0.0.0.255 any
!
! Now allow ICMP replies to echo reply, destination unreachable,
! and time-exceeded.
!
access-list 110 permit icmp any 1.4.3.0 0.0.0.255 echo-reply
access-list 110 permit icmp any 1.4.3.0 0.0.0.255 unreachable
access-list 110 permit icmp any 1.4.3.0 0.0.0.255 time-exceeded
!
! Allow replies from the ISP Name servers at 1.0.1.2 and 1.0.2.2
! back to internal hosts.
!
access-list 110 permit udp host 1.0.1.2 eq 53 1.4.3.0 0.0.0.255 eq 53
access-list 110 permit udp host 1.0.2.2 eq 53 1.4.3.0 0.0.0.255 eq 53
!
! Allow FTP servers on the Internet to open active FTP connections
!
access-list 110 permit tcp any eq 20 1.4.3.0 0.0.0.255 gt 1023
!
! Allow established sessions, sessions with the ACK bit set,
! back into the internal network. Necessary for reply traffic.
!
access-list 110 permit tcp any 1.4.3.0 0.0.0.255 established
!
! Finally, block everything else.
!
access-list 110 deny any any
```

Sample Packet Filter Router with a DMZ

The following is the second example of packet filtering with a router and a DMZ:

- No ISP hosted servers.
- All Internet accessible servers on the DMZ.
- The internal mail server polls the DMZ mail hub.
- The internal DNS server is also hidden away, and forwards requests to DMZ server.
- Router only provides packet filtering between Internet, DMZ, and internal network.

Like the first example, the packet filtering is expressed in Cisco IOS access-list syntax. This example assumes your ISP owns the 1.x.x.x address space, and you have been extended the

1.4.3.x/24 CIDR network for your internal network, and the 1.4.4.x/24 CIDR block for your DMZ:

```
!
! Access List 111 controls Outbound Internal traffic
!  applied to internal LAN interface as ip access-group 111 out
!
! First drop any spoofed internal traffic, you don't want
! to leak RFC 1918 private addresses to the world.
!
access-list 111 deny ip 10.0.0.0 0.255.255.255 any
access-list 111 deny ip 127.0.0.0 0.255.255.255 any
access-list 111 deny ip 172.16.0.0 0.31.255.255 any
access-list 111 deny ip 192.168.0.0 0.0.255.255 any
!I~DMZ servers;packet filter routers>
! Allow ICMP echos for ping tests.
!
access-list 111 permit icmp 1.4.3.0 0.0.0.255 any echo
!
! Allow Internal hosts to query the DMZ Name server at 1.4.4.130
!
access-list 111 permit udp 1.4.3.0 0.0.0.255 eq 53 host 1.4.4.130 eq 53
!
! Allow Internal hosts to reach Web Servers on the Internet and DMZ
!
access-list 111 permit tcp 1.4.3.0 0.0.0.255 any eq 80
access-list 111 permit tcp 1.4.3.0 0.0.0.255 any eq 443
!
! Allow internal mail server to reach DMZ mail server at 1.4.4.131
!
access-list 111 permit tcp host 1.4.3.131 host 1.4.4.131 eq 25
!
! Allow Internal hosts to reach FTP servers on the Internet
!
access-list 111 permit tcp 1.4.3.0 0.0.0.255 any eq 21
!
! Allow Administrative SSH to DMZ Servers
!
access-list 111 permit tcp 1.4.3.0 0.0.0.255 1.4.4.0 0.0.0.255 eq 22
!
! Finally, block everything else.
!
access-list 111 deny any any
!
!
! Access List 110 controls Inbound WAN traffic
!  applied to WAN interface as ip access-group 110 in
!
! First drop RFC 1918 private network traffic, and any spoofed
! internal traffic and localhost traffic.
!I~DMZ servers;packet filter routers>
```

```
access-list 110 deny ip 10.0.0.0 0.255.255.255 any
access-list 110 deny ip 127.0.0.0 0.255.255.255 any
access-list 110 deny ip 172.16.0.0 0.31.255.255 any
access-list 110 deny ip 192.168.0.0 0.0.255.255 any
access-list 110 deny ip 1.4.3.0 0.0.0.255 any
access-list 110 deny ip 1.4.4.0 0.0.0.255 any
!
! Now allow ICMP replies to echo reply, destination unreachable,
! and time-exceeded destined for internal network.
!
access-list 110 permit icmp any 1.4.3.0 0.0.0.255 echo-reply
access-list 110 permit icmp any 1.4.3.0 0.0.0.255 unreachable
access-list 110 permit icmp any 1.4.3.0 0.0.0.255 time-exceeded
!
! Now allow ICMP messages for destination unreachable,
! fragmentation needed and time-exceeded destined for DMZ network.
!
access-list 110 permit icmp any 1.4.4.0 0.0.0.255 unreachable
access-list 110 permit icmp any 1.4.4.0 0.0.0.255 packet-too-big
access-list 110 permit icmp any 1.4.4.0 0.0.0.255 time-exceeded
!
! Allow Internet queries and replies to the DMZ Name server
! at 1.4.4.130
!
access-list 110 permit udp any eq 53 host 1.4.4.130 eq 53
!
! Allow DMZ Web server to accept HTTP/HTTPS requests from the
! Internet.
!
access-list 110 permit tcp any host 1.4.4.132 eq 80
access-list 110 permit tcp any host 1.4.4.132 eq 443
!
! Allow DMZ Email server to accept SMTP connections from the
! Internet.
!
access-list 110 permit tcp any host 1.4.4.131 eq 25
!
! Allow FTP servers on the Internet to open active FTP connections
! to internal hosts
!
access-list 110 permit tcp any eq 20 1.4.3.0 0.0.0.255 gt 1023
!
! Allow established sessions, sessions with the ACK bit set,
! back into the internal network. Necessary for reply traffic.
!
access-list 110 permit tcp any 1.4.3.0 0.0.0.255 established
!I~DMZ servers;packet filter routers>
! Finally, block everything else.
!
access-list 110 deny any any
!
```

```
!
! Access List 115 controls Outbound DMZ traffic
!  applied to DMZ LAN interface as ip access-group 115 in
!
! First drop RFC 1918 private network traffic, and any spoofed
! internal traffic and localhost traffic.
!
access-list 115 deny ip 10.0.0.0 0.255.255.255 any
access-list 115 deny ip 127.0.0.0 0.255.255.255 any
access-list 115 deny ip 172.16.0.0 0.31.255.255 any
access-list 115 deny ip 192.168.0.0 0.0.255.255 any
access-list 115 deny ip 1.4.3.0 0.0.0.255 any
!
! Allow Internet queries and internal replies to the
! DMZ Name server at 1.4.4.130
!
access-list 115 permit udp host 1.4.4.130 eq 53 any eq 53
!
! Allow established sessions, sessions with the ACK bit set,
! back into the internal network. Necessary for reply traffic.
!
access-list 115 permit tcp 1.4.4.0 0.0.0.255 1.4.3.0 0.0.0.255 established
!
! Finally, block everything else.
!
access-list 115 deny any any
```

Sample Packet Filter Router with a Firewall and DMZ

The following is an example of packet filtering using a router, firewall, and DMZ:

- No ISP hosted servers.
- All Internet-accessible servers are on the DMZ.
- Internal mail server polls DMZ mail hub.
- Internal DNS server also forwards requests to DMZ server.
- Router provides basic packet filtering between Internet and firewall.
- The firewall provides protected access between the DMZ, the internal network, and the unprotected DMZ network connecting the router and firewall.

Like the previous examples, the packet filtering is expressed in Cisco IOS access-list syntax. This example assumes your ISP owns the 1.x.x.x address space, and because you are a large customer, you have been extended the 1.4.3.x/24 CIDR network for your internal network, and the 1.4.4.x/24 CIDR block for your DMZ.

The DMZ network block has been split into four initial subnets by extending the network mask by 2 bits from 24 to 26. You could actually increase the network mask to 28 bits giving you 16 subnets of 5 useful IP addresses per subnet, but to simplify things 4 subnets are used here.

Usable IP Addresses

Remember, although eight IP addresses are available for a 28-bit network mask, one is dedicated for the network address, one for the broadcast address, and one will be the gateway, whether it is a firewall or router.

The firewall rulebase will be enumerated in FireWall-1 on Windows NT, ipchains in Linux 2.2.x, and IP filter on OpenBSD.

Check Point's FireWall-1 is one of many commercial firewalls available for Windows NT. Check Point FireWall-1 includes all the normal features you would expect in a firewall:

- The Check Point FireWall-1 Inspection module provides stateful inspection of traffic. A significant number of existing Application protocols are available out of the box. The built-in INSPECT language allows you to extend the capabilities of FireWall-1's security rules.

- A separate management GUI can manage multiple installed FireWall-1 installations and provide consistent policy across a number of installations. The same GUI can manage FireWall-1 installed on Windows NT, Solaris, Linux, Nortel Routers, or Xylan routing switches.

- Both the Management GUI and the FireWall-1 Inspection module are multi-platform, including embedded systems such as routers and routing switches.

- Multiple authentication schemes to authenticate users to services using RADIUS, SecurID, FW-1 and Operating System password, Digital Certificates, S/Key, TACACS, and so on.

- Provides Network Address Translation services.

- Provides load balancing and high availability across multiple physical firewalls.

- Includes Content Filtering for HTTP, FTP, and SMTP protocols. This allows you to disable certain commands and remove embedded scripting languages.

If you are looking for an industrial firewall product, you should look at products such asCheck Point FireWall-1 or Network Associate's Gauntlet.

If you do not have the budget for a grand, all-singing, all-dancing firewall like FireWall-1 or Gauntlet, you can still deploy a firewall using Linux or OpenBSD.

Linux 2.2 firewall support includes ipchains, a rewrite of the previous firewalling code in the Linux 2.0 kernel known as ipfwadm, which was originally derived from the BSD ipfw. ipchains is a packet filter firewall that does not have stateful inspection support. In the Linux 2.4 kernel ipchains has been replaced by a more flexible, integrated packet mangling system known as NetFilter. Because the Linux 2.4 kernel is still in development, only the available ipchains packet filtering firewall is discussed here. TheNetFilter site has ipchains wrapper and migration scripts to ease the transition to NetFilter rules when Linux 2.4 is ready for production use.

ipchains is so named because a chain is a grouping of individual packet filter rules. Because the filtering works only with IP, ipchains is the logical name for it. That and it's much better than ipfwadm. There are three chains by default: input, output, and forward. New chains can be created to ease management.

OpenBSD 2.7 also includes firewall support in the form of IP filter. IP filter is actually available for many platforms: NetBSD, FreeBSD, OpenBSD, BSD/OS, Solaris, SunOS, IRIX, and HP-UX. IP filter is a capable firewalling package that includes all the expected packet filtering capability and stateful inspection. Like ipchains, IP filter's rules can be grouped for optimization. New alpha releases of IP filter include the beginnings of content inspection, so you could filter all Napster traffic no matter what port or server it was being sent to.

Now it's time to implement a firewall.

Minimal Router Filtering

Because a firewall is doing most of the traffic management, you can reduce your packet filtering on the WAN router. Rather than eliminate the filtering all together, however, some basic filtering for spoofed addresses and ICMP messages is included to add a layer of security and protection to the firewall, DMZ, and internal networks:

```
!
! Access List 111 controls Outbound Internal traffic
!  applied to internal LAN interface as ip access-group 111 out
!
! First drop any spoofed internal traffic, you don't want
! to leak RFC 1918 private addresses to the world.
!
access-list 111 deny ip 10.0.0.0 0.255.255.255 any
access-list 111 deny ip 127.0.0.0 0.255.255.255 any
access-list 111 deny ip 172.16.0.0 0.31.255.255 any
access-list 111 deny ip 192.168.0.0 0.0.255.255 any
!
! Make sure you explicitly allow everything else
!
access-list 111 permit ip any any
!
!
! Access List 110 controls Inbound WAN traffic
!  applied to WAN interface as ip access-group 110 in
!
! First drop RFC 1918 private network traffic, and any spoofed
! internal traffic and localhost traffic.
```

```
!
access-list 110 deny ip 10.0.0.0 0.255.255.255 any
access-list 110 deny ip 127.0.0.0 0.255.255.255 any
access-list 110 deny ip 172.16.0.0 0.31.255.255 any
access-list 110 deny ip 192.168.0.0 0.0.255.255 any
access-list 110 deny ip 1.4.3.0 0.0.0.255 any
access-list 110 deny ip 1.4.4.0 0.0.0.255 any
!
! Now allow ICMP replies to echo reply, destination unreachable,
! and time-exceeded destined for internal network.
!
access-list 110 permit icmp any 1.4.3.0 0.0.0.255 echo-reply
access-list 110 permit icmp any 1.4.3.0 0.0.0.255 unreachable
access-list 110 permit icmp any 1.4.3.0 0.0.0.255 time-exceeded
!
! Now allow ICMP messages for destination unreachable,
! fragmentation needed, and time-exceeded destined for DMZ network.
!
access-list 110 permit icmp any 1.4.4.0 0.0.0.255 unreachable
access-list 110 permit icmp any 1.4.4.0 0.0.0.255 packet-too-big
access-list 110 permit icmp any 1.4.4.0 0.0.0.255 time-exceeded
!
! Make sure you explicitly allow everything else
!
access-list 111 permit ip any any
```

Starting Free and Clear

First and foremost, flush all existing rules, and reset all existing firewall properties. This ensures that there are no existing holes, gaps, misconfigurations, or surprises that you weren't expecting.

Check Point Firewall-1 on Windows NT

Normally, you would expect a firewall to disable all traffic if the default policy is to DENY. You might be surprised, that by default, FireWall-1 accepts access to its Management ports 256, 257, and 258. Choose Policy, Properties, and then disable these ports (see Figure 10.4).

Linux 2.2 and ipchains

ipchains is part of the Linux kernel. As such, it must be enabled for you to use it. You can check for the file /proc/net/ip_fwchains. If that file exists, the ipchains is compiled into your running kernel. Most distributions install kernels that have ipchains configured. If ipchains is not enabled, you must enable that option and compile the kernel yourself. If you have already compiled your own kernels, you should already know enough to enable the appropriate ipchains options. If not, read the Linux kernel documentation on compiling kernels, your distribution's documentation, or the Linux Kernel-HOWTO available through http://www.linux.org/.

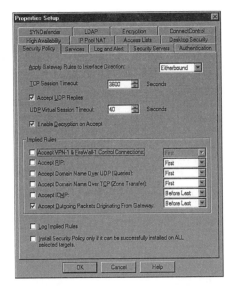

Figure 10.4   Modifying the default Security Policy, specifically Disabling Implied rules in FireWall-1.

Make sure youenable IP forwarding, or the firewall will not pass any traffic. You can do this manually by issuing the following command:

```
echo 1 > /proc/sys/net/ipv4/ip_forward
```

You can also enable it by default. For Red Hat, edit the /etc/sysconfig/network config file and change FORWARD_IPV4=no to yes. For Debian, edit the /etc/network/options config file and change ipforward=no to yes.

The default install of ipchains is to allow traffic to pass. First, make sure any existing ipchains rules are flushed. If you are building your ipchains rules interactively, or modifying them, you might want to insert explicit DENY rules until you are finished. Otherwise some traffic might pass while the rules are in flux:

```
ipchains -F
ipchains -I input 1 DENY
ipchains -I output 1 DENY
ipchains -I forward 1 DENY
Use ipchains -L to list the currently active ruleset:
Chain input (policy ACCEPT):
target    prot opt   source              destination        ports
DENY      all  ------ anywhere           anywhere           n/a
Chain forward (policy ACCEPT):
target    prot opt   source              destination        ports
DENY      all  ------ anywhere           anywhere           n/a
Chain output (policy ACCEPT):
```

```
target    prot opt   source            destination       ports
DENY      all  ------ anywhere          anywhere          n/a
```

With this ruleset in place, no network traffic, in or out, from this server will take place.

OpenBSD 2.7 and IP Filter

IP filter requires kernel support, and the default GENERIC kernel includes IP filter support. However, if you are compiling your own kernels, make sure you enable these two options:

```
option        IPFILTER      # IP packet filter for security
option        IPFILTER_LOG  # use /dev/ipl
```

Additionally, set the ipfilter flag to YES in /etc/rc.conf.

Make sure you enable IP forwarding, or the firewall will not pass any traffic. InOpenBSD, edit the /etc/sysctl.conf config file to have net.inet.ip.forwarding=1. ForSolaris, forwarding is enabled automatically if you have more than one network interface installed. However, you can control the setting by issuing the following command:

```
ndd -set /dev/ip ip_forwarding 1
```

The default install of IP filter is to allow traffic to pass. First, make sure any existing IP filter rules areflushed:

```
ipf -Fa
```

This will flush all filter rules. You can check the status of the IP filter ruleset using the ipfstat command. The output of ipfstat -io after flushing the ruleset is

```
empty list for ipfilter(out)
empty list for ipfilter(in)
```

An empty rule set for IP filter will continue to pass traffic. IP filter has active and inactive rulesets, which allows you to build an inactive ruleset while the active ruleset still protects your server. If you want to block all input, you can create a file named /etc/ipf.rules-blockall that contains the following line:

```
block in all
```

Issue the following command to invoke that ruleset and no traffic at all will enter your server:

```
ipf -Fa -f /etc/ipf.rules-blockall
```

Allow Internal Network Traffic Outbound to the Internet

To allow all internal network traffic outbound to the Internet, you allow all internal network traffic to any destination except the DMZ. Most all firewalls have the negation operator that enables you to express this rule easily.

Check Point FireWall-1 on Windows NT

The Check Point FireWall-1 Management GUI includes a Policy Editor that allows you to define rulebases. The rulebases work on objects, so you will need to define some network objects before creating any rules. Create network objects for the WAN side of the DMZ, the protected side of the DMZ, and your internal corporate network. Additionally, create objects representing your firewall, DMZ servers, and internal servers that talk to the DMZ servers (see Figure 10.5).

Figure 10.5   Create objects in FireWall-1 to represent the logical and physical networks and servers of your network architecture.

After you have the network objects defined, you can create some rules. Add a rule that allows traffic from Internal-net to anywhere except the DMZ-net (see Figure 10.6). To monitor what passes through your firewall and what does not, by default you log the acceptance and denial of packets.

Linux 2.2 and ipchains

ipchains does not operate on network objects, rather it uses IP protocols, addresses, ports, and interfaces as selection criteria. To keep things simple and more easily maintainable, this example creates specific chains that allow you to group rules specific to the direction of the flow of traffic. This allows you to modify individual traffic flows without accidentally affecting the rest of the rule groups.

First, you must create the interface pairings that will define the traffic flows. Because you have three interfaces in the firewall, that gives you a total of six possible traffic flows. Table 10.2 lists the physical interface, the descriptive ipchains interface, and the description.

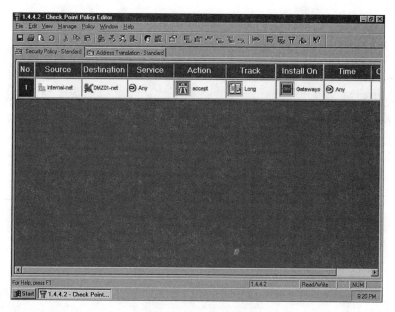

Figure 10.6 Create the rule that allows internal network traffic to any network but the DMZ network.

Table 10.2 Physical Interfaces to ipchains Symbolic Designation

Physical Interface	ipchains Designation	Description
eth0	WAN	Connects to unprotected DMZ and WAN
eth1	DMZ	Connects to protected DMZ server network
eth2	Int	Connects to protected internal network

Use the ipchains -N command to create one chain for each pairing of interfaces describing the traffic flow from the first interface to the second:

```
ipchains -N WAN-Int
ipchains -N WAN-DMZ
ipchains -N DMZ-WAN
ipchains -N DMZ-Int
ipchains -N Int-WAN
ipchains -N Int-DMZ
```

Next, insert the selection criteria for your traffic flows into the forward rule. Keep in mind that when designating interfaces for the forward rule, the interface is the one that the packet will be sent from. Each rule is added in sequence to the chain by using the ipchains -A command:

```
ipchains -A forward -s 1.4.3.0/24 -i eth0 -j Int-WAN
ipchains -A forward -s 1.4.3.0/24 -i eth1 -j Int-DMZ
```

```
ipchains -A forward -s 1.4.4.128/26 -i eth0 -j DMZ-WAN
ipchains -A forward -s 1.4.4.128/26 -i eth2 -j DMZ-Int
ipchains -A forward -i eth1 -j WAN-DMZ
ipchains -A forward -i eth2 -j WAN-Int
ipchains -A forward -j DENY -l
```

You must also create a convenience chain for ICMP replies that designates errors that you should pass. Populate the chain with the ICMP return codes themselves:

```
ipchains -N ICMP-ERR

ipchains -A ICMP-ERR -p ICMP —icmp-type destination-unreachable -j ACCEPT
ipchains -A ICMP-ERR -p ICMP —icmp-type time-exceeded -j ACCEPT
```

Finally, with the existing chains infrastructure in place, you can define the rule that allows you topass traffic from the internal network to the outside world only:

```
ipchains -A Int-WAN -j ACCEPT
```

OpenBSD 2.7 and IP Filter

IP filter, like ipchains, does not operate on network objects, rather it uses IP protocols, addresses, ports, and interfaces as selection criteria. IP filter does have a state table unlike ipchains, which will make the rulebase more manageable. Any entry made to the state table allows you to bypass the rulebase.

IP filter is not as closely tied to individual interfaces as ipchains is on Linux. To group specific rules to interfaces, you can use the group and head keywords. In addition to making the rulebase more manageable, you also gain a performance advantage of not having to process the additional rules.

> **Your Mileage May Vary**
> The interfaces listed in the table might be different than the interfaces on your system. OpenBSD, FreeBSD, NetBSD, and Solaris name interfaces differently depending on the driver used to support that card. They do not specifically differentiate between network technologies like Linux does.

Table 10.3 Physical Interface to IP Filter Group

Physical Interface	IP Filter Group	Description
dc0	101	Connects to unprotected DMZ and WAN
dc1	201	Connects to protected DMZ server network
dc2	301	Connects to protected internal network

Edit the `/etc/ipf.rules` file, which is where the rulesbase lives by default. You might want to comment out any active rules that exist there from installation. Installation default leaves two rules: `pass in from any to any`, and `pass out from any to any`. After those have been commented out, start by adding your group definitions (noted by the `head` statement):

```
block in quick on dc0 all head 101
pass out on dc0 all

block out quick on dc1 all head 201

block out on dc2 all
block in quick on dc2 all head 301
  pass in     quick on dc2 proto tcp/udp from 1.4.3.0/24 to any keep state group 301
  pass in     quick on dc2 proto icmp    from 1.4.3.0/24 to any keep state group 301
```

Notice the three pass statements. The first allows traffic out of the firewall onto the WAN interface. This statement is counteracted by the `block out on dc2 all` statement, preventing traffic that does not have a state table entry from getting into the internal network. The next two allow TCP, UDP, and ICMP network traffic into the firewall from the internal network. The keep state directive is responsible for creating state table entries allowing traffic back in.

Protect the Firewall

Drop all traffic destined for the firewall itself. You do not want people succeeding in sending traffic to the firewall proper. Here is where rule order starts to become important as this rule must go prior to the `Allow Outbound` rule. If the order were to be reversed, internal hosts could access the firewall.

Check Point FireWall-1 on Windows NT

Insert a rule above Rule #1 (the first rule listed) dropping any traffic to the firewall. Right-clicking rule #1 in the No. column invokes a menu that allows you to delete the selected rule, or add a new rule before or after. Blocking all traffic addressed for the firewall, along with disabling the implied rules, will prevent you or anyone else from managing your firewall (see Figure 10.7). This will be corrected in a later section.

Linux 2.2 and ipchains

Because the firewall will be protected when you drop all traffic from all interfaces, the easiest way to manage that is to create chains specifically describing traffic flows to the firewall itself. That way if you need to create exceptions to the rule, such as administrative traffic or DNS requests, you can do so without affecting other rule groupings.

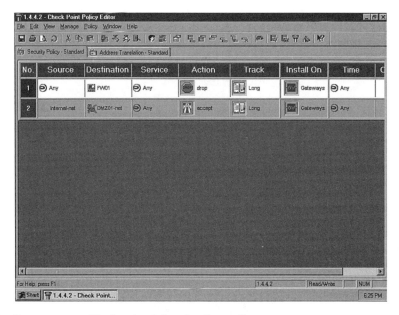

Figure 10.7 Drop any traffic destined for the firewall.

First, create chains for each interface using `ipchains -N`:

```
ipchains -N WAN-if
ipchains -N DMZ-if
ipchains -N Int-if
```

Next, because the traffic is destined for the firewall itself, and not passing through as a traffic flow, attach selection rules to the input chain:

```
ipchains -A input -d 1.4.4.2 -j WAN-if
ipchains -A input -d 1.4.4.129 -j DMZ-if
ipchains -A input -d 1.4.3.1 -j Int-if
```

Finally, you can block individual access from each interface. The ! (pronounced "not") switch negates whatever follows. So the criteria `-i ! eth0` translates as any interface but eth0:

```
ipchains -A WAN-if -i ! eth0 -j DENY -l
ipchains -A WAN-if -p ICMP —icmp-type echo-reply -j ACCEPT
ipchains -A WAN-if -j DENY

ipchains -A DMZ-if -i ! eth1 -j DENY
ipchains -A DMZ-if -p UDP -s 1.4.4.130 53 -j ACCEPT
ipchains -A DMZ-if -j DENY -l

ipchains -A Int-if -i ! eth2 -j DENY
ipchains -A Int-if -p ICMP —icmp-type echo-request -j ACCEPT
ipchains -A Int-if -p ICMP —icmp-type echo-reply -j ACCEPT
ipchains -A Int-if -j DENY -l
```

OpenBSD 2.7 and IP Filter

Add the following `block` rules to `/etc/ipf.rules`. Grouping them near the `head` rule allows you to see the flow of the rules:

```
block in log quick on dc0 from any to 1.4.4.2/32   group 101

block in log quick on dc2 from any to 1.4.3.1/32 group 301
```

You might notice there is no group to drop traffic bound for the firewall from the DMZ. Because the rule was slightly different, you'll add it later in the "Drop All Traffic from the DMZ" section.

Allow Only Internal Admin Access to the Firewall

The firewall needs to be managed, but only by the firewall administrators. Administrative access should be restricted to what machines the administrators use, and types of network traffic required to access and to manage the firewall. This rule must go prior to the "drop everything destined for the firewall" rule or even administrative traffic will be dropped.

Check Point FireWall-1 on Windows NT

Commercial firewalls, such as Check Point's FireWall-1, have specific firewall administrative ports (256, 257, and 258) that are accessed via encrypted sessions through their management console. Insert a rule above Rule #1 (the first rule in the list) allowing admin workstation FireWall-1 traffic to the firewall (see Figure 10.8).

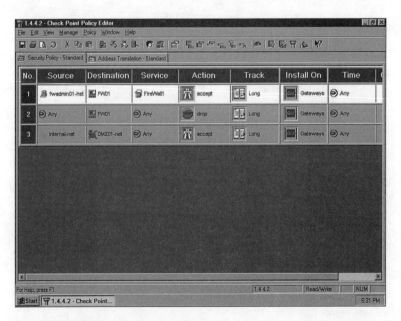

Figure 10.8 Allow FireWall-1 administrative service from the administrative host to the firewall.

Linux 2.2 and ipchains

UNIX-based firewalls should allow access by encrypted SSH sessions from the internal network only. You can modify your Int-if chain to accept SSH traffic. You do this by using the ipchains -I command to insert a rule into a specific order. Insert the rule after Rule #1, the interface check:

```
ipchains -I Int-if 2 -p TCP --dport 22 -j ACCEPT
```

OpenBSD 2.7 and IP Filter

UNIX based firewalls should allow access by encrypted secure shell (SSH) sessions from the internal network only. You can add this pass rule under the group 301 head. Add this before the rule that blocks access to the firewall:

```
pass  in log quick on dc2 from 1.4.3.0/24 to 1.4.3.1/32 port = 22 flags S keep state group 301
```

Drop Traffic You Do Not Want Logged

Broadcasts, multicasts, and other traffic your firewall sees but you do not want logged should have a rule defined that drops or rejects the traffic, but does not log. This prevents excessive, unnecessary logging that would otherwise clutter up your logfiles. Reviewing your logfiles will be difficult enough without having to wade through page after page of NetBIOS, RIP, OSPF, or DHCP requests. This rule needs to be ordered prior to the "protect the firewall" rule.

Check Point FireWall-1 on Windows NT

Insert a new rule to drop all traffic to the firewall above Rule #2. Select any source and destination of firewall, and choose the broadcast/multicast traffic that your firewall can see (see Figure 10.9). RIP traffic occurs every 30 seconds; OSPF, DHCP, and NetBIOS traffic (assuming you have a Windows-based network) are also good candidates to filter out.

Linux 2.2 and ipchains

Now you can begin to see the power of chains; you can simply insert rules for blocking broadcast and multicast traffic:

```
ipchains -I Int-if 3 -d 1.4.3.255 -j REJECT
ipchains -I Int-if 3 -d 224.0.0.0/4 -j REJECT
```

OpenBSD 2.7 and IP Filter

Insert these rules for blocking broadcast and multicast traffic before the "block all access to the firewall" rule:

```
block in    quick on dc2 from any to 1.4.3.255/32 group 301
block in    quick on dc2 from any to 224.0.0.0/4  group 301
```

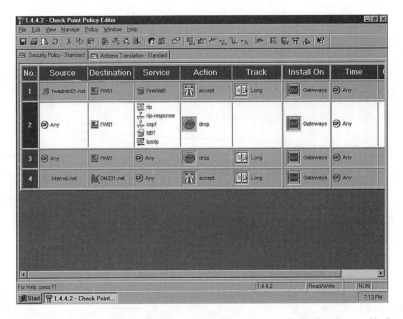

Figure 10.9 Drop all broadcast or multicast traffic that reaches the firewall that you do not want to see dropped in the logs by rule #3, drop and log all traffic for the firewall.

Services Provided to the Internet

You need to allow Internet users access to the servers and services that you are providing to the Internet. This includes DNS name lookups, Web (HTTP/HTTPS), and mail (SMTP):

- Allow DNS name lookups (UDP/53) from any network but the internal networks to the DMZ name server only. The internal users should be using the internal DNS servers. If your ISP is acting as a secondary for your external DNS name server, you need to add an additional rule allowing DNS zone transfers (TCP/53) between the ISP's name server and the DMZ name server.

- HTTP (TCP/80) and HTTPS (TCP/443), if necessary, access from anywhere to the DMZ Web server will be allowed. To enable HTTP/HTTPS access from the internal network, this rule must be before the "allow outbound to everywhere but the DMZ" rule.

- SMTP (TCP/25) access from anywhere to the DMZ mail server will be allowed. To enable SMTP access from the internal mail server this rule must also be before the "allow outbound to everywhere but the DMZ" rule.

Check Point FireWall-1 on Windows NT

Add three new rules before Rule #4 (see Figure 10.10). The first allows UDP/53 DNS lookups between the internal and DMZ DNS servers. The second allows the DMZ DNS server to do UDP/53 lookups on the Internet. The third rule allows any UDP/53 DNS lookup to the DMZ DNS server from anywhere but the internal network. Because DNS lookups occur so often, they aren't logged; otherwise, the logs would fill quite quickly.

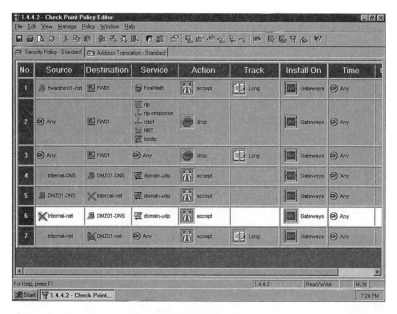

Figure 10.10   Restrict the flow and type of DNS traffic.

Add one rule prior to Rule #7, the "allow anywhere but DMZ" rule (see Figure 10.11). Allow any source to the Web server using TCP/80 and TCP/443.

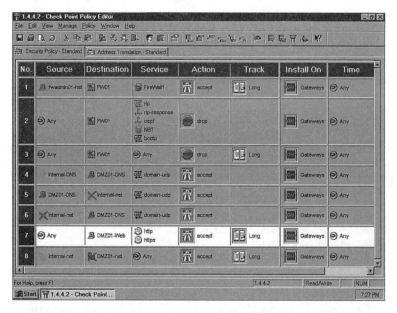

Figure 10.11   Allow and log any inbound HTTP traffic to the DMZ Web server.

Add one rule prior to Rule #8, the "allow anywhere but DMZ" rule (see Figure 10.12). Allow any source to the email server using TCP/25.

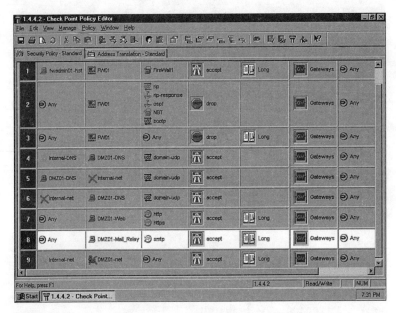

Figure 10.12   Allow and log any inbound SMTP traffic to the DMZ Mail Relay.

Linux 2.2 and ipchains

First, add rules inbound from the Internet to the DMZ servers:

```
ipchains -A WAN-DMZ -p UDP -d 1.4.4.130 53 -j ACCEPT
ipchains -A WAN-DMZ -p TCP -d 1.4.4.131 25 -j ACCEPT
ipchains -A WAN-DMZ -p TCP -d 1.4.4.132 80 -j ACCEPT
ipchains -A WAN-DMZ -p TCP -d 1.4.4.132 443 -j ACCEPT
```

Then, add rules allowing inbound from the internal network to the DMZ servers. Note how DNS zone transfers and SMTP are restricted between the servers, and other clients are not allowed by providing a source IP:

```
ipchains -A Int-DMZ -p UDP -d 1.4.4.130 53 -j ACCEPT
ipchains -A Int-DMZ -p TCP -s 1.4.3.130 -d 1.4.4.130 53 -j ACCEPT
ipchains -A Int-DMZ -p TCP -s 1.4.3.131 -d 1.4.4.131 25 -j ACCEPT
ipchains -A Int-DMZ -p TCP -d 1.4.4.132 80 -j ACCEPT
ipchains -A Int-DMZ -p TCP -d 1.4.4.132 443 -j ACCEPT
```

OpenBSD 2.7 and IP Filter

Add these rules to /etc/ipf.rules. You do not have to create separate inbound rules because you are keeping state. Notice how you can even "keep state" on a stateless protocol such as

UDP. A temporary state table entry is created with the IP address and port information that has a lifetime of 60 seconds. After that, the state table automatically expires:

```
pass out quick on dc1 proto udp from any to 1.4.4.130/32          port = 53              keep state
    group 201
pass out quick on dc1 proto tcp from 1.4.3.130/32 to 1.4.4.130/32 port = 53  flags S keep state
    group 201
pass out quick on dc1 proto tcp from any to 1.4.4.131/32          port = 25  flags S keep state
    group 201
pass out quick on dc1 proto tcp from any to 1.4.4.132/32          port = 80  flags S keep state
    group 201
pass out quick on dc1 proto tcp from any to 1.4.4.132/32          port = 443 flags S keep state
    group 201
```

Drop DMZ Initiated Traffic

The servers on the DMZ should never initiate a connection to the internal network; all requests should come from the inside. If this occurs, there is a good chance that one of your servers has been compromised. The rule that governs this activity should deny, and log the occurrence. If you have the ability to trigger an alert, that certainly is timely and valuable information to have.

Check Point FireWall-1 on Windows NT

Add one rule after Rule #9, the "allow anywhere but DMZ" rule. Any traffic coming from the DMZ network to the Internal network should be dropped and logged (see Figure 10.13).

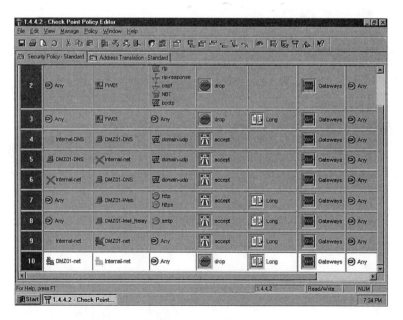

Figure 10.13   Drop and Log any DMZ Initiated Traffic.

Linux 2.2 and ipchains

Because ipchains does not have stateful inspection, it does not know when replies are part of allowed traffic. Therefore, you must allow replies back to the outside world, and to the internal network before you drop traffic.

First, allow replies back to the Internet. This is designated by the ! -y. The ipchains -y selector is a flag for only the SYN bit of a packet, therefore that does not include the SYN and ACK bits set. By saying you do not want only the SYN bit set, you are basically stopping initial connections. The last statement denies everything else:

```
ipchains -A DMZ-WAN -p UDP -s 1.4.4.130 53 -j ACCEPT
ipchains -A DMZ-WAN -p TCP -s 1.4.4.131 25 -j ACCEPT
ipchains -A DMZ-WAN -p TCP ! -y -s 1.4.4.132 80 -j ACCEPT
ipchains -A DMZ-WAN -p TCP ! -y -s 1.4.4.132 443 -j ACCEPT
ipchains -A DMZ-WAN -p ICMP -j ICMP-ERR
ipchains -A DMZ-WAN -j DENY -l
```

Next, allow replies back to the internal network:

```
ipchains -A DMZ-Int -p UDP -s 1.4.4.130 53 -j ACCEPT
ipchains -A DMZ-Int -p TCP ! -y -s 1.4.4.131 25 -j ACCEPT
ipchains -A DMZ-Int -p TCP ! -y -s 1.4.4.132 80 -j ACCEPT
ipchains -A DMZ-Int -p TCP ! -y -s 1.4.4.132 443 -j ACCEPT
ipchains -A DMZ-Int -p ICMP -j ICMP-ERR
ipchains -A DMZ-Int -j DENY -l
```

OpenBSD 2.7 and IP Filter

You create a new group here allowing all traffic from the DMZ into the firewall while keeping state. You can do this because of the block rules on the other interfaces. Notice the block rule is added here to prevent access to the firewall itself from the DMZ network:

```
pass in quick on dc1 proto tcp/udp from 1.4.4.128/26 to any keep state head 202
  block in log quick on dc1 from any to 1.4.4.129/32 group 202
```

Default Policy of Drop Everything

You need to implement the Default Stance of "that which is not explicitly allowed should be denied". This rule generally goes last.

Check Point FireWall-1 on Windows NT

Insert this final rule at the very end. Traffic from any source, destination, or service gets dropped and logged (see Figure 10.14).

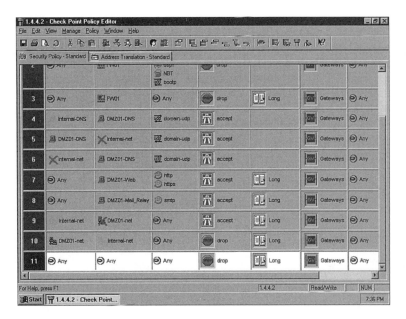

Figure 10.14   Set your default policy of "drop everything."

Linux 2.2 and ipchains

Finally, you get to block traffic that should not be passing through your firewall. You add the DENY rules to the appropriate chains:

```
ipchains -A Int-DMZ -p ICMP -j ICMP-ERR
ipchains -A Int-DMZ -j DENY -l

ipchains -A WAN-DMZ -p ICMP -j ICMP-ERR
ipchains -A WAN-DMZ -j DENY

ipchains -A WAN-Int -j REJECT
```

OpenBSD 2.7 and IP Filter

This one rule prevents any traffic entering the firewall from going onto the internal network. The only way traffic can enter the internal network is if there are already state table entries created for it using the pass statement with the keep state parameter:

```
block out on dc2 all
```

All the other interfaces already had block statements created for them when you defined the head groups.

Bringing It All Together

There are some additional tweaks and modifications that might be necessary with ipchains or IP filter. This section outlines those tweaks and why you would use them.

Linux 2.2 and ipchains

With all the individual steps for creating the ipchains rulebase, you might be interested in seeing what it looks like as a whole. You can do this by issuing `ipchains -L -n`, where the `-n` tells ipchains to not resolve addresses and ports to names:

```
Chain input (policy ACCEPT):
target    prot opt      source          destination        ports
WAN-if    all  ------   0.0.0.0/0       1.4.4.2            n/a
DMZ-if    all  ------   0.0.0.0/0       1.4.4.129          n/a
Int-if    all  ------   0.0.0.0/0       1.4.3.1            n/a
Chain forward (policy ACCEPT):
target    prot opt      source          destination        ports
Int-WAN   all  ------   1.4.3.0/24      0.0.0.0/0          n/a
Int-DMZ   all  ------   1.4.3.0/24      0.0.0.0/0          n/a
DMZ-WAN   all  ------   1.4.4.128/26    0.0.0.0/0          n/a
DMZ-Int   all  ------   1.4.4.128/26    0.0.0.0/0          n/a
WAN-DMZ   all  ------   0.0.0.0/0       0.0.0.0/0          n/a
WAN-Int   all  ------   0.0.0.0/0       0.0.0.0/0          n/a
DENY      all  ----l-   0.0.0.0/0       0.0.0.0/0          n/a
Chain output (policy ACCEPT):
Chain WAN-Int (1 references):
target    prot opt      source          destination        ports
REJECT    all  ------   0.0.0.0/0       0.0.0.0/0          n/a
Chain WAN-DMZ (1 references):
target    prot opt      source          destination        ports
ACCEPT    udp  ------   0.0.0.0/0       1.4.4.130          * ->   53
ACCEPT    tcp  ------   0.0.0.0/0       1.4.4.131          * ->   25
ACCEPT    tcp  ------   0.0.0.0/0       1.4.4.132          * ->   80
ACCEPT    tcp  ------   0.0.0.0/0       1.4.4.132          * ->   443
ICMP-ERR  icmp ------   0.0.0.0/0       0.0.0.0/0          * ->   *
DENY      all  ------   0.0.0.0/0       0.0.0.0/0          n/a
Chain DMZ-WAN (1 references):
target    prot opt      source          destination        ports
ACCEPT    udp  ------   1.4.4.130       0.0.0.0/0          53 ->  *
ACCEPT    tcp  ------   1.4.4.131       0.0.0.0/0          25 ->  *
ACCEPT    tcp  !y----   1.4.4.132       0.0.0.0/0          80 ->  *
ACCEPT    tcp  !y----   1.4.4.132       0.0.0.0/0          443 -> *
ICMP-ERR  icmp ------   0.0.0.0/0       0.0.0.0/0          * ->   *
DENY      all  ----l-   0.0.0.0/0       0.0.0.0/0          n/a
Chain DMZ-Int (1 references):
target    prot opt      source          destination        ports
ACCEPT    udp  ------   1.4.4.130       0.0.0.0/0          53 ->  *
ACCEPT    tcp  !y----   1.4.4.131       0.0.0.0/0          25 ->  *
ACCEPT    tcp  !y----   1.4.4.132       0.0.0.0/0          80 ->  *
```

```
ACCEPT    tcp  !y----  1.4.4.132      0.0.0.0/0      443 ->    *
ICMP-ERR  icmp ------  0.0.0.0/0      0.0.0.0/0       *  ->    *
DENY      all  ----l-  0.0.0.0/0      0.0.0.0/0      n/a
Chain Int-WAN (1 references):
target    prot opt     source         destination     ports
ACCEPT    all  ------  0.0.0.0/0      0.0.0.0/0      n/a
Chain Int-DMZ (1 references):
target    prot opt     source         destination     ports
ACCEPT    udp  ------  0.0.0.0/0      1.4.4.130       *  ->   53
ACCEPT    tcp  ------  1.4.3.130      1.4.4.130       *  ->   53
ACCEPT    tcp  ------  1.4.3.131      1.4.4.131       *  ->   25
ACCEPT    tcp  ------  0.0.0.0/0      1.4.4.132       *  ->   80
ACCEPT    tcp  ------  0.0.0.0/0      1.4.4.132       *  ->  443
ICMP-ERR  icmp ------  0.0.0.0/0      0.0.0.0/0       *  ->    *
DENY      all  ----l-  0.0.0.0/0      0.0.0.0/0      n/a
Chain WAN-if (1 references):
target    prot opt     source         destination     ports
DENY      all  ----l-  0.0.0.0/0      0.0.0.0/0      n/a
ACCEPT    icmp ------  0.0.0.0/0      0.0.0.0/0       0  ->    *
DENY      all  ------  0.0.0.0/0      0.0.0.0/0      n/a
Chain DMZ-if (1 references):
target    prot opt     source         destination     ports
DENY      all  ------  0.0.0.0/0      0.0.0.0/0      n/a
ACCEPT    udp  ------  1.4.4.130      0.0.0.0/0      53  ->    *
DENY      all  ----l-  0.0.0.0/0      0.0.0.0/0      n/a
Chain Int-if (1 references):
target    prot opt     source         destination     ports
DENY      all  ------  0.0.0.0/0      0.0.0.0/0      n/a
ACCEPT    tcp  ------  0.0.0.0/0      0.0.0.0/0       *  ->   22
REJECT    all  ------  0.0.0.0/0      224.0.0.0/4    n/a
REJECT    all  ------  0.0.0.0/0      1.4.3.255      n/a
ACCEPT    icmp ------  0.0.0.0/0      0.0.0.0/0       8  ->    *
ACCEPT    icmp ------  0.0.0.0/0      0.0.0.0/0       0  ->    *
DENY      all  ----l-  0.0.0.0/0      0.0.0.0/0      n/a
Chain ICMP-ERR (4 references):
target    prot opt     source         destination     ports
ACCEPT    icmp ------  0.0.0.0/0      0.0.0.0/0       3  ->    *
ACCEPT    icmp ------  0.0.0.0/0      0.0.0.0/0      11  ->    *
```

The ipchains rulebase is not persistent. This means that if you flush (`ipchains -F`) the rulebase or reboot, you will have to redo all your firewalling commands. Luckily, there are two commands associated with saving and restoring ipchains rulebases. These commands are aptly named `ipchains-save` and `ipchains-restore`. They output to standard out, so you can issue commands such as this to save and restore your rulebase:

```
ipchains-save > /etc/ipchains.rules
ipchains -F
ipchains-restore < /etc/ipchains.rules
```

The restoration of your ipchains rulebase should be done early in the bootup of your system so you don't have a window of opportunity for intruders to pass packets unabated.

One last caveat, to support FTP, in passive or active form, you must load a kernel helper module. Using the `insmod` kernel module loading command, load the `ip_masq_ftp.o` kernel module:

```
insmod ip_masq_ftp
```

It's best to place that command in the same script that restores your ipchains rulebase. There are many more kernel helper modules for difficult transports, such as CuSeeMe, IRC, Real Audio, Quake, and so on. Tosee available kernel modules, look in your `/lib/modules/<ver>/ipv4` directory, where `<ver>` is your current kernel version.

OpenBSD 2.7 and IP Filter

Linux normally has IP spoof protection on in the kernel by default. You can add that capability to IP filters with some simple statements:

```
# These may have to change if you are using RFC 1918
# addresses and IP NAT.
# Block reserved addresses in from anywhere.
#
block in log quick from 192.168.0.0/16 to any
block in log quick from 172.16.0.0/12  to any
block in log quick from 10.0.0.0/8      to any

# Block and log all Spoofed packets
#
# on WAN ...
#
block in on dc0 all head 100
  block in log quick from 127.0.0.0/8 to any   group 100
  block in log quick from any to 127.0.0.0/8   group 100

  # Prevent IP spoofing.
  #
  block in log quick from 1.4.3.0/24 to any    group 100
  block in log quick from 1.4.4.64/26 to any   group 100
  block in log quick from 1.4.4.128/26 to any  group 100
  block in log quick from 1.4.4.192/26 to any  group 100


# on DMZ ...
#
block in on dc2 all head 200
  block in log quick from 127.0.0.0/8 to any   group 200
  block in log quick from any to 127.0.0.0/8   group 200

  # Prevent IP spoofing.
  #
  block in log quick from 1.4.3.0/24 to any    group 200
  block in log quick from 1.4.4.0/26 to any    group 200
  block in log quick from 1.4.4.64/26 to any   group 200
```

```
block in log quick from 1.4.4.192/26 to any group 200

# on Int ...
#
block in on dc2 all head 300
  block in log quick from 127.0.0.0/8 to any  group 300
  block in log quick from any to 127.0.0.0/8  group 300

# Allow Localhost packets to localhost.
#
pass in  quick on lo0 all
pass out quick on lo0 all
```

Additionally, you should protect yourself from fragmented packets that are too short to process with another simple rule:

```
block in log quick all with short
```

You can enforce your kernel options of dropping source routed packets with the following two rules:

```
block in log quick all with opt lsrr
block in log quick all with opt ssrr
```

To actively monitor your firewall, you can use the `ipmon` command to view IP filter log messages in real time. Additionally, you can receive status information and statistics using the `ipfstat` command.

To support active FTP, you must use `ipnat` even if you are not otherwise using NAT. The NAT engine of IP filter is where the application-level proxy mechanism resides. Passive FTP works with the defined rulebase. Add the following `ipnat` rule to `/etc/ipnat.rules` to allow active FTP through your firewall:

```
map dc0 0/0 -> 0/32 proxy port 21 ftp/tcp
```

With all the individual steps for creating the IP filter rulebase, you might be interested in seeing what it looks like as a whole. Here is the sample `/etc/ipf.rules` in its entirety:

```
# ipf.rules for Concise Guide to Internetworking & Security
#

# Block all fragments too short to process
#
block in log quick all with short

# Block all packets with Source Routing enabled
#
block in log quick all with opt lsrr
block in log quick all with opt ssrr
```

```
# These may have to change if you are using RFC 1918
# addresses and IP NAT.
# Block reserved addresses in from anywhere.
#
block in log quick from 192.168.0.0/16 to any
block in log quick from 172.16.0.0/12  to any
block in log quick from 10.0.0.0/8      to any

# Block and log all Spoofed packets
#
# on WAN ...
#
block in on dc0 all head 100
  block in log quick from 127.0.0.0/8 to any   group 100
  block in log quick from any to 127.0.0.0/8   group 100

  # Prevent IP spoofing.
  #
  block in log quick from 1.4.3.0/24 to any    group 100
  block in log quick from 1.4.4.64/26 to any   group 100
  block in log quick from 1.4.4.128/26 to any  group 100
  block in log quick from 1.4.4.192/26 to any  group 100


# on DMZ ...
#
block in on dc2 all head 200
  block in log quick from 127.0.0.0/8 to any   group 200
  block in log quick from any to 127.0.0.0/8   group 200

  # Prevent IP spoofing.
  #
  block in log quick from 1.4.3.0/24 to any    group 200
  block in log quick from 1.4.4.0/26 to any    group 200
  block in log quick from 1.4.4.64/26 to any   group 200
  block in log quick from 1.4.4.192/26 to any  group 200

# on Int ...
#
block in on dc2 all head 300
  block in log quick from 127.0.0.0/8 to any   group 300
  block in log quick from any to 127.0.0.0/8   group 300

# Allow Localhost packets to localhost.
#
pass in  quick on lo0 all
pass out quick on lo0 all

# WAN Interface
#
block in quick on dc0 all head 101
```

```
      block in log quick on dc0 from any to 1.4.4.2/32    group 101
      pass  in           on dc0 all group 101

pass out on dc0 all

# DMZ Interface
#
block out quick on dc1 all head 201
 pass out quick on dc1 proto udp from any to 1.4.4.130/32            port = 53          keep state
    group 201
 pass out quick on dc1 proto tcp from 1.4.3.130/32 to 1.4.4.130/32 port = 53  flags S keep state
    group 201
 pass out quick on dc1 proto tcp from any to 1.4.4.131/32            port = 25  flags S keep state
    group 201
 pass out quick on dc1 proto tcp from any to 1.4.4.132/32            port = 80  flags S keep state
    group 201
 pass out quick on dc1 proto tcp from any to 1.4.4.132/32            port = 443 flags S keep state
    group 201

 pass in quick on dc1 proto tcp/udp from 1.4.4.128/26 to any keep state head 202
 block in log quick on dc1 from any to 1.4.4.129/32 group 202

# Internal Interface
#
block out on dc2 all

block in quick on dc2 all head 301
   pass  in log quick on dc2 from 1.4.3.0/24 to 1.4.3.1/32 port = 22 flags S keep state group 301
   block in     quick on dc2 from any to 1.4.3.255/32 group 301
   block in     quick on dc2 from any to 224.0.0.0/4  group 301
   block in log quick on dc2 from any to 1.4.3.1/32    group 301
   pass  in     quick on dc2 proto tcp/udp from 1.4.3.0/24 to any keep state group 301
   pass  in     quick on dc2 proto icmp   from 1.4.3.0/24 to any keep state group 301
```

Sample Packet Filter Router with a Firewall, DMZ, and VPN Security Gateway

Adding the VPN server to your DMZ is pretty much like adding any other service. The difference being the protocols it speaks. IPSec requires up to three protocols to establish and maintain connections:

- UDP/500 for IKE to do key exchanges for creating the IPSec Security Associations. This is easy because the source and destination port is UDP/500.

- IP Protocol 50 for Encapsulated Security Payload (ESP). Because ESP is a different IP protocol (like UDP, TCP, ICMP, OSPF, and so on) it has its own rules. For example, there is no concept of ports with ESP.

- IP Protocol 51 for Authenticated Header (AH). Most likely you will not be using AH, unless you would like to authenticate your ESP packets. Use of AH is mostly deprecated because it does not include data confidentiality, and ESP has the capability to do authentication. AH will most likely be used only with IPv6.

Besides modifying the rulesbase to support UDP/500, ESP, and AH, the architecture will be physically modified so that there is a second DMZ for authenticated and decrypted traffic. This allows you to distinguish authenticated traffic from possibly compromised traffic on the DMZ.

Routing unknown IP addresses to remote is handled in one of two ways depending on the IPSec implementation.

The first way is a local pool of IP addresses normally allocated by the security gateway. When a remote connection is established, its IPSec SA connection is associated with a local IP address from that pool. In that fashion, it acts very much like a Point-to-Point link.

The second way, called *extruded subnet*, is to assign the remote side an IP address that is part of the local subnet.

Either way, you will most likely need to investigate policy routing on your firewall to support the appearance and disappearance of remote hosts to route traffic to.

If you are folding your VPN gateway into your firewall, this generally reduces the problem of a separate security gateway slightly, although the remote address assignment is still handled by local address pools or extruded subnets.

Check Point FireWall-1 on Windows NT

You need to add two rules prior to the "drop everything rule". You need to allow IPSec to the security gateway from the Internet, and allow unrestricted access from the VPN DMZ network to the internal network (see Figure 10.15).

Linux 2.2 and ipchains

First, add the traffic flow chains to ease maintenance. Assign eth3 the designation of VPN. You have four traffic flow combinations. Traffic needs to flow between the Internet and the security gateway, and it needs to flow between the security gateway and the internal network. Luckily, the two flows defined between the Internet and the DMZ side of the security gateway have already been defined. So, you need to create two additional flow chains, and the forward chain selection criteria:

```
ipchains -N VPN-Int
ipchains -N Int-VPN

ipchains -A forward -s 1.4.3.0/24 -i eth3 -j Int-VPN
ipchains -A forward -s 1.4.4.192/26 -i eth2 -j VPN-Int
```

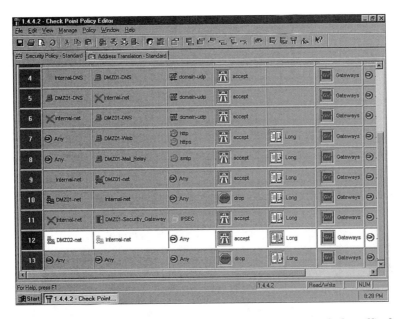

Figure 10.15 Additional rules to allow IPSec traffic, and IPSec tunneled traffic from a second DMZ subnet.

Now protect the firewall itself from traffic on the VPN DMZ. You do this the same way as before: Create a chain for that interface, add its selection criteria to the input chain, and then define the drop rules:

```
ipchains -N VPN-if

ipchains -A input -d 1.4.4.193 -j VPN-if

ipchains -A VPN-if -i ! eth3 -j DENY -l
ipchains -A VPN-if -p ICMP --icmp-type echo-reply -j ACCEPT
ipchains -A VPN-if -j DENY
```

Next, you need to allow IKE, ESP, and AH traffic to pass both from the Internet to the security gateway and back. Insert these rules before the ICMP and DENY all rules:

```
ipchains -I WAN-DMZ 5 -p UDP -d 1.4.4.134 500 --sport 500 -j ACCEPT
ipchains -I WAN-DMZ 5 -p 50 -d 1.4.4.134 -j ACCEPT
ipchains -I WAN-DMZ 5 -p 51 -d 1.4.4.134 -j ACCEPT
ipchains -I DMZ-WAN 5 -p UDP -d 1.4.4.134 500 --sport 500 -j ACCEPT
ipchains -I DMZ-WAN 5 -p 50 -d 1.4.4.134 -j ACCEPT
ipchains -I DMZ-WAN 5 -p 51 -d 1.4.4.134 -j ACCEPT
```

Finally, allow traffic to freely flow between your internal network and your VPN DMZ. Because you have separate chains, this would be the location to add access control for remote offices if you so desire.

```
ipchains -A Int-WAN -j ACCEPT
ipchains -A VPN-Int -j ACCEPT
```

OpenBSD 2.7 and IP Filter

First, add the rules necessary to allow IPSec connections to be established. In the DMZ interface group 201 specifications, you need to add two pass rules:

```
pass out quick on dc1 proto 50 from any to 1.4.4.134/32 group 201
pass out quick on dc1 proto 51 from any to 1.4.4.134/32 group 201
```

Additionally, because IP filter does not keep state for protocols other than TCP, UDP, and ICMP, you need to add matching inbound rules in group 202:

```
pass in quick on dc1 proto 50 from 1.4.4.134/32 to any group 202
pass in quick on dc1 proto 51 from 1.4.4.134/32 to any group 202
```

For IP filter, one of the many ways of doing this is to add a rule on the internal network interface that allows you to pass traffic destined for your security gateway. The routing caveats mentioned earlier apply to this rule change:

```
# Internal Interface
#
block out on dc2 all
pass out on dc2 from 1.4.4.194/32 to 1.4.3.0/24
```

Remember, because you didn't use the quick qualifier on the block statement, IP filter continues to process rules in the rulesbase. Therefore, even though you have tagged all packets to be dropped to the internal network, by adding the following pass rule you override that block for packets originating on the VPN DMZ.

Next add this rule block to /etc/ipf.rules to cover the new DMZ02 subnet:

```
block out on dc3 all

block in quick on dc3 all head 401
  block in log quick on dc2 from any to 1.4.4.193/32     group 401
  pass  in     quick on dc2 proto tcp/udp from 1.4.4.193/24 to any keep state group 401
  pass  in     quick on dc2 proto icmp     from 1.4.4.193/24 to any keep state group 401
```

11

TESTING AND
VALIDATION

Some circumstantial evidence is very strong, as when you find a trout in the milk.

> —Thoreau

Is Your Network Working Properly?

So now you've plugged everything in, some lights are blinking, and some fans are humming. So it must be working, right?

The only way to be sure is to test specifically. Never let your users be your beta testers. (Unless you're a multimillion dollar software giant, then it's okay.)

Assembling the Tools

Your network connection will be tested with both software and hardware tools. A workstation unable to talk to a router could have a bad cable in between (in which case a cable tester would be the proper tool) or it could have a faulty card, broadcasting irresponsibly, in which case a packet sniffer would be used. In either event, here are some of the tools you'll be using to test and validate your network.

Software Utilities

A lot of the most useful software utilities have either been built in to most operating systems or are available as freeware over the Internet.

Basic Operating System Diagnostics

Diagnostic programs such as ping and traceroute are included in most operating system installs because they're indispensibly useful in tracking down network problems.

Diagnosing Connections with ping

ping is a very useful little utility for checking the connectivity between two computers or the functionality of a remote computer. ping simply sends out a packet to a remote computer and requests a response (sometimes called a "pong"). By pinging various computers, you will be able to determine where connectivity problems lie. If, for example, a workstation is unable to reach foo.bar.com on the Internet, you would first ping a computer on your subnet. If that fails to work, the problem is located within your subnet; if the ping is responded to positively, you would then ping the inside of your gateway, then the outside, and then another machine on the Internet. If all these are returned successful, the problem, most likely, lies with foo.bar.com.

For more information about using ping, see the section "ping" in Chapter 1, "TCP/IP and Related Protocols."

tracert/traceroute

traceroute (sometimes spelled tracert depending on your OS) follows the path of a packet from a source to a destination. It's most useful to determine who's upstream from whom. If, for example, you're having difficulty reaching foo.bar.com, a traceroute will tell you whom the Web site is getting its service from and whom to call. For more about traceroute, see the section "ping" in Chapter 1.

netstat

netstat (network status) displays information about the current network status such as TCP and UDP ports in use and what they're connected to. There are versions of netstat for Microsoft and UNIX variants.

For troubleshooting on Windows NT and 2000 platforms, netstat can also show connections over time in the form of the following where *interval* is a number in seconds:

```
netstat interval
```

An example of netstat can be seen in Figure 11.1. See the man pages or online help for your particular install for more information.

Figure 11.1   The Windows command line version of netstat shows active TCP connections. Various UNIX versions are more capable and display information such as interface statistics, UNIX sockets, raw sockets, IP masquerading entries, and IPX and X.25 protocol information including routing tables.

ifconfig/ipconfig/winipcfg

ipconfig and its cousins (ifconfig and winipcfg) do the same thing on different operating systems, namely, show the current IP configuration; including the current IP address, subnet mask, and default gateway. ipconfig is vital for diagnosing an improper IP configuration (see Figure 11.2).

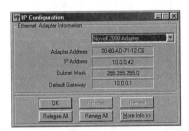

Figure 11.2   This is Microsoft's GUI version of ipconfig, winipcfg. A command line version (ipcfg) is also included with Windows 9x and NT/2000.

Packet Capture Utilities

The purpose of capturing a packet is to dissect the headers. After capture, you'll want to inspect and analyze not only the headers but also the packet contents. From the headers you can find the sending address, receiving address, and port information. But beyond that, dissecting a packet will give you information down to the link level. So apart from TCP packets, you could be examining AppleTalk or IPX packets. How could this be useful? If you're running an IP-only network that's having performance problems, running a packet sniffer may show you that 40% of your network traffic is IPX being babbled out by some printer on the third floor.

Packet capture utilities allow you to put together traffic flows by examining source and destination IP addresses along with information about the port number and TCP sequencing information. This is the three-way handshake established at the beginning of every TCP connection. Packet flows show you who is talking to whom on your network. The following sections take a brief look at a couple of packet sniffing utilities.

Microsoft Network Monitor

MS Network Monitor (NetMon) is installed by default when Windows NT is installed; however, it must be activated manually. Because it's useful and you already paid for it, take a closer look at NetMon. Network Monitor configures the adapter card to capture incoming and outgoing packets. These packets can then be analyzed. Filters can be used so that certain packets are kept and others discarded based on MAC address of the source, protocol, and so on. This filtered data is then shown in a somewhat palatable manner. The version that comes with Windows NT only shows data about the local computer (incoming and outgoing); for the full version of Network Monitor, you need to purchase SMS.

Installing and using Network Monitor on Windows NT 4.0 and Windows 2000 is pretty similar.

Installing Network Monitor on Your Windows NT Server
Here are step-by-step instructions for installing NetMon on your Windows NT 4.0 server:

1. On your Windows NT 4.0 Server computer, go to control panel. Double-click Network.
2. Click Services.
3. Click Add.
4. From the list of available services that appears, select Network Monitor Tools and Agent. Click OK.
5. Reboot.

Installing Network Monitor on Your Windows 2000 Box
Installing Network Monitor on a Windows 2000 server is very similar:

1. Open Add/Remove Programs.
2. Click Add/Remove Windows Components.
3. Select Management and Monitoring Tools, and click Details.
4. In the Management and Monitoring Tools window, select the Network Monitor. Click OK.
5. Be prepared to insert your Windows 2000 Server CD.

Using Network Monitor

After Network Monitor is activated, it appears under Administrative Tools (on both Windows NT 4.0 and Windows 2000) as shown in Figure 11.3.

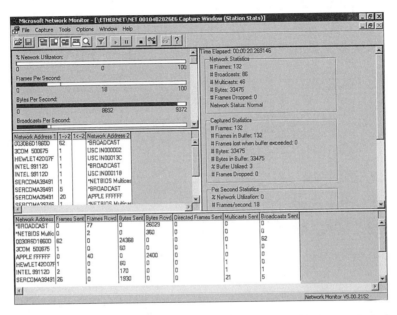

Figure 11.3   After starting Network Monitor, you can start capturing packets by selecting Start from the Capture menu.

After you've run your packet sniffing, select Stop and Analyze to show an analysis of the packets that have been captured (see Figure 11.4).

tcpdump

tcpdump was written as a portable library for capturing packets. It's a generic utility that works on Solaris and Sun OSes as well as most other flavors of UNIX. tcpdump has been ported to Windows NT as well and is available from www.tcpdump.org.

Snoop

Snoop is a built-in, command-line packet capture utility for Solaris. On its face, it's similar to a TCP dump, and does the same thing as both tcpdump and NT packet capture. The syntax is, in fact, very similar to the ever popular tcpdump. It allows you to capture data from the Link Layer up based upon filtering criteria.

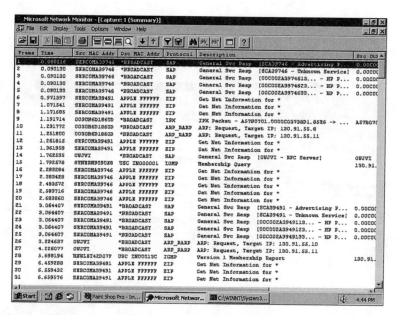

Figure 11.4   An analysis of the captured packets is provided by Microsoft's Network Monitor.

nstreams

nstreams is a utility that works with tcpdump. By itself, tcpdump will only capture or display packets. It won't put them together into individual flows. This is where nstreams comes in, taking data collected by tcpdump and assembling it into useful packet streaming information.

netcat

netcat is a packet assembly and diagnostic tool. netcat is not only a good diagnostic tool, but it's also something that an intruder might use to try and damage your network. Basically, Netcat allows you to specify and generate traffic packets of an arbitrary type. It is useful as a diagnostic tool to send various types of packets to see how your network will respond. That's what your intruder will be doing, too.

Hardware Sniffers

Hardware sniffers are larger buffers for capturing all the traffic without dropping packets; they include a LAN adapter that can be set in promiscuous mode.

Network Analyzers/Protocol Analyzers

Network analyzers grab network traffic and display it for you in a readable format. They do this by putting the network card into promiscuous mode, whereby it listens in on all network traffic rather than just traffic destined for that particular card. There are two types of network analyzers: software and hardware. As you might guess, hardware works better, software is cheaper. There are many different varieties of both available, some free, some expensive. The following are a few to consider:

- **Sniffer Pro from Network Associates**—Combination of hardware and software from www.sniffer.com.

- **Sniffer Basic aka NetXray from Network Associates**—There's also a software only version of Sniffer Pro at www.sniffer.com/asp_set/products/tnv/snifferbasic_intro.asp.

- **Etherpeek from AG Group**—Very powerful and expressive, Etherpeek is a software only network analyzer available from www.aggroup.com/products/etherpeek. It allows you to analyze packet information from the Link layer up. Also, it allows you to perform a variety of built-in diagnostic tests, including analyzing traffic flows to see who's talking to whom. It's rife with graphs and charts, such as the protocol distribution graph, which will allow you to see how much IPX your network is passing in contrast to how much IP.

- **Ethereal**—This is the Swiss Army knife of packet sniffers. Ethereal is a free, cross-platform packet analyzer available from ethereal.zing.org. It's open source and runs on just about any modern UNIX/Linux variant and Windows 98/NT. It can read a variety of capture file formats, including libpcap/tcpdump, snoop, LanAlyzer, Sniffer (compressed and uncompressed), MS Network Monitor, AIX iptrace, NetXray, Sniffer Pro, RADCOM, Lucent/Ascend debug output, output from Toshiba's ISDN router, HPUX nettl, and the ISDN4BSD "i4btrace" utility.

Testing Your Routing

You can test routing using some of the tools you've already looked at, including ping, and traceroute, which will tell you if a host is reachable across a network and what path is being taken to get there. Make sure you get a list of pingable resources from your ISP including the upstream router, a couple of servers, and the access point at the NAT, to help diagnose where a problem is.

Using ARP

You can also use the arp command, which will display the contents of the ARP cache. This is important to determine that IP addresses are being resolved into MAC addresses properly. See Figure 11.5 for a look at an ARP cache.

Default Route

The default route, otherwise known as the "gateway of last resort," is the route your traffic takes to get to your default gateway. If data has no other direct route, it's sent to the default gateway, which then forwards it along *its* default route to its own default gateway.

Figure 11.5 The arp command can be used to show the contents of the ARP cache, which lists IP address and Ethernet addresses.

Your workstation has a routing table. In that routing table is information on how to get to other computers on your internal network, which will be contained in a direct routing table entry. If a packet comes along for a destination for which it has no route, it will generate a no route to host error, *unless* there is a default route specified. If there is, the packet will be sent along that route to the default gateway and forwarded along its merry way from there.

Both your clients and your edge router should have default routes set up, from the clients to your edge router, and from your server to your ISP.

Border Gateway Protocol (BGP4)

BGP is an EGP (exterior gateway protocol) that aggregates multiple route advertisements into a single routing table entry. This makes load balancing traffic across multiple links to a single ISP far easier.

Follow the Traffic Flows

By following traffic flows, you make sure that data is able to get where it's supposed to get and not where it's not supposed to. It's sort of like going around the house at night and making sure the doors are locked. There are some doors that you do want locked at night and others that you don't. So you go around and make sure the front door and the back door are locked and that the bathroom door is unlocked. The same goes for your network. Traffic should be able to get from the Internet to your Web server and from your desktop workstation to your Web server, but no traffic should be able to get from the outside world to your desktop computer.

Initiate traffic in the following directions and make sure it works:

- From your internal network to your WAN/Internet connection
- From your internal network to your DMZ

- From your WAN/Internet to your internal network
- From your WAN/Internet to your DMZ
- From your DMZ to your WAN/Internet connection
- From your DMZ to your internal network

Testing Your Required Services

Testing services is a simple matter; make sure that allowed services (such as HTTP requests) can get out and that unallowed services cannot.

Testing Your Exposed Services

Testing your exposed services means trying to reach components of your network that are available to the outside world. You should be able to reach these from inside. Telnet is a handy tool for checking the path to a particular computer, especially for mail and HTTP server inspection.

You also need to make sure that you cannot reach other services running on the servers that you should not be able to reach from the outside. Pretend you're trying to break in.

Also, make sure that you cannot reach your internal network from the outside.

Testing Your Security

Security is difficult to test thoroughly, especially if you're not well trained in it. There are two ways around this (well, three if you count waiting for intruders to test it for you by erasing your corporate data and serving warez off of your site): One is to hire somebody who does know how to test your security, and the other is to use canned security validation tools. Some of these prepackaged tools are considered in-depth in Chapter 12, "Managing Your Internet Connection." Ideally, you should be using a combination of a knowledgeable security auditor and software together.

## 12

MANAGING YOUR
INTERNET CONNECTION

Does a good farmer neglect a crop he has planted?
Does a good teacher overlook even the most humble student?
Does a good father allow a single child to starve?
Does a good programmer refuse to maintain his code?

—Geoffrey James, "The Tao of Programming"

Evaluating New Services

Every network should have a paranoid administrator. By virtue of your site
being on the Internet, it is a target for nefarious characters from the outside
world. Even, and perhaps especially, if your operation is innocuous and
small enough that you don't think that you attract attention, agents of various malevolent ilks might attack you. Disgruntled employees (or former
employees) with an axe to grind or crackers on a power trip might target a
large corporation or government institution to show off their ability to
defeat security. While at the same time, people looking for a safe place to
store pirated software, run IRC "bots," or relay spam will pick a small target in the belief that security there is low.

Any new protocol that your users want to allow through your network
should be evaluated before it is permitted. If you don't posses the skillset
necessary to evaluate the protocol, you can rely upon the expertise of others
by subscribing to the BUGTRAQ mailing list or the Windows equivalent,

NTBUGTRAQ. BUGTRAQ goes over security holes in detail, and because it explains how to exploit security flaws, it's important that your security officers or engineers are reading it, because the people who are trying to break into your system certainly are.

Sign Up for BUGTRAQ

BUGTRAQ uses the LSoft LISTSERV list management software. If you are unfamiliar with using LISTSERV mailing list software, you can read the online user's guide at `http://www.lsoft.com/manuals/1.8d/user/user.html`. Some simple commands are provided here to get you going.

BUGTRAQ is hosted at `securityfocus.com`, so all LISTSERV commands dealing with administration of your subscription should be sent to `listserv@securityfocus.com`.

To subscribe to BUGTRAQ, email the following text in the message body to the address in the previous paragraph:

```
SUBSCRIBE BUGTRAQ Lastname, Firstname
```

To unsubscribe, it is just as easy:

```
UNSUBSCRIBE BUGTRAQ
```

Suppose you are taking a leave of absence to study the mating habits of the migratory Madagascar hissing cockroach as they pass through the tropical swamps of Costa Rica. When you return you don't want to wade through hundreds, or thousands depending on how long you stare at some bugs of a different sort, of BUGTRAQ messages. You can abate the ensuing tide of the BUGTRAQ deluge with the following:

```
SET BUGTRAQ NOMAIL
```

This command temporarily suspends BUGTRAQ email delivery of your subscription. Don't forget to put a hold on your newspaper as well.

To re-enable delivery of BUGTRAQ messages, use this command:

```
SET BUGTRAQ MAIL
```

There might come a time when your email address will change, like your company was acquired while you were on vacation. Upon your triumphant return from the tropical swamps of Costa Rica, all outbound email is now automatically readdressed. You will no longer be able to manage your account from this new address, even though you might still be able to receive. In this case, you will need to send email to

```
listadmin@securityfocus.com
```

The list administrator will be able to rectify the situation.

If you don't like to get all those individual BUGTRAQ messages, you can enable BUGTRAQ digests to be sent by emailing the following command:

```
SET BUGTRAQ DIGEST
```

To re-enable individual message delivery, use the following logical command:

```
SET BUGTRAQ NODIGEST
```

The list is moderated, meaning that all messages pass through an overseer who ensures that the content is appropriate to the list. Moderated lists tend to have the best signal-to-noise ratios around. So, when you submit an email to the list, it goes to the following address:

```
BUGTRAQ@securityfocus.com
```

The moderator actually receives and reviews the email first before the list members get to see it.

Finally, if you want to go back and read some of the exploits, how they were developed, fixed, and other general IT security history, you can read the BUGTRAQ archives. The archives can be read at `http://www.securityfocus.com`.

Sign Up for NTBUGTRAQ

If you don't have time to be concerned with network gear, UNIX/Linux, and other security concerns outside your core focus, there is an NTBUGTRAQ list that has a much more narrow focus. The LISTSERV is hosted at `listserv@listserv.ntbugtraq.com`, and not at `securityfocus.com`.

Because the mailing list manager is LISTSERV, all your favorite commands work with NTBUGTRAQ. To subscribe, send an email the to the address in the previous paragraph with the following text in the body:

```
subscribe ntbugtraq firstname lastname
```

If you want to remain anonymous, you can do that as well. Subscribe in the following manner:

```
subscribe ntbugtraq anonymous
```

To actually submit messages to the list, send mail to the following address:

```
NTBugtraq@listserv.ntbugtraq.com
```

All the other commands work the same way, except you need to replace BUGTRAQ with NTBUGTRAQ as appropriate. If you prefer reading rather than subscribing, you can read the NTBUGTRAQ archives. The NTBUGTRAQ archives are kept at `http://ntbugtraq.ntadvice.com/archives`.

Someone should also be reading the security alert information at the SANS institute (www.sans.org). Be sure to at least audit your systems for the "Ten Most Critical Internet Security Threats" as defined by "the Expert's consensus." This list, and the methods used to plug the holes, is outlined in a living document found at http://www.sans.org/topten.htm.

Checking for Security Breaches

There are two ways to test the security of your system. You can either do it yourself or a hacker can do it for you. In the latter case, it might be too late if your quarterly reports are replaced by pirated copies of Tomb Raider and gigabytes of MP3s.

Periodic Vulnerability Assessment

You can hire an independent auditor or consulting company to test your systems from the inside and outside. If someone's breaking into your system, it's a lot better if you're paying him to do it because you get a full report in the end rather than having your Web page changed to endorse an intruder's cracking skill.

Use the guidelines in Chapter 6, "Consulting, Consultants, and Contractors," for selecting your security auditing firm. There are several key points to keep in mind:

- Get references. Talk to previous clients to build up a comfort level with the firm and the individuals they are proposing to deploy.
- Define the scope of services. Be as explicit as possible with regard to what is tested and deliverables you are expecting. Many firms will gather information through social engineering or dumpster diving. If you don't want that aspect of your company tested, make sure you define those stipulations.
- If the budget allows, hire multiple firms to do the procedure at once. That way you can validate and compare the results in the same timeframe. After you have selected a trustworthy company, you can move forward with them.
- Periodically means as often as you can afford it. Exploits come out daily. You might have been audited and come out clean to all known exploits. A month later an exploit can be found that leaves all your servers exposed.

Security expert Bruce Schneier once said that "security is a process, not a product." There is no known magic to keep the intruders away, only due diligence.

Tools for Simple Intrusion Detection

Aside from hiring a contractor, there are several tools you can use to perform simple intrusion detection yourself. These won't replace a meticulous and full audit, but they're better than not doing anything and will help you quickly seal the obvious holes.

Shields Up!

The easiest way to run basic intrusion detection on your computer is with Steve Gibson's Shields Up! (www.grc.com), which tests for some of the more obviously bad things your computer might be doing—sharing printers over NetBIOS, for example. Shields Up! Is free to use and is shown in Figure 12.1.

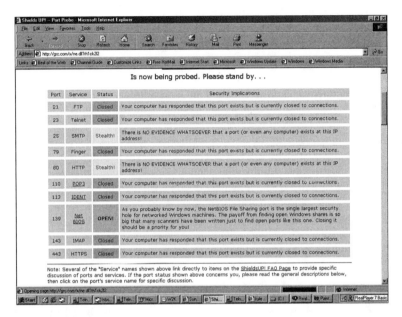

Figure 12.1   Shields Up! Provides an analysis of your security by performing port scans and notifying you of weaknesses.

Snort

You can perform simple intrusion detection yourself with Snort. Snort is a svelte network intrusion detection system that runs on most variants of UNIX and has been ported to Windows 2000, Windows NT, and Windows 9x. Snort can both sniff and log packets. You can also use it to detect various types of attacks and probes, port scans, buffer overflows, and so on. It can also alert system admins in real-time. Snort is freeware licensed under the terms of the GNU General Public License.

Intrusion detection signatures for Snort can be found in several locations. The stock signatures' rulebase is released periodically, roughly every month, at Snort's homepage. Additionally the arachNIDS attack signature database (www.whitehats.com) receives updates and is refreshed hourly. You can retrieve the Vision.conf signatures from
http://dev.whitehats.com/ids/vision.conf.

Snort is also extensible; using a plug-in architecture, it can be extended with additional features without bloating the core codebase. Two promising plug-ins are ACID, the Analysis Console for Intrusion Databases, and SPADE, the Statistical Packet Anomaly Detection Engine.

ACID was developed at the Carnegie Mellon University and the Software Engineering Institute and is a PHP-scripted Web interface. According to ACID's Web site, ACID allows you access to real-time statistics, such as the following:

- Percentage of traffic for each protocol
- Alerts such as the number of source and destination per IP, and last/first arrival time
- Graphs of the number of arrived alerts over a period of time
- A definable last number of alerts by protocol

Information on the ACID plug-in and its continuing development can be found at http://www.cert.org/kb/acid/.

SPADE is actually one component of an evolving architecture being designed to detect and correlate distributed port scans. One of the many problems encountered in today's Internet environment is that port scans from the intruder's point of view can be done in a slow, distributed fashion so as to not raise any flags on an Intrusion Detection System. Using many compromised hosts over a period of days, the intruder can collect information and potential opportunities without you being alerted.

SPADE attempts to profile your traffic patterns and then creates alerts when anomalous traffic is detected. The alerts themselves don't mean a whole lot individually, and might actually just be false positives. It's the job of an event correlator to group the alerts into a cohesive summary. However, with enough information, you can do this manually, even though the correlation engine to take advantage of SPADE's alerts is not yet available as of publication.

Information on SPADE, and SPICE, the Stealthy Probing and Intrusion Correlation Engine, can be found at http://www.silicondefense.com/spice/.

Nessus

Another free vulnerability assessment tool is Nessus (www.nessus.org). Nessus is an excellent open source UNIX-/Linux-based vulnerability assessment scanner that is updated often.

Nessus has a series of "families" of vulnerabilities that it checks, including backdoors, CGI abuses, denial of service, finger abuses, firewalls, FTP, gain a shell remotely, gain root remotely, general, misc, NIS port scanners, remote file access, RPC, SMTP problems, and useless services. In each of these families are specific lists of vulnerabilities tested, which is updated as necessary.

Although the Nessus server runs from a UNIX/Linux server, there are clients for Windows based machines.

ISS SAFEsuite

Internet Security System's (at www.iss.net) SAFEsuite product line includes ISS Internet Scanner, System Scanner, and Database Scanner. Each product is tailored to a specific task. ISS's product offerings are often considered the flagship vulnerability assessment tool for those who do not compile their own exploits database.

Internet Scanner pricing varies depending on amount of network devices scanned. The suggested price for a 30-device license is $2795 and $4995 for a Class C (254-device) license.

System Scanner is priced at $695 and the suggested retail price of a 10-server license is $6,250.

Database Scanner has a starting list price of $995 per database server for Microsoft SQL Server, and $1995 per server for Oracle and Sybase database servers.

The SRP of RealSecure Newtork Sensore is $8995 for a single perpetual license and $900 for RealSecure Server Sensor for a single perpetual license.

SAFEsuite Decisions has a starting U.S. suggested list price of $25,000 and is based upon the size of a customer's protected network.

ISS also offers its RealSecure intrusion detection suite—RealSecure Manager, Network Sensor, and OS Sensor. The OS sensor is a platform-specific agent that resides on the server listening for specific traffic signatures or patterns. The Network sensor product listens for those signatures and patterns on the wire, and thus must be able to hear all traffic to be effective. This might prove difficult in a fully switched environment. Finally, the RealSecure Manger correlates all events from the network and OS Sensors.

Most ISS products are designed for Windows NT 4.0 Workstation or Windows 2000 Professional. As expected, there are many architectures and operating systems supported by the OS Sensor product.

CyberCop

Network Associates' CyberCop product line (www.nai.com) includes intrusion detection in CyberCop Monitor and vulnerability assessment in CyberCop Scanner. There is an additional offering known as CyberCop Sting that is their honeypot product.

CyberCop Monitor is currently available for Windows NT 4.0 and Solaris, which are two very popular platforms for Internet application deployment.

CyberCop Scanner is currently available for Windows NT 4.0, Windows 2000, and Linux/Intel. CyberCop is more reasonable in price than ISS ($35 per node at 254 nodes and $16 per node at 1,000 nodes), and includes a trial download.

QualysGuard

QualysGuard from Sunbelt-Software (http://www.sunbelt-software.com) is a vulnerability assessment tool. It provides a mapping of your network and performs numerous white-hat hacking techniques against your security to pinpoint weaknesses. Security flaws are then ranked on a scale of 1 to 5. QualysGuard can be automated to run at specified intervals.

One interesting thing about QualysGuard is that it is run from a browser over the Web and the security holes it looks for are updated daily at the server side. Unfortunately, QualysGuard doesn't have a downloadable demo. Pricing is tailor-made (i.e. how much can you afford?) with base pricing starting at $166 / month for one IP with a minimum 12 month commitment.

BlackIce Defender

BlackIce Defender from Network Ice (www.networkice.com) is a popular single-node intrusion detection and active "personal firewall" product that businesses might want to consider for Cable/DSL users who are constantly connected to the Internet doing remote/telecommuting work.

BlackIce Defender is a firewall paired with an intrusion detection system geared toward the home user with a dedicated, high speed Internet connection such as a cable modem or DSL. The corporate version, BlackIce Agent, provides similar protection to desktops across an internal network. Pricing on BlackIce Defender is $39.95.

There are plans to make a vulnerability assessment agent called IceScanner will work similar to QualysGuard.

Monitoring and Baselining

Monitoring of the network is ongoing and not glorious. However, it is critical to the operation of any organization. Before you can judge abnormal behavior on your network, you need to define *normal* behavior with baselining.

Baselining involves monitoring network usage over a period of time to produce a record of normal trends—both high and low usage. This snapshot of "normal" network use will then be compared to future snapshots to determine if the network is being strained and, if so, in what way.

What to Baseline

When baselining, pay attention to the bandwidth usage, number of users, network applications, and, obviously, if you're using applications for which you have a limited number of licenses, monitor the max number of copies of that application running at any given time. Also, keep track of things such as number of collisions and frames per second being sent.

How Long Should Baselining Last?

Ideally, you'll be able to baseline over a week or two weeks. If your organization goes through seasonal changes (if, for example, you're at a university), baseline at different intervals so you know what's normal during the summer, at the start of the school year, and during finals.

Peaks Versus Averages

There are two types of things to look for during baselining: your *peak* usage, and your *average* usage. Peaks might occur at the beginning and end of a day, on a particular day.

Identify the Sources of Peaks

Determine what is causing your peaks. In the spring of 2000, universities across the country began to discover that as much as a third of their Internet bandwidth was being consumed by .mp3 traffic. Eliminating peaks such as these can free up space for legitimate business.

Log Monitoring

Log monitoring is tedious; however, it can be valuable for managing your network's health. In theory, you should be looking at your security logs daily. In practice, network engineers often have more pressing problems.

By itself, a log entry isn't a terribly exciting piece of information. The following log entry, for example, comes from a Microsoft Internet Information Server log and documents the downloading of a .gif file from a Web server:

```
10.0.0.236, -, 3/4/00, 0:00:04, W3SVC1, BIGPROXY,
10.0.0.32, 71, 522, 183, 200, 0, GET, /scripts/proxy/w3proxy.dll, 03ce8008,
http://underfoot/exchange/Navbar/public.gif,
```

As you can imagine, hundreds of similar log files are written every day. The question then becomes how to analyze the enormous amounts of data generated in log files.

Through careful manipulation with log analysis programs, the logs can be summarized—digested if you will—making it more likely that the logs will be looked at and incursions detected.

Windows NT

A bevy of log files are generated by Windows NT. From Security logs to application logs to event logs to the logs generated by Internet Information Server, your Windows NT/2000 box is keeping track of everything that's going on. The problem with many of these logs is that they're difficult to manage with the native Windows tools. There are several useful third-party products for managing Windows NT/2000 log files. Some of them are described here.

Log Analyzer

Log Analyzer from Web Trends is a terrific way to make sense out of your IIS log files. Log Analyzer will create usage reports on multiple Web sites and subdirectories within those Web sites. It will also do reverse DNS lookups, and present everything in an attractive manner in numerous formats from Word to HTML. Log Analyzer can be scheduled to provide daily stats for different users. If you have users concerned with hits to their Web pages, Log Analyzer can really make you a hero. See Figure 12.2 for an example of one of the automatically generated reports.

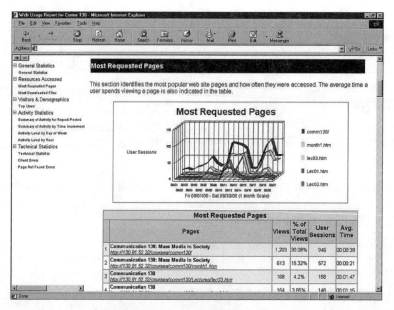

Figure 12.2 Log Analyzer by Webtrends creates many useful graphs and charts summarizing your Web activity.

DumpEL

DumpEL (Dump Event Log), from the Windows NT/2000 Resource Kit, allows you to take an event log on a local or remote computer to which you have the proper access, and dump it to a file. You could then import that file to a program such as Excel or into a scripting language, which you could use to strip out certain events.

NTOLog

NTOLog from NTOBJECTives (`www.ntobjectives.com/ntotools.htm`) is a free tool that can back up and clear the Event log. This tool is useful for moving to a different partition or machine for processing.

To automate the task of backing up and clearing event logs you can make use of the built-in AT command to schedule the execution of NTOLog. Using AT from the command-line allows for the editing and general maintenance of scheduled jobs from both the command-line and the GUI interface. AT jobs submitted from the Graphical Wizard in Windows 2000 or Windows NT with IE5 (which shouldn't be installed anyway) cannot be managed from the command line. Unfortunately, there is no CRON equivalent on NT for running commands periodically throughout the day/week/month.

Because Windows NT has no native remote logging service such as syslog, you can purchase a third-party syslog service from Adiscon Software (`www.adiscon.com/EvntSLog/main.asp`). In a mixed environment, you can then point all your Windows NT servers using syslog to a UNIX server and process the logs on a centralized box.

UNIX/Linux

UNIX/Linux has always had strong logging support. Almost every modern UNIX variant has logging facilities generally centralized in one place (`/var/log`), and often includes support for logfile rotation, compression, and archival storage.

Through the use of various log processing utilities and built-in scheduling (via `cron`), the task of monitoring your systems and user activities can easily be simplified.

syslog/syslog-ng

syslogd is the program that provides support for system logging, known as syslog, and, in many cases, kernel message logging. syslogd has similar field discriminators to the Windows NT applications System and Security logs, although they are more flexible. The syslogd discriminators are often called selectors, and are comprised of a facility field and a priority field. The facility field could be any one of the following keywords: auth, auth-priv, cron, daemon, kern, lpr, mail, mark, news, security (an alias to auth), syslog, user, uucp, and local0 through local7.

The priority field scales from low to high using the following keywords: debug, info, notice, warning, err, crit, alert, and emerg.

Even though there are significantly more selector combinations in syslog than in Windows NT's EventLog, with the remote logging of multiple services from multiple servers to the same logging server, you might still find logs to be crowded with information.

There is a solution, a syslogd replacement called syslog-ng. syslog-ng has several features beyond the normal syslogd, including the capability to filter messages on message content, not just `facility.priority` pairs. Using regular expressions, you could log hosts information to individual logs. syslog-ng might already come with your UNIX/Linux distribution, but if it doesn't, it can be found at the following location: `http://www.balabit.hu/products/ syslog-ng/index.html`

Abacus Project's Logcheck

Logcheck (`http://www.psionic.com/abacus/logcheck/`) is part of the Abacus project (`http://www.psionic.com/abacus/`), an initiative to provide free system intrusion detection software to the Internet. Logcheck periodically reviews your system logs and attempts to identify problems and security violations in your logfiles. The results of those analyses are automatically sent to you in email.

swatch

The Simple WATCHer, or swatch (`http://www.engr.ucsb.edu/~eta/swatch/`), was written to actively monitor messages as they are written to a log file via the UNIX syslog utility. It can search configurable patterns in log files and perform designated action based on the pattern matched.

Log Surfer

Log Surfer (`http://www.cert.dfn.de/eng/logsurf/`) was designed to monitor any text-based logfiles on your system in real-time. The program has been developed because of some limitations of swatch. Two major limitations that have been removed are the inability to parse a single message line at once and the inability to pass substrings of the message as arguments to external programs.

Why Monitor Logs?

There are all sorts of applications to help you look at your logs, but why bother? There are obvious reasons, such as when you want to know how many times your Web server was hit after your TV commercial came out. Then there are more subtle reasons, such as checking to see if unusual requests are being repeatedly made to your servers, or to see if your users are running unauthorized applications which could jeopardize the security of your network.

Your Clever Users Tunneling Over HTTP

Although some of your users might appreciate all you're doing to protect their data, others might find your firewall blocking some of the services they want to run. And, if they're clever, they might install something such as Httptunnel (www.nocrew.org/software/httptunnel.html) which will allow them to create a virtual bidirectional data path hidden inside HTTP requests. A user can use this to Telnet or PPP outside of your firewall. And, of course, it might also let someone in.

Your Clever Users Tunneling Over DNS

Tunneling over DNS is both possible and a pain in the rump to prevent your users from doing. An example of tunneling over DNS is NSTX (nstx.dereference.de/nstx), which allows you to tunnel from behind a firewall to a DNS server; both machines must be running the tunneling client software. Currently it's only available for Linux.

The only way to prevent your users from tunneling out over DNS apart from specific network policy strictly forbidding it is to perform content inspection to strip out the TXT records in the replies, which, of course, might break other services that are expecting intact TXT records.

Monitoring Usage

Monitoring the use of systems will prevent unhappy users by allowing you to enlarge portions of your network at the appropriate times, and as your budget allows. Additionally, it will allow you to make more accurate predictions as to what new applications will do to the performance of your network and Internet connection.

Monitoring the use of your infrastructure should be designed in from the beginning. Network monitoring and analysis tools should be part of every operating network. How can you quantify the screams of "the network is slow" if you have no way to measure what is going on?

There are many very large, very expensive network monitoring frameworks available. HP OpenView, Cisco CiscoWorks, Nortel Optivity, and Cabletron's Spectrum shouldn't be unknowns to a network admin. Use these tools if available. Use RMON collectors and SNMP statistics. Baseline your network, and then constantly gather information, so you can perform capacity planning.

There are also not-so-expensive options, such as Network Associates Sniffer Pro Lan (www.sniffer.com), which runs about $1,500. There's also Wizard Baselining from Wavetek Wandel Golterman (www.wwgsolutions.com) for about $3,500.

There are several free tools available as well, so there is no excuse to not monitor use of your network infrastructure.

MRTG (Multi-Router Traffic Grapher)

MRTG is a collection of utilities that monitors and graphs the traffic load on network links. The output is generated HTML pages containing live graphs of the monitored links. MRTG works with most UNIX/Linux operating systems and Windows NT/2000. MRTG requires a recent version of Perl to be installed. MRTG can be found at `http://ee-staff.ethz.ch/~oetiker/webtools/mrtg/mrtg.html`.

RRDtool

RRDtool is a graphing and logging engine originally designed to be a replacement for the components used in MRTG. The main difference is that RRDtool can monitor anything, not just network link use. You can monitor just about any numeric metric that can be retrieved. This means you can monitor network link use and any metric that can be quantified in a numerical value. This includes, but is not limited to, memory use, outside temperature, server room particulates, CPU load, disk use, cache hits/misses, port scans, emails sent/received, wind speed, and cups of coffee made (if supported by your coffee maker).

RRDtool is not a replacement for MRTG, and has to be used in combination with either customized scripts or any number of existing front-ends. RRDtool and many of the front-ends work on most UNIX/Linux operating systems and Windows NT/2000. RRDtool can be found at `http://ee-staff.ethz.ch/~oetiker/webtools/rrdtool/`. A list of front-ends is linked off the main RRDtool page.

Cricket

Cricket is an example of front-end wrapper to RRDtool that provides a high-performance, yet flexible system for monitoring trends in time-series data. Cricket works on UNIX/Linux operating systems and Windows NT/2000. Cricket can be found at `http://cricket.sourceforge.net/`.

Bronc

Bronc is another Web-based front-end to RRDtool but aims to be a replacement for MRTG using RRDtool as the core graphing component. Although Bronc's dependencies all work on UNIX/Linux operating systems and Windows NT/2000, at the time of this publication, Bronc itself is specific to the Apache Web server using `mod_perl`, and has only been developed and tested under UNIX/Linux. Bronc can be found at `http://bronc.blueaspen.com/`.

Planning for the Future

As soon as your Internet connection is stable, it's obsolete. But you knew that already. When you have time to breathe, start looking toward the next goal. This might involve a redundant connection to the Internet to prevent network outages, or it might involve new cabling or transmission media breakthroughs. Unlike a bridge, your network connection cannot sit unmodified for years while traffic crosses it. Planning for your next expansion far ahead of time will allow you to prepare your users and, perhaps more importantly, the people who control the money, for the next great thing.

What's Going to Break First?

Baselining will give you the opportunity to tell what parts of your system are being used the hardest. These are the primary candidates for upgrades. Are you running at your max bandwidth? Are you running out of ports in your data closet? Are your users downloading MP3s left and right and crunching your disk space? Your network is a chain; that chain has a weak link, and every day you should be replacing the weakest link.

Appraising New Technologies

Every few years a new technology comes along that turns Internet bandwidth requirements upside down. It happened when the World Wide Web became popular and it happened again when Napster started taking up a third of the available bandwidth at some universities. Keeping abreast of trends can keep you from getting caught with your bandwidth down. Whether this means installing caching devices, faster connections, forbidding certain types of services, or limiting what might be done on your network at certain times of the day, there's no substitute for reading trade magazines and talking to your colleagues.

13

MOVING TO A NEW ISP

"My problem lies in reconciling my gross habits with my net income."
—Errol Flynn

Nothing lasts forever and eventually your Internet service provider (ISP) might go away for one reason or another. The ISP might close down, you might close down, or you might hate the ISP. In any event, it's possible that some day you will have to pack up your domain name and move along.

There are several things that you need to take care of for this to happen.

Equipment Return

Are you leasing equipment from your ISP? If so, this will need to go back and you'll need to settle. Is any of your equipment co-located? Co-located equipment should be itemized, disconnected, and carefully moved to the new location. Don't leave Marketing's development server behind. Redundant equipment might need to be installed and brought up at your new ISP to minimize downtime.

Has your ISP been backing up your data? You might want to ask for those backup tapes. Or at least be sure that you will be able to get restores from them in the future should you need to.

IP Addressing—The Return of Leased Numbers

Any non-RFC-1918 address space is normally leased to you by the ISP. Unless you were directly allocated an IP address block by ICANN, the IP address block belongs to the ISP. Sadly, that means any Internet accessible addresses must be renumbered with your new IP address space. This can be a real pain if you're using a huge block of real IP addresses. Network Address Translation (NAT), DHCP, and BootP can all help in re-allocating your internal IP address structure.

DNS Modifications

If you are not running your own DNS—which is heartily recommended after the resources are available to you—you will need to coordinate the transfer of your DNS authoritative servers from your old ISP to the new ISP with your registrar of record. This must be done by an administrative or technical contact. It will usually take 24 hours, but could take as long as 48 hours for all cached entries to be updated. Your new ISP and your old ISP have to make sure that your DNS information changes properly so that traffic continues to get to your site from the outside world.

New Equipment Purchases

Will your existing CSU/DSU equipment work with your new ISP? Do you have the redundant equipment necessary to exist on both ISPs during the changeover? It's probably time for an on-site visit by someone from your new ISP to go over the changeover. The last thing you need is to discontinue service with one ISP and then find out that your router isn't compatible with your new ISP's equipment. (For example, is it doing Frame Relay or T1 serial encoding? Will you need to use PPP?)

Transition Period

To reduce downtime, you will be testing the new ISP concurrently before disconnecting the previous ISP connection. Make sure you can run a battery of tests. Do an acceptance test plan. Validate that the new connection is working, routing, and so on prior to network cutover. Do not immediately disconnect the previous ISP until everything is working and burned in! The new ISP might be leasing you equipment or you might want to buy new equipment; you need to be sure this is compatible with your new ISP. You'll also want to make sure that your router software is up-to-date.

Security

Was your old ISP handling your security? Will your new ISP be providing a DMZ or security infrastructure? Will you be reusing your old one? Evaluate what you have and what exactly your ISP was doing for you in this regard.

Mail Servers

If your company has been using the email services of the ISP, make sure everyone has downloaded their email (and removed it from their server!) prior to DNS cutover. This will be more disruptive and painful the more email accounts the ISP is handling. Again, this is best handled if you are running your own mail server. Your old ISP should be able to forward email to the new mail server on a short-term basis for you.

Upgrades

Often it is better to install new equipment (and take the opportunity to do upgrades in the same process) than it is to move old equipment. While old equipment is off, you are offline. You cannot burn in the old equipment in the new environment without affecting your uptime. It is difficult to run old and new production environments in parallel while conducting acceptance testing. Often, upgrades are delayed because it would affect the uptime of your services. This process provides a valuable service window to affect changes. Plus, the equipment you've already deployed is insufficient and outdated.

INDEX

help desks, Internet service
providers (ISPs), 110
hierarchies, Dedicated Digital
Services (DDS), 33-35
High Definition Television
(HDTV), 54
High Security for Workstations
(HISECWS.INF) template, 196
High-Speed Digital Subscriber
Line (HDSL), 50
hiring consultants and
contractors, 125-137
HISECWS.INF (High Security
for Workstations) template,
196
HKEY LOCAL
MACHINE\SOFTWARE key
moving log files, 212
Windows NT, 192, 194
HKEY LOCAL MACHINE\
SYSTEM key
moving log files, 211-212
Windows NT, 192-194
honeypots, 80, 83
hop counts, 16
hop limits, Internet Protocol
(IP) version 6, 27
hopping, frequency, 67
hops, next. *See* gateways
hosting
email, Internet service
providers (ISPs), 110
local vs. Internet Service
Provider (ISP), 92, 96
servers, 172
servers off-site, 98
servers on-site, 96-98
services on-site, 163
Web sites, Internet service
providers (ISPs), 110
hosts.allow file, 201
hosts.deny file, 201
hotfixes, 162, 189
HTML. (Hypertext Markup
Language), 21
HTTP. *See* Hypertext Transfer
Protocol
Httptunnel, 267
Hypertext Markup Language
(HTML), 21
Hypertext Transfer Protocol
(HTTP), 21, 166
tunneling over, 267
user access to, 230

I-J

ICMP echo request broadcasts,
ignoring, 209
ICMP echoes, 169
ICMP redirect messages,
209-210
ICMP replies, creating
convenience chains, 225
ICMP timestamp request
broadcasts, 210
ICMP. *See* Internet Control
Message Protocol, 71
ID. *See* identification;
identifiers
identification
packet headers, 20
process, winmgmt command,
195
sources of peaks, 263
identifiers, Terminal Endpoint
(TEI), 47-48
IDS (Intrusion Detection
Systems), 82-83
IDSL (ISDN Digital Subscriber
Line), 51
ifconfig, 247
IGMP (Internet Group
Management Protocol), 119
IHL (Internet Header Length),
packet headers, 19
IIOP (Internet Inter-Orb-
Protocol), 158
IIS (Internet Information
Server)
installing, Windows 2000, 189
removing applications installed
by default, 198
IKE (Internet Key Exchange)
protocol, 154
impact analysis, 134
Implementation stage,
projects, 137-138
in-band signaling, 33
in.fingerd command, inetd
services, 200
in.named command, inetd
services, 200
inbound server connections,
File Transfer Protocol (FTP),
159
indecision, controlling in
projects, 134-135
inetd services, disabling on
UNIX and Linux servers, 200
info keyword, 265
Information Collection stage,
projects, 136

Information field, 48-49
informational messages,
Internet Protocol (IP) version
6, 27
infrastructures
adaptability, 151-152
network, co-located systems,
117
Initial Sequence Number, 13
input chains, attaching
selection rules, 227
insmod kernel module
command, 238
inspection, stateful, 84, 181-182
installation services, Internet
service providers (ISPs),
109-120
installing
firewalls, 81
Network Monitor (NetMon),
248
proxy servers, 141-146
tcp wrappers, UNIX and Linux
servers, 201
Windows 2000, server
hardening guidelines, 194-195
Windows NT, server hardening
guidelines, 188
WINS, Windows NT, 189
insurance, contractors and
consultants, 130-131
Integrated Services Digital
Network (ISDN), 42-45, 149
integrated solutions,
evaluating, 100-101
integrity, data, 74
interfaces
access, blocking, 227
Basic Rate (BRI), 43-44
grouping rules to, 225-226
Local Management (LMI),
59-60
Physical, IP Filter, 225
internal access, firewalls,
228-229
internal clocking, 184
internal CSU/DSUs, 182
internal traffic, allowing
outbound to Internet, 222-226
International Standards
Organization (ISO), 6
International
Telecommunications Union
(ITU), 41, 64
Internet
accessing services, 156-158, 166
allowing internal traffic
outbound to, 222-226

Other Related Titles

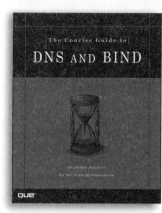

The Concise Guide to DNS and BIND
Nicolai Langfeldt
0-7897-2273-9
$34.99 US/$52.95 CA

The Concise Guide to Microsoft Windows 2000 DNS
Andy Ruth
0-7897-2335-2
$34.99 US/$52.95 CA

Upgrading and Repairing Networks, 2nd Edition
Terry Ogletree
0-7897-2034-5
$49.99 US/$74.95 CA

Special Edition Using Microsoft Active Directory
Sean Fullerton
0-7897-2434-0
$39.99 US/$59.95 CA

Special Edition Using Microsoft Windows Millennium Edition
Ed Bott
0-7897-2446-4
$39.99 US/$59.95 CA

Special Edition Using Red Hat Linux Millennium Edition
Alan Simpson
0-7897-2258-5
$39.99 US/$59.95 CA

How Networks Work
Frank Derfler
0-7897-2445-6
$29.99 US/$44.95 CA

Special Edition Using TCP/IP
John Ray
0-7897-1897-9
$29.99 US/$42.95 CA

Think Unix
Jon Lasser
0-7897-2376-x
$29.99 US/$44.95 CA

Platinum Edition Using XHTML, XML, and Java 2
Eric Ladd
0-7897-2473-1
$59.99 US/$89.95 CA

Tangled Web: Tales of Digital Crime from the Shadows of Cyberspace
Richard Power
0-7897-2443-x
$25.00 US/$37.95 CA

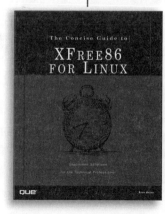

The Concise Guide to XFree86 for Linux
Aron Hsiao
0-7897-2182-1
$34.99 US/$52.95 CA

www.quecorp.com

All prices are subject to change.